Princess
Secrets to Share

www.transworldbooks.co.uk

Princess
Secrets to Share

Jean Sasson

Doubleday

LONDON · TORONTO · SYDNEY · AUCKLAND · JOHANNESBURG

TRANSWORLD PUBLISHERS
61–63 Uxbridge Road, London W5 5SA
www.transworldbooks.co.uk

Transworld is part of the Penguin Random House group of companies whose
addresses can be found at global.penguinrandomhouse.com

Penguin
Random House
UK

First published in Great Britain in 2015 by Doubleday
an imprint of Transworld Publishers

A CIP catalogue record for this book
is available from the British Library.

ISBN 9780857523372

Typeset in 11/14½pt Sabon by Kestrel Data, Exeter, Devon.
Printed and bound by Clays Ltd, Bungay, Suffolk.

Penguin Random House is committed to a sustainable
future for our business, our readers and our planet. This book
is made from Forest Stewardship Council® certified paper.

MIX
Paper from
responsible sources
FSC® C018179

1 3 5 7 9 10 8 6 4 2

This book is dedicated to Raif Badawi,
a brave man who has given up his freedom
to fight for freedom for all.
Such a worthy man should be known by the world.
The hearts of so many are with you, Raif Badawi.

All that is written here is real.
Some of the stories are very happy while some are tragically sad.
But all are true.
A few names have been changed to protect those who would
come to great harm should their true identity be known. But the
names have been revealed of many others.

– Jean Sasson and Princess Sultana Al Sa'ud

Contents

A Note from Jean Sasson

Human beings are complex, diverse, creative and often inde-cipherable. Whether genius or ordinary, disappointing or inspir-ational, kind or evil, the human mind, with its eighty-six billion nerve cells and innumerable nerve fibres, is incomparable in the known universe.

Exploring its complexity and power in all its colours, shapes and furrows will hopefully lead us to an understanding of our world and our place in it. There is one thing I know for certain: if human beings survive for a billion years, writers will never run out of material, due to the strangeness, beauty and unique nature of our marvellously intricate minds.

I am pleased that readers walk this path of discovery with me.

So, turn the page and let us begin this latest journey into the lives of some remarkable human beings.

SAUDI ARABIA

Foreword

The Challenge of Keeping Secrets

A good Muslim must keep secrets.

For non-Muslim readers who may feel surprise at hearing this disclosure, I will briefly explain the motivation for secret-keeping in Islamic societies.

For readers who do not know, the Muslim world is unique when it comes to secret-keeping. Certainly, no human secret is safe in most societies. For those who have read newspapers and magazines published in Great Britain or America, you have likely been scandalized at the malicious articles. Such stories are written with the sole intent of vilifying high-profile celebrities, or even ordinary people who are so unfortunate as to snag the notice of journalists. Many innocent lives have been damaged by such disagreeable media attention.

While there are many negatives in my own society, there are positives, too. One is that you will never read slanderous reportage in Saudi newspapers or magazines. Muslims are taught that anything told to others that does not serve a virtuous purpose is considered backbiting, which is highly improper conduct for any follower of Islam. Thus, it is essential to conceal secrets that protect us and those we know. This wisdom came from the

Prophet Muhammad (Peace Be Upon Him), who once told a companion, 'Whomever sees a defect in a Muslim, and overlooks that defect, is the same as one who saves the life of a young girl who has been buried alive.'

For readers familiar with Saudi Arabia, you know that female babies born in our country once faced the peril of being buried alive. Before the Prophet Muhammad prohibited the heinous practice, there was widespread acceptance that fathers or mothers could end the life of a female infant thus. Even after the Prophet's command to cease the custom, some unfeeling parents and unfaithful Muslims defied his ruling. They accepted the custom of freeing a family of a female child who might possibly bring dishonour upon them. This is a fear that still inhabits numerous parental hearts in my country, where mothers and fathers still endlessly fret that a daughter will witlessly conduct herself in such a manner as to bring them shame.

Truthfully, during the time of ignorance, most families believed that there were no beneficial aspects of birthing a daughter. Thus tiny girls were taken to the soft sands, where the father scooped out a small grave, placing the innocent and trusting infant in the ground to be buried alive, to die a terrifying, gruesome death.

But those fathers, or other male family members, who heeded the wisdom of the Prophet to take action to save the lives of innocent female infants were considered the best of men. And thus believers take the Prophet's words to mean this: that to keep secrets that will expose others to idle gossip or societal reprimand is the same as saving a life.

Although I have been one of the first to acknowledge some of the undesirable facets of my society, I also take pleasure in revealing the advantages of life in Saudi Arabia. One such benefit is related to the Prophet's words against backbiting and telling lies. If one is born a Saudi Arabian, there will be no fear that others will fabricate falsehoods about you or those you love. If such should happen, that person will be harshly punished. Such disapproval, and guaranteed punishment from society, stills the tongues of many gossips.

In my Muslim society, the loss of one's reputation is considered as serious as physical death. This means that there have been several legal cases in Saudi Arabia where those found guilty of slandering others have earned a term in prison, topped by public and painful flogging. Potential backbiters take heed!

As a young girl, I often sat listening at the knee of my beloved mother, a Muslim woman who lived a life of devotion to all things Islamic. I clearly remember the day she made her point about secret-keeping, when she gently grasped my small tongue between her fingers and slowly pulled, telling me, 'Sultana, the Prophet once took hold of his own tongue, saying, "Keep this under control."'

During those long-ago babyish years, I felt a rush of pleasure to be encouraged by my darling mother to keep my tongue quiet from spilling secrets. Those declarations from her own impeccable mouth illuminated the truth that nothing good would come of publicizing mischievous behaviour. Truthfully, though, due to my youthful inability to judge my own actions in a mature manner, I applied her counsel to self only, meaning that while I took care to guard and keep secret my own naughty behaviour, the wicked ways of my nemesis, my brother Ali, were told to all.

As all of you know from the stories of my youth and adult life, there is no denying that I never fully absorbed my mother's heart-felt guidance when it came to my brother.

And for those who will say that I have exposed many secrets about my own society, I will not disagree, but I caution any who criticize by reminding all that my conduct was, and is, discharged by my most cautious handling of the subjects: I have taken the greatest care to shield the real names of those whose actions I expose, although if one's name has already been revealed in the courts of Saudi law, or in Saudi publications, the world already knows their secrets prior to my own disclosure.

Due to the teachings of the Prophet, all the Muslims I have

known take deep satisfaction in keeping secrets. I am no exception to this rule when it comes to secrets I wish to keep. My secretive deeds have been noted by my husband Kareem, who has often remarked that no Muslim he has ever known could personally match my propensity for secret-keeping. When he says these words to me, I smile politely, never admitting to Kareem that I feel little remorse when I keep important secrets from him, the man who is my husband. Then I acknowledge to myself that while I am a loving person who cares for others I am an imperfect human being.

For all who follow the news, you know that these days there is tremendous instability rippling across the Arab world. During such chaotic times, secrets explode in huge numbers, most kept from public scrutiny. In the past year, I have been told secrets kept by the men who are the highest officials in our Saudi government. I have also been privy to secrets withheld by royal cousins and, most importantly to me, I have known of secrets hidden by members of my own family. But most dear to my heart are the secrets told me by abused and unhappy women. These distraught women have unburdened their confidences to me. Many have pleaded for me to reveal their secrets to the world. Their purpose is a fine one: they believe that if attention is drawn to their plight, other women in jeopardy of receiving the same ill treatment might be saved.

Catastrophically, the Middle East is burning, with extreme violence and war raging across Syria, Iraq, Libya and Yemen, ending many lives and threatening others. In times of conflict, women and children bear the brunt of men's violence. Those women who are raped and brutalized carry their own heavy secrets, and are willing to share their darkest moments with other women only. Do not believe they are not courageous, for they are the most heroic of the brave just to continue living. They would shout their outrage from the highest mountain if not for compelling justifications. Most importantly, they are struggling to ensure that their small children will not be left without a mother.

Tragically, in ultra-conservative cultures women must live in apprehension of the men of their own family, as well as in dread of the fierce condemnation of a strict Muslim society that sides against any female who finds herself a victim of a man. Alas, when innocent women are raped in my corner of the world, they will often be held liable for their misfortune. This is true, and I will tell you stories that confirm this outrage.

Although I will reveal important secrets in this book, I will carefully divulge only those that will cause no harm to innocents. I will keep the names of girls and women anonymous, where they have requested this. Should I reveal names or secrets already disclosed by other sources – sources who have labelled the secret-keepers by their true names – I am not the one who has caused the harm.

An important secret I kept was told to me by my husband Kareem, who warned me of the bombings soon to commence against Yemen. I nervously kept the secret, for our entire country's safety was at stake. But now the whole world knows that our new king, Salman, is sending Saudi pilots to war against the Houthi fighters in neighbouring Yemen. Those of you who have read the history of Saudi Arabia will know that it is uncommon for us to go to war against any nation, or any fighting group. While it is true that my warrior grandfather, Abdul Aziz, used combat against various opposing tribes to consolidate the vast lands of our country, once Saudi Arabia was formed as a viable nation, he tossed his sword to the side and employed his wisdom to pursue diplomatic approaches to solve political dilemmas.

But now my country is at physical war against rebels striving to occupy and control Yemen, our southern neighbour, with whom we share affection through our ancient ties and personal relationships. This troubling conflict is intertwined with a verbal dispute with Iran – a country that created no problems for its neighbours during the rule of the Shah but since the 1979 revolution, when the clerics devoured the country and looked beyond Iran's borders to arouse the anger of many, a sense of dread of what would one day come has flickered in all our Saudi hearts.

Now it seems that the day we feared has arrived. With Iran and Saudi Arabia at odds in Yemen, with Iran supporting the Houthi rebels while Saudi Arabia is fighting them, perhaps our two countries will end up physically at war. Should this frightening scenario occur, the entire region will burn, threatening all of the Middle East and beyond. Due to the enormous ramifications of total war in the Middle East, every rational person living should pray that this simmering conflict does not erupt into a fully fledged war – one that will adversely affect our entire world.

For the moment, however, Yemen and the countries of the Gulf Corporation Council (GCC), consisting of Saudi Arabia, Bahrain, Kuwait, Oman, Qatar and the United Arab Emirates, are those most affected by the simmering battle.

While I care about all who suffer, my thoughts dwell on the women and children, for those are the ones most harmed in times of chaos and war. Nothing is more important to me than the right for women to live in dignity and freedom.

The personal problems of Yemen's women and children were always challenging, as females suffered greatly from raging gender discrimination even before the Houthi rebels assumed government control of the county. Now, with full-blown war, women's lives are nearly unendurable.

These shattering times in Yemen have greatly affected my life and the lives of those in my family. Kareem and I have agreed and disagreed, according to the incidents creating alarm throughout the region. I am sorry to say that we have kept secrets from each other, which have created turmoil in our home. But through it all we remain a family, and nothing can change the love we feel for one another.

Chapter One

Yemen Is Burning

THERE ARE TIMES WHEN we are so tightly aligned with a person, or with a country, that we overlook the importance of its presence, sometimes forgetting that it even exists. This happened to me. For the past twenty years, one of the principal countries adjacent to Saudi Arabia faded from my thoughts. The nation of which I am speaking is Yemen, a country with whom Saudi Arabia shares a 1,800-kilometre (1,100-mile) border. The crossings between our two countries remained porous for many years, with Yemenis and Saudis moving at will, but after the upsurge in radical uprisings and violence in the Middle East my country began building a physical wall, known as the Saudi–Yemen Barrier. This structure is ten feet high, and has been filled with concrete and outfitted with electronic surveillance. The wall has been a point of contention between our two governments, with Yemen claiming it is as ruinous for Yemenis as the Israeli West Bank barrier is for Palestinians. This stinging rebuke, comparing Saudi Arabia to Israel, caused the men in my family to stop and start wall-building in bursts of activity. But, with increasing tensions in Yemen, they refuse to allow emotion to temper their plans. The Saudi–Yemen Barrier has now become a reality for our two countries.

With the continuing eruptions of violence in my region of the world, it is heartrending to admit that perhaps every country would benefit from such a barrier.

Now the Saudis are at war, and perhaps this much-criticized barrier will help to save the lives of some people.

For certain, with all that has happened, those reflections on Yemen and its people which had been waning of late have recently been ignited to become a mental obsession.

It was on Jumada t-Tania 1436 (25 March 2015, Gregorian calendar) that I felt my passion first burn again. This was the crucial day that my uncle Salman – the new king of Saudi Arabia after the death of King Abdullah on 2 Rabi'ath-Thani 1456 (23 January 2015) – commanded Saudi fighter pilots to unleash their bombs over the disruptive Houthi rebels in Yemen. From the first moment of Saudi military action, memories collected over a lifetime sparked in my mind, flaring as brightly as those exploding bombs.

While I will not elaborate regarding the lengthy history of the Houthi rebels in Yemen, I will reveal some facts about these insurgents that rarely make the news reports in other countries, for I know that readers of my books frequently correspond with the author and even send second-hand messages to me to say that they enjoy the history behind the events that affect my life and the lives of other women in the area. I respect the reader's preference, for it is good to know the background of important current events.

The Houthi insurgency has been battling the Yemeni regime for a decade. This rebellion, named after Hussein al-Houthi, is causing enormous despair in Yemen and apprehension in Saudi Arabia and other Gulf countries. Hussein al-Houthi's life and history are noteworthy, despite the fact I am not in agreement with his sayings or teachings.

The current troubles did not stem from the usual Sunni/Shia problems, although al-Houthi was a pious Shia religious leader who became well known in Yemen, and in Saudi Arabia, in 2002, when he chanted a sarkha, or the slogan of the Houthi. The cleric's words were his song: 'God is Great. Death to America. Death to Israel. Curse the Jews. Victory to Islam.' While I fully agree that God is great, the remainder of al-Houthi's provocative sarkha is unnecessarily confrontational. This hostile slogan is the symbol of the Houthi – words, fighting words, that they emblazon on their flags. By their slogan alone, one can presume that the rebels are fractious negotiators and thus far no one has been able to convince them to relax their combatant attitude.

Furthermore, Hussein al-Houthi gave a speech in 2002 that divulged his boiling hatred for America. In his defiant speech (which was very popular with the masses), he asked: 'Why did America come to Yemen? Under the pretext of spreading democracy and fighting terror? Did they come to be briefed on the situation in Yemen, and then decide what kinds of projects were needed for Yemen's development? Or did they come to plough the lands? Did they come to make beehives? Did the Americans come to work with us, or did they come for something else? America is the greatest devil and lies behind every evil in the world.'

Although America, like every other country that has ever existed, is not perfect, only the ignorant would say that one country is behind every evil in the world. Such foolish statements create disrespect for the person who utters them. Ask yourself only one question: were there no evils on this earth prior to the formation of America in 1776?

Although Hussein al-Houthi is the face of today's rebels in Yemen, the roots of the Houthi movement snake back through the country's modern history, although there are some minor differences between the current rebellion and the original one, which began in 1986, prompted by the religious sheikh Salah Ahmed Feletah.

Feletah's passion for change attracted Hussein Badr al-Din al-Houthi, a cleric with similar ideological leanings. The small rebellion led to great unease in the region. When a civil war in Yemen broke out in 1994, Feletah and al-Houthi cast their lot

with south Yemen. When north Yemen won the conflict, Feletah
and his party lost their power.

I shall try to make the history of a long revolution short for
my readers. Hussein al-Houthi was the physically attractive and
personally charismatic son of Badr al-Houthi. Hussein became a
man under the tutelage of his father. But unlike his father and
Feletah, he believed that he could bring change if he participated
officially. He ran for office and served in parliament. After a
series of disappointments with a government that was moving
towards the West, Hussein came to the conclusion that he could
not successfully reach his goals as part of the regime, so in 1997
he resigned, establishing a political organization, the Believing
Youth.

The people of Yemen easily followed this handsome man with
a magnetic personality. Instantly popular with the masses, he
gained many followers. Instantly unpopular with the government,
he was proclaimed a dangerous reactionary. His enthusiastic
supporters flooded nearby governorates, calling for the most
conservative interpretation of the Koran. Tensions mounted as
al-Houthi's support surged. Believing Hussein al-Houthi a true
threat to the legitimacy of their authority, full-blown war finally
erupted between the government and al-Houthi in 2004. The war
became so costly that various government leaders met with al-
Houthi, asking him to list his demands so that negotiations might
result in the end of the rebellion. Al-Houthi replied that he had
no demands. He wanted nothing more than for Yemeni youth to
be taught the true principles of Islam, and for Yemeni officials
to move away from cooperation with the West, in particular the
United States.

Neither side could find their way to peace. Physical fighting renewed. That's when government soldiers bombarded al-Houthi's
home with missiles, injuring many family members and killing
him and some of his guards.

As is the case with so many rebellions, when the leader is killed,
the spirit of the rebellion swells. Hussein al-Houthi's brother,

Abdul Malik, assumed leadership of the spreading movement. Fighters following Abdul Malik called themselves Ansar Allah, or Supporters of God.

At this stage, the Yemeni government realized that the Houthi rebellion was bigger than its deceased leader, for it threatened even more unrest without him than it had with him at its helm. The rebellion became so detrimental for the government that the president of Yemen offered a pardon, if only the rebellion would end. Abdul and his fighters declined the peace offering.

Fighting was intermittent over the years. Like a wild fire that would not go out, the fighting crept near our own Saudi border in 2008. By 2009, Saudi armed forces and Houthi fighters battled one another across the border. Alarm bells began to sound in Riyadh.

Now to return to the long-dead Hussein al-Houthi. When Hussein was killed in 2004, the government feared that his grave would become a shrine. And so they refused the pleas of his family to return the body of their martyr for a proper burial. Instead, authorities unceremoniously buried his body in a prison yard. Their act caused such bitterness with the Houthi that finally, in December 2012, eight years later, the Yemeni government allowed the family to claim the body. The government hoped that their benevolent gesture would encourage national harmony.

They were wrong. The burial stimulated the rebellion. And so, from that time until the present, battles have erupted alternately between Houthi fighters, the Yemeni government and various other groups. Then after several years of unflagging fighting, the rebels finally toppled the Yemeni government and assumed control of Yemen.

Most tragically, many innocent Yemenis have been caught in the line of fire, with thousands dying and many more losing their homes and becoming refugees.

With the rebels making threatening moves towards our own country, the men in my family felt that there was no option but to go to war for the purpose of booting the Houthis from power and reinstating a less aggressive leadership.

And so Saudi Arabia has entered a new and most unpleasant period in its history, when we feel we must defend ourselves against a neighbour with whom we have generally enjoyed close ties since ancient times. Our king sought a coalition of other Arab states, and with the United Arab Emirates, Kuwait, Qatar, Egypt, Morocco, Jordan, Bahrain and Sudan the air strikes began. While no thinking person applauds war, I will not deny that the all-Arab military intervention sparked a sense of pride in many Saudis, a people whose government has been accustomed to looking to America and other Western allies for defence. Most Saudis calculate the enormous amounts of money spent on military might for the kingdom and believe that the correct course for our land is to defend ourselves, whenever feasible.

And so the day arrived that Saudi Arabia and other Arab nations joined forces to solve their own problems in the neighbourhood.

*   *   *

Although my privileged husband, Kareem, is privy to many of the secrets known only to the male rulers of my land, from the first day of war he joined me in watching endless television news reports, as well as reading internet articles, about Saudi Arabia's military intervention in Yemen. When Kareem first informed me that the intervention's title was codenamed Operation Decisive Storm, I was stupefied.

'Husband,' I said, 'this is not prudent. Most Saudi citizens will connect our military action with Operation Desert Storm.' This, of course, was the military reaction to Saddam's invasion and occupation of Kuwait. Surely our Saudi military minds could do better than imitate the Americans.

Kareem shrugged without answering, as such a thing had not entered his thoughts.

I exhaled noisily, reminding myself that female minds often see dark corners not visible to male minds. All who live in my country remember that Operation Desert Storm left a sour taste on the tongues of nearly all Saudi Arabians. There was jittery instability in the country for many years after that time of war, for ordinary Saudis found it objectionable that, after many years of spending many millions of Saudi oil money on military hardware, their rulers felt our own Saudi military was incapable of defending our country.

Yet I said nothing more, for I saw Kareem's jaw clench, bracing for my retort. I chose to surprise him with silence. I like reacting in ways unexpected to my husband, as I do not wish to be a woman easily read. Rather than argue, I gave my husband a pleasant smile and asked if he might like a nice coffee with a sweet. Kareem agreed and was pleased to have a piece of Arabic honeyed dessert, which our kitchen staff had made especially for the men in my family, who greatly fancy such things. Still, even as he nibbled the sweet, Kareem failed to conceal the vexed, and slightly confused, look on his face, for rarely do I give in so easily or miss a chance to make my full point.

As time passed, I concluded that men and women will never think alike. As I listened to my husband applaud our military successes, I felt increasingly gloomy, wondering if there was a less physical way than war to solve the problem. I am not ashamed to admit that as Kareem crowed, my tears flowed. I could only think of the Yemeni civilian heads poised unknowing beneath those falling bombs. With more than 200,000 Yemenis displaced, and the number of lives lost climbing higher every day, my unease increased. Once, when Kareem leapt into the air and clapped his hands in glee upon hearing the damage done in Yemen, I looked at my husband in dismay and fled to my bedroom, locking the door and ignoring his appeals to allow him entry.

*   *   *

As I collapsed in abject misery, I asked myself: Sultana, how could you have forgotten our southern neighbour and its inhabitants? Since I was a child, Yemen and its people have been interwoven in nearly every aspect of family life. When I was a small girl, my first knowledge of the country came from my father's Yemeni tea boys. There were always two or three of the boys in our palaces, as in most Saudi royal households.

Accustomed to seeing Saudi men dressed in the white thobe, a shirt-like garment that reaches the ankle, I was astonished by the attention-grabbing attire of those tea boys. On the first occasion I was of an age to become aware of non-family members around me, I stopped and stared at the short futa they wore, a wraparound skirt topped by a dark-coloured jacket. Most appealing to my unaccustomed eyes was the famous jambiyya, a Yemeni curved dagger, tucked comfortably into the skirt waistband. The tea boys topped off their native dress with a meshedda, a shawl that is wrapped around the head or shoulders, while they slouched around with simple sandals on their feet.

While it was their national dress that first attracted my notice, it was their attitudes and faces that drew my attention. For some reason, every Yemeni tea boy I have ever seen has a painfully thin body. Those thin bodies loiter tenaciously, sagging with the tediousness of standing in wait for many hours on end. While the tea boys' postures showed hopelessness, their faces were generally arched in hopeful expectation, anxious that someone in the family would request a cup of sweet tea or bitter coffee. If there is a more wearying duty than anticipating thirst in others, I do not know of that occupation.

But I was only a child at that time, with no concern for the dilemmas plaguing others. I remember spinning around, rushing to tell my sister Sara about the captivating spectacle I had seen. But my noisy enthusiasm drew the attention of my mother. My beautiful mother looked at me in quiet disappointment before gently reminding her youngest child that female children should keep their eyes down, to count steps, anything to cease the temptation to stare at those different from us, and most particularly when observing the opposite sex. I tried to obey my mother's teachings, but I never ceased ogling those waif-like boys in our home, although I trained myself to look around to ensure no one in my family might see my bold stares.

Later I remember political discussions between my father and his brothers regarding a few troubling circumstances with our neighbour Yemen. I recall something of their worries, for they felt the problems stemmed from the fact that our neighbour was very poor while Saudi Arabia was, and is, very rich. Such variance in economic resources means that the government of Yemen and the Yemeni people have looked to Saudi Arabia for generosity since the early days of the oil wealth. Yet the people of Yemen are very proud and will never accept humiliation. Therefore I have never known of a Yemeni who felt reduced in the presence of wealthy Saudis. No nationality of people is as self-respecting as them.

I sighed and slipped into something comfortable, for I had no intention of seeing my husband again that evening. After settling in bed and calling for a glass of cold apple juice, my mind settled on two specific Yemeni women whom I had come to know during my adulthood. Their names are Italia and Fiery.

No two women on earth could be more different from one another. Italia was born into stark poverty, her early life marked with fear and constant need. When she became a great beauty from the age of ten years, she suffered abuse due to the gift that had freed her from poverty.

Fiery, however, was born into completely different circumstances, hers being a respected, middle-class family; her father was a scholar seen as a wise and fair man to those who knew him. Her father's position in life spilled deference over to his two sons and three daughters. Fiery was always ordinary in appearance, but with a colourful personality; those who know her well often say that the physically plain Fiery has achieved a certain female splendour reserved for those of magnificent beauty in my country, where what is on the outside is what defines women, not intelligence or personality. Despite her lack of beauty, Fiery was esteemed as much as a woman could, and can, be in Yemen, a country that has fallen below Saudi Arabia in terms of its treatment of women, in 2006 being named the worst country in the world to be a woman by the World Economic Forum (WEF).

While I am pleased that Saudi Arabia and other neighbouring Gulf countries have moved up on this respected listing, I am not so happy that women in Yemen cannot climb the ladder of freedom with other Arab women to enjoy more independence and greater prosperity.

I came to learn much about Yemen and the women who live there by getting to know beautiful Italia and intelligent Fiery. Their lives are meshed fully with the good, and the bad, of our neighbour.

I believe that there is no truer way to discover the most significant aspects of a country and its people than through the private lives of the native women.

Chapter Two

The Beauty from Yemen

FOR MY ENTIRE LIFE, I have measured female beauty against that of my older sister, Sara. So physically magnificent is she that the first time Kareem's brother, Assad, accidentally saw Sara in the women's garden of my father's palace, he was, temporarily, speechless! For those who have read the first book of my life, you will know the full details of Assad and Sara's courtship and marriage; it has been a wonderful love story from the first day until now, and promises to last for their lifetimes.

Assad's reaction was no surprise to anyone in our family, for all so fortunate to see Sara's unveiled face never fail to declare that nowhere have they ever seen a more beautiful woman.

It is especially agreeable that my sister Sara's beauty is not limited to its physical form. Sara's heart and mind are as exquisite as her physical self.

Assad, her husband of many years now, frequently emphasizes that there is perfection in all aspects of his wife. Truthfully, Assad would become wearying with his repeated exclamations if all did not love Sara completely. We are in agreement with Assad that our precious Sara is a perfect woman in every way.

But when I first saw Italia, a woman from Yemen so striking

that I openly stared, I was nearly as stunned as Assad had been upon viewing Sara. My own eyes beheld a great beauty – and while Italia's physical splendour did not surpass Sara's, it at least equalled it.

The occasion I first met Italia was some time ago at the palace of Ameera, a royal cousin who is the daughter of my father's youngest sister. Ameera was hosting an intimate party of eight royal female cousins to specifically confer about several scandals that had erupted in our royal midst.

While the Al Sa'ud men are the public face of the royals, the women often quietly solve problems from within our family circle so that they do not reach the world at large. Sometimes there are royal princesses who travel abroad and behave badly, their conduct known only to the women of our family. When such things happen, a group of older princesses endeavours to counsel the young women, discouraging them from misbehaving in future and thus avoiding the severe punishment meted out by the men of the family.

With a large royal family whose numbers are expanding by the week, there are many such human complications. There are times when our humiliations are intentionally leaked to the Western press. For example, many readers will recall the episode when one of my cousins was arrested in Europe for physically assaulting one of her maids. We could do nothing to solve that specific problem, for her vicious conduct was splashed across numerous foreign newspapers, embarrassing those in our family who treat our domestic help properly.

And so some of we more modern royal princesses use our energy to solve tribulations in our innermost circle. But the purpose for the gathering at Ameera's home was more political than usual, so I was surprised to see the elegant stranger sitting quietly, turning the pages of a large, illustrated book about the most picturesque gardens in the world.

I instantly knew that the beauty was not a Saudi woman, for there are identifiable indications of our nationality. I cannot describe them precisely, but as a Saudi woman I am rarely mistaken when presuming whether an Arab woman is a Saudi or not. While I could not guess the woman's exact nationality, I knew she was not 'one of us'.

Then our hostess introduced her, gently coaxing our unknown visitor to her feet. 'Dear cousins,' Ameera said, 'Italia is a special guest in my home. I wanted to present her to you before she retires, as she is quite exhausted from a tiring journey.'

Italia smiled with a distinctive sweetness, nodded, then spoke gracefully in her soft voice, revealing a conspicuous Yemeni accent. I was more than surprised. Despite Italia being the most physically striking woman at the gathering, it was rare for women from Yemen to be part of our social gatherings. There had been occasional instances when the wife, daughter or sister of the ruler of Yemen might visit Saudi female royals while her husband, father or brother conferred with the Saudi king or high-ranking Saudi government ministers, but I could count those events on the fingers of one hand. But perhaps this was the case with Italia, I thought to myself, for at that particular time in our history I had little knowledge of the sisters and daughters of the rulers of our neighbouring country. Nonetheless I felt strangely drawn to Italia. As I smiled at the woman, I made a mental note to ask Ameera later to share something of what she knew about her unconventional guest.

Our family gathering ended once we made plans on how to solve a few important problems and I sat quietly, intentionally lingering as my cousins exited the palace. Once alone with Ameera, I encouraged her to share details of Italia.

'Ameera, dear, I am intrigued by your guest, Italia. Can you tell me something about her?'

For some reason, Ameera was shy to provide personal particulars about the young Yemeni, saying that her brother, who was considering marriage to the woman, would be annoyed. But she did accept an invitation to bring Italia to my palace the following day, so that we might have a private lunch. 'Italia is free to tell you whatever she likes, but I must keep private what I have been told.'

Ameera's words spiked my curiosity, but I did not push my cousin to break her brother's confidences. As I was saying my farewell, Ameera did reveal something of what I had already guessed. 'But I will tell you that Italia is from Yemen.'

'That I assumed from her speech,' I acknowledged.

Not least, Italia's name intrigued me. Traditionally, Arabic names are mostly given to offspring, with Mohammed and Ali being very popular for male children, yet Yemeni parents sometimes name their children after an event, a country, a dream or even a memory. Never have I heard more peculiar names than those bestowed on Yemeni children. I was keen to discover where Italia's unusual name originated, guessing that the story was bound to be fascinating. But just as I was posing my question, Ameera was interrupted by two of her three daughters, who had finished their school studies and wished to speak with their mother. The young princesses were obviously not privy to Italia's personal story, for uneasiness streaked Ameera's face. She hastily redirected our conversation, enquiring about the health of my father, for he had been unwell for the past few weeks.

My father was still relatively young at that time, but he had suffered what was feared to be a stroke. Strokes are common with the men in our Al Sa'ud family, so there was reason for worry.

'He has not left his bed for many days, and I admit I am nervous,' I acknowledged with a resigned shrug, for my father's physicians would never confer with me, the daughter from whom he had been estranged for so many years.

However, Sara and several of my other sisters were at his palace for a visit at that very hour. Suddenly recalling that I had asked Sara to stop by my palace on her way home so we might discuss my father's deteriorating condition, I quickly gathered my abaya, veil and handbag, but not before reminding Ameera that I would be expecting her and Italia at my palace the following day.

I departed Ameera's home with a giddy sense of anticipation, feeling a very strong magnet pulling me into Italia's life. I did not fight the urge to better know this appealing Yemeni woman. How could I know that many lives in my family would be altered by our meeting?

*　　*　　*

When I arrived at my Riyadh palace, I was frustrated to learn that Sara had come and gone. I would have to wait until the following morning to learn of my father's health. I had cheerfully antici-pated Sara's visit, as she is the closest of my sisters, and has been my most trusted confidante since childhood. Kareem was unavail-able for a late-night visit, as he was in the company of several high-ranking prince cousins. My children were not yet married but all were in Europe on a skiing holiday with one of my older sisters and her family.

Our huge home was bustling with the activities of our palace staff, as there is someone in attendance twenty-four hours a day, but I was the only member of my family present. I remember feel-ing quite lonely, as I wished to see my family, but that was not to be. I asked for a cup of tea and a basket of sweets from one of the nicest and most bashful of our Indonesian servants.

After my tea and sweets arrived, I sat alone in the sitting room, my thoughts drifting to the one person I have missed for my entire adult life. That person is my mother. I was only a young girl when Mother died and I had missed her every day since the moment she breathed her last. I closed my eyes, daydreaming, visualizing how the evening would be so special if only Mother could be sitting with me, sipping tea, laughing lowly, discussing my children, giving advice about my marriage and guiding me through my young adulthood.

However blessed I am, my life would have been much sweeter with my mother by my side.

Although she would have been considered elderly in my Arab society, at that time, in fact, she would have only been sixty-two years old. Though lost in a reverie, thinking of Mother and how much I needed her, and how she would have loved my children, I forced my thoughts to return to the present, to consider my father's health crisis and wonder if he might die long before expected.

I did not want my father to die.

I had not acknowledged my feelings to anyone, but I had become amenable to an improved relationship with a man I had once feared, and disliked. The years had passed and, despite the fact he was not yet old, I had noticed a surprising shuffle when I had last seen him, a reminder that he was many years my senior, for my father was in his fortieth year when I was born. Sara had recently confided that his hearing had diminished. His ageing touched my heart, increasing my affection for the man who had given me life.

I sighed as I recalled the unpleasant stages of our relationship.

I hated my father when I was a child, for I truly felt that he disliked me. My independent character does not allow me to love someone who does not love me. As an adult, I became accustomed to his disregard and convinced myself that I was indifferent. But as he aged, I matured, and I wished for a better relationship, despite the fact my father did not appear particularly keen to become the father for whom I had always longed, a father whose eyes would light with pleasure at the sight of his youngest child by my mother. With news of a possible stroke, however minor, I knew that the time was passing and the chance of a better relationship was slipping from my grasp.

'It is impossible to befriend a corpse, Sultana,' I reminded myself.

Little did I know that my father was experiencing similar feelings at that time. How could I know that one day our relationship would rekindle when he bequeathed a picture of my mother as a gift to his youngest child by his first wife. But that memorable occasion was some years away, so I retired to bed feeling lonely, unloved and quite miserable.

I was awakened late the following morning by the persistent ringing of my private telephone, which is easily reached from my bed. I was not quite awake, but I was pleased to hear Sara's voice, and listened carefully when she told me that our father had not suffered a stroke but instead had been ill with food poisoning from a fish dinner. The food poisoning had created pains in the top of his head that alarmed Father's physician, who chose to explore all serious possibilities.

My expressed relief surprised Sara, but she did not enquire further when I changed the focus to tell her about the beautiful Yemeni woman named Italia. I hoped that Sara might join us for lunch, but my sister declined, saying she had some pressing work to do with a committee of royal women who were working in private to write a convincing presentation to offer to several of our younger male cousins who were in line for powerful positions in government. These modern-thinking male cousins were in agreement with their female cousins, who wanted to make it illegal for any Saudi Arabian girl under the age of eighteen to marry.

I believe it is inexcusable that there is no legal age limit set for girls to marry in Saudi Arabia. Although most families do not push their girls to marry before they become sixteen, should a father decide to accept a proposal for his eight-year-old daughter no one in the government, or in our society, will attempt to block the marriage. Such decisions, regardless of how detrimental they might be to a child, are considered private matters and are under the full control of the child's father or legal guardian.

Such marriages have caused unending anguish and life-threatening health emergencies. Many young girls who know nothing of adult life and the sexual relationships between men and women are terrified and brutalized when forced to have sex with adult men. Tragically, many give birth long before their young bodies are properly matured, creating lifelong health complications.

Sara had a special reason for waging war against child marriages. Prior to becoming Assad's wife, the teenage Sara had been compelled by our father to marry a much older man; as a consequence of sexual assaults upon her youthful body, she had experienced grave mental and physical problems. Due to her personal experience, Sara and her husband Assad had made it their life's work to push for a law to protect young girls from early marriage.

Theirs is a daunting task since there are many powerful men in Saudi Arabia working against such a law, saying it is the right of a Muslim man to marry a child.

There is no more important work being done in my country.

I wished Sara success before ending our call and preparing for my guests. Several minutes prior to the time I expected Ameera and Italia, I received a second telephone call, this time from my cousin Ameera, who called to say she'd had a change of plan, as her seventeen-year-old daughter was hysterical after being told by her father that she was too young to attend school in Paris the following year. I could hear the young princess screeching in the background, along with crashing and banging that I assumed was the result of a full-blown teenage tantrum. Ameera lowered her voice and confided, 'You know how we have spoiled these girls. All three of my daughters are accustomed to having all wishes granted.'

I replied with true empathy, 'Yes, I understand.'

Most Saudi royal children are shamefully overindulged, either from the love of wealthy parents who want their children to have everything they desire, or from parental laziness. I have discovered that it is much easier to be a lax parent than a vigilant one, to give in to my children's requests rather than explain the reasons they cannot and will not be allowed certain privileges. I suffered a fleeting image of a similar noisy performance thrown by my own two daughters. At such times only their father could put an end to their childish commotions. Thankfully, my son Abdullah had never once given his parents heartache with such childlike feats.

I felt disappointment mounting that the luncheon I had planned was not to be, but then Ameera added some good news: 'If you are fine with Italia coming alone, she is free and quite pleased to accept your invitation.'

Since meeting and talking with Italia was the purpose of the luncheon, I felt cheered. 'Yes, please send Italia over. I will be waiting.'

'She is extremely shy, though, Sultana,' Ameera confided.

From Italia's reticent demeanour the previous day, I believed my cousin's words. But Italia's reserved appearance had been misleading, as I was soon to discover.

When Italia disclosed her true motive for travelling to Saudi Arabia to meet with Saudi royals, I realized that the way she presented herself was very clever and she was destined to achieve her objective.

* * *

Italia's arrival was announced by our doorman, an Egyptian man named Mahmoud whom Kareem had recently met, liked and promptly lured away from one of the finest hotels in Cairo. We had never before had a doorman, but Kareem believed that in addition to our staff of guards we needed a physically strong man whose only task was to watch our doorway and be accessible to protect our family. I was unconvinced at first but was soon pleased with the situation, for Mahmoud was a jolly man who could also be bold and very tough when necessary. I walked briskly from the sitting room to the entrance to our palace, and thought little of it when the unceasingly cheery Mahmoud turned to me with eyes twinkling with amusement when opening wide the heavy metal door so that Italia might make her entrance into our home.

I quickly understood the reason for Mahmoud's merriment. I inhaled sharply when Italia stepped into the vast entrance hall; smiling broadly and dressed in a designer gown that was more suitable for the most exclusive royal wedding than a lunchtime visit, she looked elegant and poised. Her long hair was twisted into an intricate braid, with what appeared to be diamonds looped delicately through her dark tresses. She appeared even more beautiful than the day before, even though her elaborate attire was shockingly inappropriate. She failed to notice that I was wearing a simply designed yellow silk dress suitable for an ordinary luncheon.

The previous day the young woman had looked every inch the educated daughter of a powerful Yemeni family. But her present ensemble put my previous opinion in doubt. She was garbed in the most costly and luxurious clothing available, in a manner most people routinely associate with the Saudi royals – though this is not the case.

Her guileless appearance brought my curiosity to the surface.

I realized that Italia's former timid conduct had vanished, along with her serene and elegant manner, the moment she gushed a joyful greeting and pulled me eagerly to her bosom to deliver several enthusiastic kisses on my cheeks.

I patted her shoulder with my hand, pulling away and inviting her to follow me into the small sitting and dining area that provides a lovely view to our glorious Olympic-size pool, decorated with five large cascading fountains. Kareem had built this for our son, Abdullah, who is an accomplished swimmer.

While sampling our lunch of fresh fruit and small tea sandwiches, I focused my attention on my guest. 'Italia, please tell me about yourself.'

'No, Princess, please do tell me about yourself,' Italia said with a blinding smile, for her teeth were perfectly aligned and brilliantly white, causing me to wonder if she had undergone the kind of dental treatments common to Hollywood actresses who intentionally whiten their teeth.

I'm discomfited to admit that I sat speechless for a long moment, openly staring at Italia, for rarely does one see a perfect physical human specimen. Italia's thick black hair shone and framed her flawlessly formed oval-shaped face. Sparkling amber eyes were set far apart, fringed by generous, dramatic brows. Her enviable nose could have been sculpted by Michelangelo, the incomparable

Italian sculptor and painter who lived during the Renaissance, and who changed the world for all time with his immense genius for creating beauty. Italia's lips were full, and her chin was feminine but strong. The tawny skin on her face and neck was soft and smooth like cream.

Now that I had the opportunity to scrutinize her features more closely, I reluctantly conceded that Italia was even more beautiful than Sara.

Filling the silence, Italia smiled once again. 'I am very fascinated by your life, Princess.' She glanced at our pool and gestured towards some expensive furnishings in her sight, revealing that her interest was most likely related to our wealth and what our abundance provided.

'There is little to tell, Italia,' I answered, for I had no desire to go into detail about my life. 'I will tell you my story in brief. I was born into the royal family and have many sisters and one brother. I married a royal cousin. I have three children. I am involved in pushing for reform for women and girls. This,' I said with a light shrug, 'is my life.'

'What a marvellous life,' Italia said flippantly. 'You must be envied by everyone you meet.'

'I hope not,' I declared, with a sense of dismay that my visitor might be feeling envious of my lavish home.

Most Arabs do not seek envy out of fear that it will trigger the evil eye, bringing misfortune on one's head. Few people in the Western world realize that a large number of Arab women believe in the evil eye. Remember, from the time we are young children we are fed the theory that such a force exists.

Wishing to change the subject, and thinking to calm her excited nature, I took Italia's hand in my own and was not surprised to feel smooth skin and see long willowy fingers. Was it possible that this woman did not have one physical flaw? Even Sara has an imperfection. My sister's big toes are inconsistent, with one toe large and unattractive and the other strangely small and misshapen. Our mother once told Sara that one of Father's prize horses had trampled on the smaller toe when Sara was a child. Whatever the reason for the disfigurement, Sara rarely wore sandals due to the conspicuous unsightliness of her disproportionate toe.

Unless there were hidden physical flaws under Italia's clothing, everything of her physical self would spark admiration.

'Italia, you have prompted a great curiosity in me. Please do tell me everything of your life.'

Italia's expression darkened, but only for a moment. 'Everything, mistress? Are you sure?' she asked.

'I want you to tell me all that does not make you feel uncomfortable, Italia.' I slowly smiled. 'Let me tell you this. I am a woman with a passion to seek the truth of women's lives, whether the truth reveals sorrows or joys. It is my life's work to explore, then study, and finally to analyse the lives of women from wherever I find them. I accumulate information so that I can speak knowingly of every country and culture, and to know precisely how much these countries value their women. Only then can I work with accurate knowledge to help achieve equality for every woman. While I am familiar with Yemen, and with the Yemeni people, I have lost touch since adulthood. But now I am striving to discover the changes that have come to your country, in particular the changes that affect its women.'

My words obviously struck an emotional chord, for Italia's eyes brightened, threatening to tear. I soothed her, 'But, Italia, tell me nothing that will create an unpleasant feeling in your heart.'

Italia stifled her tears and began to talk, choking with emotion, telling me, 'I feel very badly, Princess. I can see that you are a genuine person, unlike many in your Saudi royal family.'

She stared at me for a long time, until I nodded my head and said, 'Go on,' choosing not to take offence at her disagreeable view regarding other members of the Al Sa'ud family, for even I have critical opinions concerning certain relatives.

'Princess Ameera has been so kind to me. Now you are generous to invite me to your home and to have such an interest in me, for Princess Ameera told me that you might ask many questions. I must tell you the truth.' Her tawny skin blushed a deep red, then she confessed, 'I am a pretender, mistress.'

Never had I expected her words and it took me a moment to respond. 'How are you a pretender, Italia? Are you not Yemeni, as you claim?'

'Oh yes, yes! I am pure Yemeni,' Italia said with a touch of pride. 'I am not a muwallad. There is no foreign blood in our family.'

The term muwallad means 'an Arab who is not purely an Arab'. The expression is often used in Yemen to humiliate someone, to remind that person that he or she is not an authentic Yemeni, something shameful in that culture.

Although the people of Yemen are very welcoming to visitors, there is a noticeable discrimination whenever Yemeni men marry women from other cultures, and specifically if the bride is from Africa. Yemenis tend to express admiration for light-skinned Yemenis.

As a woman with olive skin, married to a man with the same, together creating two beautiful daughters and a handsome son, all with olive complexions, I am baffled by the Yemeni idea that lighter is better. Although many people in our world prize very white skin, I can truthfully say that some of the most beautiful women, and handsomest men, that I have personally seen have exquisite olive skin.

I have travelled to many countries and have known human beings of every shade, and I know that there is beauty in every colour.

Italia continued, 'Here is the issue. While I am truthful when I say that I am a Yemeni, I am pretending to be someone I am not. Honestly, Princess, for many years now I have been imitating a wealthy woman I once met. I assumed her personality, which is several sizes too large for me, for she was real and I am not. Since I was a young woman, there have been important reasons for me to convince others that I am of a wealthy family. I do not have to say that I am wealthy, and those words do not form on my tongue. I act it. I act wealthy. I had very little education as a child, but as an adult I have self-educated by reading newspapers, magazines and books belonging to others. To give my character authenticity, I have accumulated lovely clothes and a few good jewels from previous marriages. It is easy enough to convince people who do not know my background that I am an influential woman with great wealth. So, when people assume this persona is true, I go along and never deny. No one ever questions me as to my wealth, but I intentionally make them feel my wealth.'

Italia's head bent low, nearly to her chest, and her voice lowered. 'Princess, I cannot look into your eyes when I tell you my truth.' Her previously strong voice had become a light whisper. 'Princess, I was born a deprived child of an impoverished Yemeni farming family.'

She hesitated, raising her eyes to peek at my face, obviously assuming that I would shout for Mahmoud to come inside and escort such an unimportant woman of modest means from my palace.

Italia did not know me well or she would have known that I do not judge anyone by the size of their bank account or the circumstances of their birth.

I smiled.

She gasped in surprise at my reaction.

'Italia, you are right about one thing. I assumed by your wardrobe and by your manner that you came from wealth.' I nodded knowingly, speaking from my heart. 'Dear Italia, here is a good lesson for you. Every human being who has ever lived, and who will ever be born, is born in circumstances determined by God. No human being has ever had the opportunity to select a family, country or culture.'

I chuckled. 'God's decision to place me in my mother's womb so that I might be born a wealthy Saudi princess was out of my control. I could have easily been born destitute, weak and ugly in a small village in a poor land.' I gestured with my hand at our opulent surroundings. 'All of this was given to me.

THE BEAUTY FROM YEMEN

Did I create the oil that finances the lavish palaces, luxurious buildings and infrastructure of Saudi Arabia? No. I have contributed nothing to make Saudi Arabia what it is today. My wealth is unearned, so I cannot take credit for a single Saudi riyal issued or spent in this country. But I do help many young girls by spending my wealth to guarantee their education and the possibilities for a good life.' I stroked the back of her hand. 'Just as God gave you great physical beauty, he gave me great wealth. We are to thank God, and to accept everyone we meet as an equal in life.'

For a few moments, Italia did not speak, although she appeared to be absorbing my words. Then, unexpectedly, a burst of words broke through. Emotional declarations suddenly flowed from Italia, a woman finally free from fear of condemnation for the circumstances of her birth.

I was soon to realize that her journey had been far more fascinating, and challenging, than that of the wife, daughter or sister of an influential man. A number of people whom I admire greatly have taught me that being born poor often takes a person on a stimulating journey of discovery, for destitution frequently creates great energy – the kind of energy required to pull oneself out of the deep dark sea of poverty.

'Let me tell you everything, Princess,' Italia said.

'Yes, I have all afternoon to be with you and to hear your story,' I replied, then suggested, 'Let's move from the table and sit in an easy chair.'

Italia followed me to relax in a more comfortable seating arrangement, smiling easily for the first time. I believed that she felt relief to be hurling aside a burden she had carried for so long. As soon as we settled comfortably, she began her story.

'Princess, my unusual story begins with my name. Italia was suggested by Mother's favourite brother. That brother had had the pleasure of travelling to Europe with an English capitalist who had spent time in Yemen, where he had become affiliated with a prominent Yemeni entrepreneur. The Englishman became rich after connecting a local Yemeni manufacturer with vital English business contacts.

'My uncle began his employment as a tea boy, but his clever nature was soon evident and he rose in rank, assuming a middle-tiered position in the Yemeni company managed by the English-man. This gentleman grew to depend upon his Yemeni sidekick, and when he, the Englishman, chose to return to Europe, specific-ally to purchase a home in Liguria, Italy, my uncle was surprised with an invitation to visit Europe as well.'

I knew something about Liguria, for Kareem and I had travelled to that area with Sara and Assad a few years previously. We had stayed in the famous resort town of Portofino and had explored the entire region. That area of Italy is famous for its beauty – even in one of Europe's most beautiful countries. Incomparable Tuscany is part of the vicinity, as well as Genoa, the home town of the famous seagoing explorer Christopher Columbus.

'As you know,' Italia continued, 'in those long-ago days, ob-taining a tourist visa to Europe or to America was not so difficult a task as it is in today's fearful world.'

'That is true,' I replied.

'Anyhow, my uncle became so besotted with the area, and with Italy, that he made use of his resourceful disposition to acquire an Italian sponsor so that he might remain in the Tuscany region. He was a man who could get along with anyone, and so he lived and prospered in Italy for more than twenty years. After his father died of old age, he returned to Yemen. He cared for his mother, as he was the only remaining son alive, and took charge of the family.

'His return coincided with my birth. My mother, who had been a baby when her older brother left for Italy, was astonished that my uncle took such a keen interest in her first child, particularly since I was a girl. There was another reason, as well.

'Prior to my birth her brother could speak of little other than the great beauty he had encountered in Italy, the astonishing land-scape of rolling hills; he talked, too, of the native people, who seemed to be so happy in this sunny land. Indeed, he praised Italy and Italians so much that many villagers began to avoid him; they grew tired of hearing about a paradise on earth that they knew they would never see or experience for themselves.

'But after I was born, my uncle became obsessed with the name to be given to my mother's first child. Now that I think of it, my uncle was a man who was easily obsessed, first with Italy, and then with me.

'Finally, he persuaded his brother-in-law, my father, to name his newborn daughter Italia, after the country of Italy. My uncle assured my parents that if they bestowed the name Italia on their daughter, I would personally benefit from the splendour that was Italy. With such a name, he claimed, the girl was certain to be a great beauty who might attract the attention of a wealthy land-owning Yemeni, who would take me as a wife.

'My parents assumed that my uncle knew everything. They were believers in his power only because he had knowledge from years of travel and a nice amount of money he had saved from his years working abroad. After arriving in Yemen, he had built his mother a new home and had taken her to Saudi Arabia to be treated for cancer at a large hospital. She was cured, in fact. There was a lot of respect for such a generous man, with enough money in his pocket to help out his family and friends. My parents were not particularly keen on the odd name Italia, but they were superstitious and very afraid that if they did not listen to my uncle's advice I might grow up ugly.'

Italia laughed loudly. 'Despite the name, the great irony is that I was ugly!'

'You were what?'

'Ugly. I was ugly.'

'Do not tell me that lie!' I exclaimed.

'It is true. I was an ugly baby and an ugly child. But because they respected my uncle, I was crowned with the name Italia. My poor uneducated parents anticipated that I would change from a red-faced, unattractive baby into an astounding beauty.' Italia raised her dramatic brows high. 'That did not happen. I was ugly at birth and remained ugly for many years.'

'I really do not believe that you could ever be called ugly, Italia!' I said with a chuckle.

Italia's voice was suddenly a falsetto. 'Yes, I was. Ugly.' She grimaced and began gesturing with her hand, pointing to her face. 'In my early years, I was small and bony, with outsized teeth, a nose too large for my skinny face and feet so big that even my uncle said that they looked exactly like the miniature skis he had seen in Italy – the Italians would secure pieces of wood to their feet before rocketing down the snow-covered mountains.

'Princess, to this day, when I look at my feet I see skis!'

We both laughed loudly because it is easy to laugh at one's feet when they are perfect, as were Italia's.

'My poor mother. My poor father. They were devastated by the catastrophe of my ugliness. They knew that I would never fetch even a small dowry. In fact, they reconciled themselves to the possibility that I would die a spinster, supported by my parents until they died of old age.

'Poor darlings. Their dreams of future wealth faded into the crush of daily anxieties over money. The story went around the village that my uncle had promised my parents that I would be a great beauty. Of course, with my ugliness in plain sight, people were merciless. Even the children in the village cruelly labelled me a little monkey. Most appallingly for me, one of the old men in the village verified their taunts, saying that indeed I was nearly indistinguishable from some small brown monkeys he had seen swinging in a forested area of Yemen. In fact, he said with certainty, he had found the monkeys to be much cuter than the skinny girl with the big nose.'

I felt my heart plunge in grief for the childhood Italia had known. 'Did your parents not protect you from this cruelty, Italia?'

'No. They had four other children. My four growing brothers were always hungry, and it took all my parents' hard work and energy to feed the family. They told me to hide in the house to escape the children's insults.' Italia's memory drew tears. 'Believe me, my parents cared about their only daughter, but I was not developing into the beauty who would beguile a moneyed husband. My uncle had planted that seed in their minds as surely as my father planted the terraced crops.'

With a catch in her voice, Italia continued, 'For most of my childhood, I was so very miserable. But there were a few times that I felt greatly loved. Our family was so poor that meat was served rarely, those times being two specific occasions, the festivals of Eid al-Fitr and Eid al-Adha. Those were happy festivals, as we remembered God and showed our gratitude to Him. The only time I felt special was during the festivals. This was linked to my father. Although after the first few years of my life my father paid little heed to me, during feast times he always singled out his only daughter. He made a big show of slipping me the fatty tail of the slaughtered sheep, although my four eager brothers desired that tail. The joy of that one moment fed my sagging confidence for the entire year, until the occasion of the next festival, when once again my brothers would stare at me in puzzlement – my parents had many times claimed that I was a great disappointment to the family, as I was far from the great beauty they had expected.

'For sure, the old dreams popped into their minds on occasion, for I did have a few good qualities. When I became an adult, my mother brought up an old memory, telling me that even when I had had that ugly look, my almond-shaped eyes flashed like liquid chocolate and my skin was so smooth that some of the older women in the village wanted to stroke their palms against my skin.'

Poor Italia sighed. 'Princess, if anyone else spoke of small signs of potential beauty, the vision of a smitten suitor glimmered like gold for my parents. But for years nothing came of the fantasies they so eagerly pictured in their minds.

'As their dreams faded, my parents lost their glorification of me, frequently expressing their opinion that I was the biggest disappointment of their marriage. I was the unattractive child who was supposed to have been such a beauty that I could have changed all their lives, my promised beauty whisking them from a life of backbreaking work on those steep terraced gardens so common in Yemen to wealth so great they would sleep on silk sheets and eat at tables laden with delicacies.

'I was so miserable. I cried so loudly that neighbours sometimes complained, shouting at my mother that she should have buried me in the sands when I was born.'

'Oh, Italia. I am so sorry. And I can imagine how disagreeable it must have been to lose the coveted position of the child christened with hope.'

At this point, I asked myself: how many bones of unwanted baby girls are buried in the sands of Arabia? I shuddered with the knowledge that it would be impossible to put a number on the crime.

Italia brought me out of my contemplations. 'Yes, and you know how it is in Yemen, Princess, more than in most countries, where the birth of a girl is considered a stroke of bad luck.'

'When did the little ugly monkey turn into a beautiful girl, Italia?' I asked, knowing that this had happened because I had the proof sitting before my eyes.

'Oh, there was a big miracle, Princess. It happened when I was about to enter the eleventh year of my life.'

The breath left my body, for I had always been enthralled by surprising stories that could only be explained as miracles. 'Oh? A miracle? Tell me everything.'

'I don't remember the exact details because there were no mirrors in our home. The only time I had ever seen my ugly face was when Mother took me to the small stream to fill the water jugs and once I looked in the small pool and saw something fearful looking up at me! I thought there was an evil jinn in the water. I started to scream and shake, hiding my face in my mother's dress. Then I really cried when my mother told me not to worry, that the ugly jinn I thought I had seen was not a jinn at all but was me! I was really ugly, much uglier than I had ever imagined, even when people were telling me I looked like a monkey!'

'Oh, Italia.'

'Do not worry, Princess. My mother soon returned to that same pool to show me a beautiful image.'

'Tell me. Joyful endings make me the happiest,' I quipped.

'The miracle was rather rapid, or that is what I was told. Yet neither my parents nor I noticed anything different, at least not at first. I supposed that my parents looked "through me" rather than "at me". As for my brothers, well, they never noticed anything about me, whether good or bad. Then one week my uncle invited us for a meal, saying that he had bought some plump chickens at the market and we would have delicious meat for our meal. We were all very excited about eating a plump chicken because the only chickens we had knowledge of were the village chickens. Every one of those chickens was pitifully skinny. They had little to eat, living off a few weeds and dirt; in fact, our village chickens tasted like mud,' she giggled.

Again I thanked God that I had been blessed with wealth; I was never concerned with the quantity or quality of the food put on my table because it was always the best and I could eat to my content. Kareem has always said that money has no importance unless there is none.

'Also, I wanted to look as nice as an ugly girl could look for my uncle, who had so kind-heartedly predicted that I would be beautiful. So I worked for hours to comb out the tangles in my thick and curly hair, which by this time was so long it reached my knees. I had a full bath for the first time in my young life, scrubbing my face until it glowed. I asked my mother if she might put some kohl on my eyelids, which she did. I then pleaded to wear her only real gold earrings, which were large gold circles. She indulged me, letting me wear the earrings from the Riyadh gold souk, which had been purchased by my uncle when he had travelled to Riyadh with his mother.

'So with the kohl-coloured eyelids, and with my long curly hair and dangling earrings swinging as I walked, I felt confident for the first time in my young life. I was also thrilled by the thought of eating a juicy, fat chicken. I was so happy that I laughed as I followed behind my parents, skipping gaily all the way to my uncle's home. Still my parents detected nothing physically different about me, possibly because they were so distracted by the prospect of the delicious chicken feast that awaited them!

'But my uncle noticed me, and when he greeted the family he gulped and said, "Italia? Is that you, Italia?"

'I stood in silence as my mother teased her brother, something unusual for her to do, but I supposed that she was in a good mood, thinking about that delicious chicken waiting to be placed on her plate. "Who would it be if not Italia, brother? A good little jinn who came to take Italia's place? Or perhaps a beautiful jinn, my brother?" Both my parents laughed, poking a little fun at my uncle's long-ago prediction.'

I smiled, imagining Italia's mother at that instant, enjoying a moment of jest. Impoverished women in Yemen rarely have reason to joke about anything. Yet I knew that Italia's mother was on firm ground with her words, according to the teachings of the Prophet Muhammad. Jinns are mentioned fairly often in the Koran. While these creatures are most often described as being made of smoke or fire, jinns can assume a physical body and communicate with people. They can be good, or bad, but are usually bad. Most Arab parents characterize jinns as frightening beings to terrify their children into good conduct, much in the same manner I have overheard parents in other cultures trying to frighten their children with warnings of a bogeyman.

Italia continued with her captivating tale. 'I do remember that my uncle did not laugh. He did not even smile. I was afraid that my mother had gone too far with her teasing. Then my uncle brushed past my parents and knelt down before me, staring into my face before saying in his quiet voice, "My sister, tell me, what happened to that big nose? And look at her huge eyes. They are beautiful! Those unattractive baby teeth are gone, too!" Never had I seen my uncle so excited, other than when he was sharing his tales of Italy.

'That's when I was rushed by my parents, who stooped beside my uncle. They both stared at me as though they had never seen their only daughter before.

'"Look, sister, your daughter's legs are no longer scrawny like those chickens in the village." Then he laughed happily, scaring me into pulling away from him. That's when he leapt to his feet and looked to the heavens, crying out, "Thank you, Allah, for this miracle. She is a beauty!"

'I remember little more of that evening for I became embarrassed by the favourable attention. I was accustomed to ridicule, never to praise. I did not like it so much, to tell you the truth, although my life changed radically and in many ways for the better from that moment on.

'The following morning the visitors to our home began, all wanting to verify what they had heard through the rapidly moving village gossip. Everyone said that they must see me so that they might stroke my long hair that they had never before noticed, to debate how the little girl had transformed from an ugly monkey into a beautiful woman. I tried to hide under my parents' winter blankets, but they forced me to stand to be scrutinized, to show the villagers that my uncle's prediction had come true.

'Truthfully, that morning is stamped upon my memory as if it happened yesterday. There were bellowing voices, praising God that such an unattractive little girl had blossomed from a twisted vine into a blooming flower, a rose that would tempt the strongest man. Even an old auntie who was half-blind shouted, "Look, even her toes are beautiful." I hopped about, trying to see what she saw. Looking back, I wonder why no one noticed my physical changes as I was developing. I can only speculate that an ugly little girl was considered of such little value that, while people glanced in my direction, no one ever really took the time to look at me properly. I was not only the ugly little girl but the invisible little girl as well, I suppose. Even today, this makes me very sad because it highlights how females are judged in our society.

'A man, known as Haji, who was considered the wisest man in the village because he had made the hajj pilgrimage to Mecca and had seen things others could not imagine, speculated that perhaps a good jinn had visited me during the night, removing all my unattractive features and replacing them with flawless parts. Such things were believed to happen. In fact, he said, when he was visiting with other hajis in Mecca, he had heard of a number of similar miracles, where good-looking women were transformed into hideous humans, while unpleasant specimens of women became breathtaking beauties. He said that obviously this had happened to me because only the day before there was no sign of beauty on my face or my body.

'Suddenly everyone wanted to befriend our family. All the mothers with appropriately aged sons thought that I should be matched with those men. Several began to speak of well-to-do relatives who lived in the capital. There would be huge dowries offered, they said. Some of the old men already wed to several women wanted me as their newest bride.'

At this, Italia's shoulders slumped with the burden of built-up memories. 'That is when I discovered that great beauty has its own special curse,' she confided.

'I appreciate what you are saying, Italia,' I stated, struck unexpectedly with the recollection of Sara's early marriage; her beauty had attracted much attention. In Saudi Arabia, female social gatherings are organized for mothers or sisters of Saudi men who are looking for brides for the men in their families. The primary goal is to find a woman of great beauty, an important quality. The second objective is wealth and influence. Therefore, beautiful females of the royal family are the most coveted brides in the kingdom.

To Sara's future despair, the sister of an older man looking for a young, beautiful and moneyed bride attended such a function. The man was exceedingly wealthy and influential, and after hearing of Sara's unique beauty he became a determined suitor and had no difficulty persuading our father to agree to Sara's marriage, even though it was far too early for her to wed. Neither my mother's heartfelt pleas nor Sara's virginal innocence could touch my father's heart.

'What happened next, Italia?' I questioned.

'Well, my parents were overjoyed when word of my beauty spread throughout the region. Soon they were accepting the dowry offered by a wealthy Yemeni businessman, who promised them the moon if only they would accept his proposal over the twenty or more proposals they were considering. Although the dowry offered was modest by his standards, it was huge to my parents – it was enough money for my parents to pay off some debts and to feed the family for at least a year. Additionally, he promised to send farm animals to my father, and I was to receive gold necklaces and bracelets.

'Princess, I was not yet twelve years old. That man was forty-three.'

'Oh, no,' I uttered quietly, aware of the pain and horror the young girl Italia had endured.

'At first I was excited to hear details about the village party that would be given in my honour, and the fact that I would receive some dolls for play. I had always wanted a doll after a friend told me about seeing one when she went with her family to Sana'a.'

I knew that Sana'a was the capital of Yemen, as well as the largest city in the country, a place few village women would ever see.

'Such a luxury was beyond my parents' means. I played with dolls in my dreams only. When I heard that I would be eating meat frequently, my mouth watered, imagining a table laden with lamb and chicken. Truthfully, I was eager for this new life my parents were describing. What small girl, who had never known wealth or abundance, would not be thrilled by the prospect of dolls and toys and plenty of food?

'Of course, I was unaware that I was being sold into sexual

bondage. I was the most innocent of girls, never having been away from my mother, other than to play in the dirt path bordering our mud home.'

'Oh, Italia. I don't know what to say, other than I am so, so sorry. I know that Yemen, as in Saudi Arabia, does not have an age limit set for marriage. I have been told several stories of young Yemeni girls no older than eight or nine years being wed to men in their forties, men who so brutally raped the girls that they died on the wedding night. This is a crime that should be stopped now. Such marriages also happen in Saudi Arabia, although there is little media coverage since the Saudi authorities do not allow newspaper reporters to write about such scandals.'

Italia nodded. 'There is talk of various women pushing for that in Yemen too, but the clerics have such power that a law like this will never pass. Many of the poor in Yemen are uneducated; they are stuck in the past, where the happiness of females means nothing. They will go with the opinion of the clerics. Even the mothers of young girls don't give the well-being of their daughters a thought.'

'Yes, I agree. Many women in Yemen and in Saudi Arabia are so steeped in our authoritarian patriarchal cultures that they truly believe that the only purpose for females is to serve the man, whether in the kitchen or in the bedroom. Without the unwavering support of enlightened mothers, young girls will always be used as sexual bait to capture some of the wealth of those disgusting paeodophiles.'

Just then Italia's gaze rested upon an expensive golden clock, a very special present from Sara's husband Assad, who had given it to me for my birthday. 'The time is getting late, Princess. Should I take my leave now?'

'No, no. My husband is in Jeddah until tomorrow and my children are in Europe on a holiday.' Ordinarily I would never sit and listen to such a lengthy tale in one afternoon, regardless of my interest in every woman's life. Generally I learn about others over the course of many visits. But I was alone in my big palace and I had a genuine interest in Italia, for she was in many ways a mystery. I was intrigued by this dazzling woman from a poor Yemeni family who spoke like a highly educated woman, although I doubted she had been schooled as a child.

I encouraged her, 'Please stay a while longer. I must hear the rest of your story, Italia.'

Italia suddenly had a dazed look on her face. Her voice gradually raised in pitch, something I had noticed happened routinely when she was surprised or excited. 'Is that clock solid gold, Princess?' she asked.

I smiled, telling her, 'I have never asked, Italia. The clock was a gift from two very special people in my life, so I am sure it was costly. However, I doubt it is solid gold. Perhaps it has a gold layer.' I had little concern whether the clock was real gold or fake, so long as it gave the correct time. Years before I had lost my desire for expensive possessions, although various family members still paid premier prices for all purchases, as owning the finest was gratifying for many Al Sa'ud family members, including Assad.

'Tell me about your marriage, Italia,' I suggested.

'Which one, Princess?' she replied, as she reluctantly pulled her gaze away from my gold clock before clicking her perfectly mani-cured nails together, waiting for my reaction.

'How many times have you been married?' I asked.

'Seven. Seven times, Princess. But I am divorced at present.'

I did not ask for details, but my face must have shown my astonishment. Although many men in my culture marry frequently, as Muslim men are allowed four wives at one time, I have never known a woman to have been married more than two or three times.

'Princess, when men hear about me from the women in their families, or see me for the first time, they feel they must marry me. Once they have me in the marriage bed, they wear them-selves out enjoying me, but they tire of me after a year or two and then send me back to Yemen with a few good jewels and a little money.'

Italia then revealed a new, interesting detail. 'In fact, I am in Saudi Arabia looking for a new husband, princess. This time I want to marry a member of the royal family. I have yet to marry a prince.'

'Oh?' Remembering what Ameera had said, I asked, 'Are you thinking to marry Ameera's brother?'

'Perhaps,' Italia replied. 'It is according to the dowry he offers.'

'He is married to two other women at the moment, Italia. Did you know that?'

'Yes, I know.'

'And you are not concerned?'

'No, Princess. I am accustomed to being the new wife in a family of other wives.'

I am a believing Muslim woman, and acknowledge that our religion allows a man to marry more wives than he needs, yet I had physically fought my husband over his scheme to take a second wife. My strong reaction had changed Kareem's plan and from that day my husband has never again mentioned the possibility.

Now I held my tongue, although I desperately wanted to advise Italia that it was important for all women to stand together, to fight against such customs, which I do not believe fit into our modern world, but I did not. I moved on.

'Well, for now, tell me about your first marriage, Italia, when you were a child bride.'

Although I would warn Sara never to mention Italia's name, I knew she might refer to Italia's experience as a child bride in some of her documents. Personal accounts were the most compelling of all.

A sad expression crossed Italia's face. 'The engagement was fun. The marriage was bad. I was excited during the short engagement because everyone was making an enormous commotion over me. My groom dispatched three dolls from Egypt, along with my dowry of gold coins, bracelets, ten cows, fifteen goats and twenty sheep. He also sent a wagon filled with food. Never had we seen such an array of food, and all of it was purchased from a big store in Sana'a. There were packages of food stored in plastic wrapping – my youngest brother nearly died after he ate the clear wrapper along with the food. He said later that it was not very flavoursome, but he thought he might develop a taste for it, so the fool kept eating. My other three brothers ate until they were almost sick.

'My mother told me nothing of what to expect regarding my duties as a wife. The wedding was very expensive because the groom paid for everything. In fact, hundreds of people came from neighbouring communities. They still talk about that wedding in my village.

'I was very tired when the time came for my mother and aunties to dress me in a frilly nightgown which my groom had sent prior to the wedding. I felt pretty and pampered in that new clothing, for I had never before worn anything so fancy. After arranging everything just so, they left me alone in the marriage bed. I honestly believed that I was being put to bed to sleep. I snuggled in for the night, but within moments my eager groom entered the room. I was puzzled at first, thinking that he might be there to give me another doll. I quickly told him that three dolls was plenty. He was so excited that he could not stop grinning. Then he started taking off his clothes and I was so shocked I could not speak, for I had never seen a naked man. I remember shaking and whimpering with fear, but nothing I did discouraged him. I even told him that my father, brothers and uncle would kill him if he didn't leave. I knew that men out of the family were not allowed in the rooms where women slept. Of course, my naive manner made him merry because those kind of brutish men like to rape young and innocent girls under the guise of marriage.

'That man was big and powerful. In his eagerness to take me, he leapt clear across the room and into the bed. He began ripping my pretty new gown off, and before I knew what was happening, he was in. I was a very young virgin, too small to endure sex. As I screamed, he laughed. I remember the wild look in his eyes and the foam that came from his mouth and onto his lips. He was like a mad dog and I was his prey. He raped me more times than I could count. Knowing what I now know of men, I have no idea how he could have sex so many times so quickly long before the days of sex pills.

'This is the story of my first marriage. He was a man with lots of money in comparison to most men in Yemen, yet he was not nearly as wealthy as some men I later married. His only thought was to have sex. I was raped every night for two years, then he heard about another young girl, supposedly a blonde Yemeni girl whom many men wanted. That poor girl was only nine years old, but he got her. Once she was in his home, I knew some peace. That's when I began my studies. He agreed to hire a female teacher to come to our home daily to give me some lessons. Once I learned to read, I read everything available, and still do, to this day.'

Now I understood where Italia had acquired such an extensive vocabulary for a girl whose education was limited.

My thoughts at that moment returned to the horror of Italia's early marriage. I felt a great anger flooding my mind, for nothing is more upsetting than to brood over the plight of young girls forcefully married to grown men. Such young brides are nothing more than helpless children at the mercy of brutish men who have no compassion. I decided at that moment to join Sara in her efforts to bring change to my own country, so that an age limit for marriage might change the lives and futures of many young Saudi girls.

And at this moment Kareem unexpectedly arrived from Jeddah. I was surprised to see my husband a day early, but more surprised to see his father, as it was not common for my father-in-law to visit our home. Shielding Italia's exposed face with my hands, I protested: 'Kareem! I have company!'

Kareem would never have entered the room had he known that

I was entertaining a woman not of our family. Such conduct is out of respect for the woman. While some Muslim women do not object to strange men seeing their unveiled faces, other women react visibly with tears and protests. Saudi men learn early in life to announce their entrance into their own homes.

My protest was too late. Both Kareem and his father were noticeably startled by the vision of Italia, for rarely does one see a woman so beautiful.

Italia pushed my hands aside and peeked at Kareem and his father, seemingly pleased to see the admiration displayed on the faces of two men she did not know.

Kareem quickly recovered his composure, but his father was rendered speechless, much in the same manner that his son, Assad, had reacted to Sara's beauty many years before. Kareem grabbed his father by the arm and both hurriedly exited the area. Thinking that the crisis had passed, I helped Italia slip into her abaya and fastened her veil over her face. I apologized for my husband and his father, although Italia was not concerned.

'Never mind, Princess,' she said. 'I am not like so many Muslim women who blush at the sight of a strange man.'

'I am glad not to have offended you in my home, Italia,' I told her, as I walked her towards the entrance. I then asked Mahmoud to escort my guest to her car, where her driver could return her to Ameera's palace.

Although I would have been pleased to have learned more of Italia's story, I assumed that I would never see the beautiful Yemeni woman again. Even if she had married Ameera's brother, as was her plan, I might never have see her again because I am not particularly close to that part of the family

But I was wrong.

Italia's story, and her connection to my family, did not end at that luncheon. Kareem's father is a serial husband and marriage addict. While still married to Kareem's mother, Noorah, and his second wife, a Lebanese woman, my father-in-law marries and divorces a new and young woman every few years. His behaviour is a great shame for Kareem and Assad, but no Saudi man will confront his father over anything. In light of this, by inviting Italia into my home I had started a family crisis that would affect all our lives in ways we could never have imagined.

Chapter Three

Female Power in Yemen

ONE WEEK AFTER MY meeting with Italia I heard heavy footsteps running through the house and towards the area of our private quarters. I was instantly on high alert and for a moment I felt certain that insurgents had seized our palace and that soon I would find myself a hostage. I've always been quick on my feet and particularly when I sense danger. Before my bedroom door was flung open I was safely sequestered in the panic room connected to my private bedroom, one of three in our palace made of bullet-resistant fibreglass, with thick steel doors. I was in the process of entering the special code to lock the door when I heard my husband's voice. Thankfully the safe rooms had been built so that the occupants of the safe room could hear what was being said on the outside.

'Sultana!'

Worried that he might be a hostage already, I remained silent. We had devised and practised a reaction to such a situation several times and I had been warned by our security team that should I ever be suspicious of anything that hinted of danger, I was to stifle all sounds so as to keep my location secret until I heard Kareem, Abdullah or one of our security specialists provide me with a special password that we had agreed upon.

'Sultana! Where are you?'

I did not speak. I did not shift my position.

My husband repeated his cries: 'Sultana! Where are you?'

Kareem was undeniably agitated, causing me to feel certain that he was being threatened with a gun or a knife. I was safe inside, so I very quietly removed the receiver from the secure telephone line that was linked only to our safe rooms and quickly dialled Sara's private number. When she answered, I paused before communicating, remembering being told that I should suppress or disguise my voice or I might alert any hostage-takers to my presence. But when I went to speak I was too afraid to utter a sound.

'Hallo, hallo,' Sara said several times. Raising her voice, she asked, 'Who is this?' When there was still no answer, she hung up.

I heard my husband calling my name again, as he exited my bedroom. I supposed he was going to look for me in other areas of our palace. But only a few minutes passed before he returned with my personal maid, Babette, who was anxious because she had left me in my quarters seconds before Kareem had burst in the door.

Babette sounded hysterical. 'Madam? Are you here? Madam? Sir, she was here. Madam was here, deciding upon her dress for the day, when I left to go to the galley to bring her tea. That is when I saw you running down the hallway.'

I heard furniture being moved. 'She is not here, sir.' Babette's shaky voice indicated that she was ready to weep. 'Madam has disappeared!'

By this time I understood that I had no worries about terrorists looking to harm us. But now there was a second complication. Our safe rooms were top secret. The only employees who were privy to our security arrangements were our security team. Kareem had warned me never to trust anyone, even favourite maids who had been with our family for many years. I remember that he had touched my lips and ordered, 'No matter how much you want to make your presence known, never expose your hiding place to any employees. If so, these panic rooms will be useless, Sultana, for we could not expect anyone to undergo torture to protect us.'

Kareem was correct. Should any insurgents think to torture our servants, I am certain they would find it impossible to keep our security secrets. And there would be a chance that I would cry out for their pain and all would be lost, for everyone. We all know that if ever taken hostage by rebels, there would be no mercy shown to Al Sa'ud royals, or to the people who work for us.

Kareem is so cautious about secrecy that when the panic rooms were installed we sent our house servants to Jeddah for the week to ensure that our security would not be compromised. Since they did not know of the safe rooms, threats against them to disclose our whereabouts would hopefully bring no harm to them, or to us – for they truly did not know anything about our main security strategies.

I was in a predicament, for I knew that something important was happening or Kareem would not be in such an emotional state. My husband is normally a very calm man. Yet if I made my presence known, then our safe room would be exposed. Babette, although nearly perfect in every way, had been known to speak freely when she should not have. She was certain to share the secret with her friends in the palace at some point.

Not knowing what I should do, I sat down and waited for events to unfold. It was then, for the first time, that I fully appreciated the plans made by Kareem to ensure our safety should murderous rebels break into our home. I studied my surroundings carefully. There were many cartons of water and other packaged food items we might need if we were trapped in our safe room for several days.

I was suddenly distracted when I heard Kareem shout to Babette as he left my quarters, telling her to wait in the room. 'When the princess returns, tell her that I am waiting in my study,' he instructed her.

'Oh no,' I whispered, wondering how long I might be confined. Babette would do as my husband commanded, so I knew she would not leave; yet I could hear that she was distressed from her muffled crying.

Moments seemed like hours. I gathered several large pillows and moved to the furthermost corner of the room, holding the pillows over my head so as to muffle the sound of Babette's sobs, then I dialled Sara's number once again. When she answered, I whispered my dilemma. Sara was initially confused, but soon understood, as she and Assad had also had safe rooms installed in their palace. Through her low laughter, she said she would have her husband call Kareem and explain the situation. I started to feel a little foolish.

Moments later I heard Kareem re-enter the room and tell Babette to wait outside. 'I will call you later, once I find the princess,' he said.

Poor Babette made no reply, but I heard the door to my quarters close.

Kareem walked to the entrance of the safe room. His voice was soft, as he told me the password, although it was not necessary at that point. I was so flustered, though, that I failed to remember the key code to release the locks on the thick steel door. Kareem whispered it to me. Finally, my husband was in, taking charge by pulling me outside and closing the heavy door, hiding evidence of a secret entrance.

With a big smile on my face, I said, 'Husband! Thank goodness Sara reached you.'

Kareem was not amused. In fact, he was so incensed that his face was red and his eyes were inflamed. He made no mention of the safe-room fiasco, instead yelling, 'Sultana, my mother is going to kill you this time.'

I was so confused that I stammered, 'What . . . what did you say?'

What was my husband speaking about? Although his mother, Noorah, and I would never be a devoted 'mother-in-law and daughter-in-law' unit, we had overcome our difficulties years ago. We were both unfailingly courteous to one another on every family or social occasion.

Just then Babette came into the room, looking as though she had seen a ghost. Evidently she had not left her place at the door from the moment she had walked outside. Now she was entirely bewildered as to where I had been, as she and Kareem had thoroughly searched my quarters.

'Madam,' she cried out, 'where were you?'

Kareem's harsh expression hardened. 'Babette, are you deaf? I told you that I would call you.' He gestured towards the same door she had entered. 'Leave now, please.'

Poor Babette burst into tears and fled the room.

Kareem turned his attention back to me.

'I cannot believe what you have done,' he roared.

'What are you talking about, husband?' I shouted back, for I was weary of the mystery. 'What have I done?'

'That woman! Italia! Did you send her to seduce my father?'

'Italia?' While I had thought of the Yemeni woman several times since she had left our palace, I had not contacted her. I had telephoned Sara the day after Italia left my home to ask if she might meet with the woman to hear her story. But Sara had not yet returned my call to advise me of her decision on the matter, as she was very busy with a variety of other important things. 'I do not know what you are talking about, Kareem. Please tell me what has happened. I know nothing of your father, or of his dealings with Italia.'

'Sit down.'

I sat. Dread was forming in my mind and in my heart, as I strongly sensed that I was about to be told something I would not like to hear.

'Mother called. She was distraught. She asked that I pay her a visit without telling me the problem, so I rushed over, fearful that someone was dying. When I arrived, she was wailing. She had heard that Father was set to marry a beautiful Yemeni woman named Italia. Mother told me that her husband has lost his mind over the woman. He has already divorced Amina, his third wife, and has ordered the servants to pack her things to make ready for Italia to live in her villa.'

Italia? Marriage? Amina divorced? Too shocked to think calmly, I could only utter one word: 'Truly?'

I felt a heat wave spread throughout my body. Although I recalled that Kareem's father had reacted favourably to Italia's great beauty, as had Kareem, who would have thought that he would pursue the Yemeni beauty and propose marriage? Wealthy royals travel the world and routinely see beautiful women of every nationality. The most exquisite women in the world are usually available for marriage when a Saudi prince makes a proposal. Al Sa'ud men can be arrogant and can afford to be very selective when it comes to choosing wives.

Kareem's father had briefly married many women during his adult life, and had divorced most of those women, keeping only his first and second wives since marriage.

Yet it was not a huge surprise that he was taking another wife. The jolt came from knowing that he was going to marry Italia. How had he found her, to court her and to make a proposal? I had told no one that she was staying at Ameera's palace. No one but Sara.

'When Mother learned that Father had met Italia at home, she became incensed; she believed that you were scheming to bring trouble into her life. You know how she likes Amina. You also know that Amina is the only wife my father has taken that met with my mother's approval. They have become good friends, and now Amina is being sent back to Syria.'

'Really? Kareem, I am astonished! Such a thing never once came to my mind. I met with Italia only because of the mystery that surrounded her, and because the story behind her change in circumstances intrigued me. Once I discovered her history, and the fact she was an abused child bride, I thought that Sara might like to meet her too.'

I suddenly remembered something important: 'Listen, husband, I believed that she was going to marry Ameera's brother. That is what I was told.' Caressing Kareem's shoulder, I added, 'Please, husband, please revisit to your mother and tell her that I did not meet with Italia for the purpose of setting up a marriage to anyone. After your father came into our home and saw Italia, he did not contact me for any reason. I have no knowledge of how he located her after she left my side.'

'Are you telling me the truth, Sultana?'

'On the lives of all those whom I love, I am telling you the truth, Kareem.'

With my strong words, my husband knew that I was not lying.

Kareem stood quietly, thinking. 'Did you reveal Italia's connection to Ameera to anyone else?'

'Only to Sara.'

Kareem's eyes met my own. At the same moment, we both said, 'Assad!'

Kareem promptly called his brother to ask if their father had requested information on the Yemeni woman he had met in our home. Assad admitted that he had visited with his father on the same evening Kareem brought their father into our home, and only a few hours after he had accidentally seen Italia. Assad had been surprised when his father spoke so passionately of the woman's great beauty. He had even asked Assad if he knew of the woman. Assad had said no, other than that Sara had talked about learning about the poor woman from Sultana, and how Sara might meet with her later in the week. He admitted relating to his father that the Yemeni woman was going to be in the kingdom for another month as the guest of our cousin, Ameera.

I was relieved to hear this verification, which would relieve me of the guilt my mother-in-law had so quickly hung on my shoulders. 'Go to your mother now, Kareem. It is important that she knows the innocence of all. She needs to feel confident that no one was conspiring to introduce your father to a beautiful woman. Even Assad's information was accidental, for he had no idea that his father was looking for Italia, or had plans to so quickly propose marriage.'

I knew that Noorah would never become angry with Assad or Sara, but the thin veneer of our affability could be easily pierced. Our friendly greetings and farewells at family socials went no further than the surface. I had no desire to battle with Kareem's mother over anything, and certainly not my father-in-law's appetite for beautiful women. Such in-law conflicts were too consuming. As the years have passed, I have grown wiser about such matters.

* * *

The next time I saw Italia was at a gathering of Kareem's female family members. If possible, Italia appeared even more magnificent than she had done the previous month when she was a guest in my home. She was more self-assured, too, for she had her prince, despite the fact he was old with a wrinkled face, hunched back and weak knees. Kareem learned from Assad that his father had sought out the most renowned physicians in the kingdom to prescribe the most potent sex pills, without concern for the age or health of the man. Kareem's father had very high blood pressure and was on powerful medication. Kareem and I read about the pills on the internet and we were alarmed. When my husband read the warnings – for a man with his father's health condition and history there was a slight danger of blindness – he shot into action and approached his father with a fervent warning.

Kareem's father was uncommonly rude, telling his son to shut his mouth and mind his own business. Kareem could do nothing more, for our culture does not look agreeably upon a son who argues with his father.

Kareem blamed me once again for creating the problem, but after I criticized my husband for bursting into the room without announcing himself, he quietened, for he knew that if he had only heeded the social restrictions of our society, his ageing father would never have seen the beautiful Italia.

I was sad to hear the story of the sex pills for a second, very important reason. Tragically, nothing had changed for Italia from her first marriage to her eighth. She had been used as a sex toy by every husband.

That's when I acknowledged that Italia's beauty was a curse. Her appearance was so blinding that men could think of nothing but physically conquering her. No man she had ever known had respected the mind beneath her stunning face and body, for I had no doubt that Italia was a smart woman hindered by her external appearance.

I glanced at the various women at the party to see if Kareem's mother was in attendance, but she was not. Noorah had gone into near isolation since her husband had wed Italia, refusing to meet with me. Inexplicably, she still adored Sara, despite the fact that Sara clearly supported me and had assured my mother-in-law that I was innocent. Sara had told her that it had been Assad who had unintentionally led his father to the beauty from Yemen. I was sad and sorry because Noorah's ill feelings were based on something that had not happened, but I knew Noorah had spent years feigning friendship, when in her heart she had always disliked me. Now, in her eyes, there was no need for such pretence.

For certain, Italia had disrupted the dynamics of our family, but when a person wishes to be angry, as Noorah was demonstrating, there is little one can do.

Before walking over to speak to Italia, I stood silently to consider her performance. After a few minutes, I grasped that I was not watching an act. Italia was indisputably happy. Her laughter was sincere. Her smile was wide and her eyes were lit with joy. Perhaps her happiness had to do with marrying a prince and having unlimited wealth to purchase the best of everything. Italia's designer gown was a shining shade of gold, and the wide diamond and gold necklace draped around her neck matched the fabric nearly perfectly. Her clothes, hair and jewels heralded great wealth.

Kareem had also confided that his mother had not exaggerated: his father had indeed lost his mind over Italia's beauty. He catered to her every wish.

I sighed, feeling bad for what I knew was in Italia's future, for I understood from my father-in-law's history that his affection and favour for Italia would fade. To Kareem's father, all Italia had to offer was great beauty – like the works of art displayed in the finest European museums, to be admired and praised. Certainly, when a woman is as beautiful as Italia men can often see nothing else.

I thought of Sara. Thankfully, my gorgeous sister had miraculously escaped Italia's fate, but only because she had met and married a man who fully appreciated all her characteristics and qualities, including her brilliant mind.

For the first time in my life, I thanked God that I was not born a celebrated beauty. Although I am pleased that those who know me find me attractive, with some saying I am very pretty, my looks, whether good or bad, have not determined my place in life. As I have grown older, I have grown wiser and now know that physical beauty should not be the standard by which we appraise women. Nothing is more important than intelligence, wisdom and kindness, characteristics that remain with a woman while beauty fades. I am one who believes that all societies delude our young when we focus attention only on physical appeal. May the day come when such flawed thinking is erased from our minds.

The greatest pleasures in my life have had nothing to do with the way I look, the clothes I wear, the jewels I possess or the palaces I own. Other than the joys I have derived from being a wife and mother, my greatest satisfactions in life emanate from the ideas I have in my mind and the assistance I have given to help girls and women escape abusive relationships and achieve their life goals.

I sauntered to Italia's side. When she saw me, she shouted in delight, pulling me close so as to kiss my cheeks and whisper in my ear. 'I told you, princess. I told you that I would get a prince.'

I forced a smile, for I have learned in life that some people will never change. From the day she had matured into a great beauty, Italia had been nurtured by her family, society and culture to use her looks to their greatest advantage, as surely as her father had nurtured the crops he grew on the terraced mountains of Yemen.

Italia, I believed, would do nothing more than devote her life – and her beauty – to marrying wealthy men. Or at least that was my belief at the time.

*   *   *

In the years that followed her marriage, I built a friendship with Italia, but it was only when Kareem's father grew bored with her that her true plans emerged. I discovered that Italia was more thoughtful and intelligent than her actions had implied. After Kareem's father mentioned that he was planning to divorce, for a scrumptious feast every day soon loses its appeal, Italia outwitted her husband, inducing him to award her vast riches as a divorce settlement, something he had never done before. While he had not once sent his ex-wives away destitute, never had he given many millions of dollars to a woman with whom he had grown weary.

But Italia was triumphant where his other wives had not been. At the end of her eighth marriage, the beauty Italia returned to the country she had never forgotten, and the people she loved, with $30 million, a vast sum of money for a previously impoverished girl from Yemen.

Although I lost contact with Italia once she moved out of Saudi Arabia, Sara was in occasional communication, for they had made an association in their work devoted to the plight of child brides. Never was I more astonished and proud than when I discovered that Italia had become a mighty force in the arena of educating and saving abused girls in a number of countries where they were being held in sexual bondage. Italia was using her divorce wealth to further the cause of such girls and free those poor unfortunate victims, so I knew that wherever she might be, she was happy, for nothing guarantees happiness more than helping others.

In early 2015, when Saudi Arabia launched its military action, bombing Yemen, it was not surprising that Sara had difficulty reaching Italia, for the entire infrastructure of the previously destitute country was acutely affected. A worried Sara was fearful that Italia had been trapped by the intense bombing and was no more. When Sara spoke of her worry, Kareem and Assad exchanged amused glances before laughing heartily at Sara's fears.

'Darling,' Assad told his wife, 'Italia is the sort of woman who can catch a bomb with her teeth and send it back to the pilot.'

Sara did not find their witticism amusing and raised her concern again because it was as if Italia had disappeared from Yemen. After numerous attempts, Sara located Italia through the investigative endeavours of a Yemeni tea boy who had worked for Kareem's father while Italia had been one of his wives. The young man had been treated kindly by Italia during her time living in the palace and through his Yemeni contacts he located her on the outskirts of Sana'a. It seems that courageous Italia had moved from her village to be near the main conflict so that she might help others.

Resourceful as ever, Sara succeeded in placing a call through to Italia in Yemen, something exceptionally difficult due to the bombing campaign against the Houthi rebels there. Sara set the phone on loudspeaker, so that we might both hear Italia's words. She answered quickly, touched that our thoughts had turned to her. Thankfully, Italia claimed to be safe, despite the chaos in Yemen.

I easily envisioned the melodramatically disposed Italia as she excitedly made conversation. 'Royal ladies,' she laughed, 'I am unharmed. At least for the moment. God is saving my head from those bombs. However, I had some very difficult experiences with a few of those woman-hating rebels. Did you know they claimed to be ready to curb male domination? But no, they are trying to push women even further into the abyss.'

Sara interrupted, 'Italia, tell us if you are all right. We have been worried.'

Italia laughed again, more loudly this time. 'I am good. But let me tell you a funny story. One day when I went to visit a good friend, I forgot to pull my long hair back, so a few hairs escaped from beneath my shawl. One of those illiterate men glared at me, in the same manner as those excessively intense Mutawah used to do in the Riyadh souks when they looked so mean, giving the impression that they yearned to pound your head with their long sticks. Anyhow, that silly rebel had the impudence to ask if I was married. I said, "None of your business," and he shouted, "Get married! Stay at home!" I shouted back at him, "I have been married more times than you can count."

'That ruffian had no knowledge of how to react to a strong woman. He scowled some more, and then stomped off to pursue a woman less spirited. Yemeni women are forced to live like mice, sitting quietly in the corners, nibbling on the cheese when no one is looking. But not this woman.'

I interjected before she could get into another story that told us nothing of what we wanted to know. 'We want to know if you need anything, Italia.'

'Yes, in fact. There is something I need desperately. I need electricity.'

'Electricity?' I stammered.

'Yes! Electricity! I have become an electricity refugee. My millions are not helping me now. There are no generators to be bought in this country. Now I spend much of my day being driven from one establishment to another, looking for a generator so that I might have some electricity to power up my phone and computer. Electricity! Tell that old prince of mine to instruct those Saudi pilots not to drop their bombs on the electrical plants.'

'I would give you a generator if I knew how to get one to you,' Sara replied sweetly.

'I know you would, Sara. You are a gem.' Italia coughed loudly. 'Those bombs are making rubble out of this neighbourhood. My lungs are aching even now.' And then she laughed as she said, 'If only you could tell that old prince of mine that I would appreciate it if they discontinued bombing in this neighbourhood!'

She knew Kareem's father was no longer in a powerful position, as his advanced age kept him confined in his home more often than not. But Sara and I exchanged woeful looks, for both of us felt terrible that in this war, as in all wars, civilians were too often harmed, were too often the victims.

'Ladies, I am so pleased you cared enough to call. But I must go now. My friend Fiery has organized a meeting at the university to discuss women's rights under the Houthis. I am giving my support to this woman because she is fearless. Fiery the Fearless is what we call her.'

'I have not heard of this fearless Yemeni woman,' I said, although since the bombing war began I had greatly increased my knowledge of everything that was going on in Yemen, and most particularly how the girls and women were faring.

'I am not surprised. Fiery does not come from the wealthy class. Her father was a professor at Sana'a University until he dropped dead of a heart attack. Such people never meet Saudi royals. Or any royals, for that matter. But she is educated and resourceful and determined. I believe that she will change the history of women in Yemen.

'All right. I must leave you. Please call later. If my phone is charged, I will answer. If I do not answer, send a generator!

'Do not worry about your beautiful friend Italia. The rebels have less time to scheme these days, so they are leaving the women alone, at least temporarily. They are busy shoring up their defences. The fools believe that the GCC armies are going to invade the country. I told them that I know the Saudi royals better than anyone in this country and the attacks will be limited to the sky.

'I leave you now . . .' – then Italia startled us by making an unexpected promise –'but before long I will bring Fiery to visit you in Saudi Arabia. You shall meet this fearless woman for yourself.'

The telephone connection died. Sara clicked off her cell phone, a look of approval on her face. 'Sultana, it appears there was more to Italia than good looks. I believe she can take care of herself much better than any of us had expected.'

I nodded in agreement. My thoughts were with Italia in Yemen, and the friend she called Fiery the Fearless. I doubted that I would ever meet this fearless Yemeni woman, although I was titillated by the idea, as nothing intrigues me more than talking with women who fight for freedom against archaic societies and within patriarchal-controlled countries.

But once more Italia would surprise me with her gifts of persuasion; she was a woman who could make the impossible possible.

Fiery the Fearless

Through Italia, Sara and I soon met the woman known as Fiery, a woman unlike Italia in so many ways but as similar as a twin in others.

Fiery was born into a conservative Yemeni family who held dear the female tradition of obedience to men. Her father, Jamil, was a highly respected scholar in the Faculty of Education at Sana'a University in Yemen. The university was first opened in 1970 as the primary university in the Yemen Arab Republic, now known as the Republic of Yemen.

Jamil was hired in 1974 with a satisfactory salary that meant he could offer an appropriate dowry to wed a colleague's sister. The two men were professors in the same department and had similar pursuits, which were a love of reading and of travel, although Jamil had never journeyed further than neighbouring Saudi Arabia. Neither man was married, even though both were seeking a virtuous woman to wed, as they had been raised with conservative values, in harmony with the majority of Yemeni citizens.

After Jamil's associate mentioned that he had three beautiful sisters who were of an age to marry, Jamil eagerly investigated further, as his parents were both deceased and he had no sisters or aunties in the area to seek information about potential brides, as all had married men from small villages well outside Sana'a. But after his colleague said that his eldest sister, named Pearl, was not only beautiful but also a good woman without ambitions for education or a career, Jamil plunged into marriage negotiations without seeking an intermediary to discover additional personal information regarding the woman with whom he would spend the rest of his life, for he was not the sort of man to divorce or to take a second wife.

Living in one of the most conformist countries in the Arab world, Jamil never saw his bride before the wedding night. He was excited, though, to meet her and could think of little else in the days leading up to the wedding. But once alone with his bride Jamil plunged into disappointment. When he at last saw his wife unveiled, he could not conceive why his friend and colleague had called his sister beautiful; his new bride was so homely that there was simply no beauty to be seen. But Jamil was an honourable man and there was nothing to do but to accept that he had been duped into marrying a woman so physically unattractive that she would tempt no man.

Jamil felt despondent, although he kept his emotions suppressed when his colleague, who was now his brother-in-law, boasted about his good fortune to marry an exceedingly beautiful woman from a family with important connections at the university.

Ironically, over time Jamil became attracted to his wife, for she was a good-natured woman with a sense of humour; she made him laugh and was pleasant to be around. In fact, Pearl had many qualities that suited Jamil. She was frugal, buying nothing more than what was needed for daily life, and she kept an immaculate home. Most importantly, she was an attentive wife and mother. Jamil was quickly a contented man. His contentment at home extended to his place of work, where he soon became known as one of the most cordial professors on the university staff, with his personality gaining him many devoted friends. As time passed, he was promoted into a high position in his department and his salary was increased.

The very kind-hearted Jamil took no comfort from his brother-in-law's marriage of misery when he learned from Pearl that her brother's salary was not sufficient to purchase the fine clothes, jewels and house furnishings that his overindulged wife demanded, for she had been accustomed to an extravagant lifestyle when living in her wealthy father's home. There were also difficulties with children, or the lack of them, for the couple had failed to conceive. In Yemen, nothing is more important than the birth of a child.

Pearl's brother was a miserable man, married to a beautiful but manipulative woman.

Jamil felt so pleased that his brother-in-law had misled him into marrying Pearl that he did not condemn his brother-in-law when he complied with his wife's demand for a divorce. Jamil did not believe in divorce, but he saw his brother-in-law's point of view in this case.

Jamil and Pearl took enormous pleasure in their children, two sons and three daughters. All were obedient children, for they had been raised to obey God's commands, given to all Muslims through the Prophet Muhammad. None of the children were acknowledged for good looks, although the two sons were moderately attractive, and two of their three daughters were pleasing enough to look upon, with smooth skin and attractive features.

Fiery, their second daughter, was nearly identical to her mother in appearance and was known by everyone in the community as the 'homely' daughter. Clearly, she was no beauty, and neighbours cruelly predicted that this child would be the daughter to tend to her parents in their old age, for no man would seek her for a bride. Fortunately, though, Fiery inherited her mother's fun and dynamic personality. The child was well liked by everyone who met her. She was also the most intelligent of the five children, with an obvious high IQ.

Although Jamil thought it best that women remain in the home and support their husbands by assuming responsibility for home and children, after observing his daughter, Fiery, he felt the urge to make an exception. Fiery, he knew, was an unusual girl who would do well to pursue education and a career. When speaking about Fiery, Jamil always commented that the girl was born with a book in her mouth. Indeed, Fiery was so curious about the world that she devoured more books than the family could afford to purchase, furthering Jamil's intentions to ensure that Fiery received the best education he could afford.

Jamil often expressed amusement when he told Fiery how uncomfortable he had been with the name given to her by her mother. But he had agreed with Pearl that if he was going to select the names given to any sons they might have, she could name their daughters. Jamil was not a man to go against his word, so he endured Pearl's choice when it came to Fiery.

Jamil had reacted as expected, giving his sons traditional names, Mohammed and Abdullah. Pearl had chosen Nadeen for their eldest girl, and Marwa for their youngest. But Jamil thought that Pearl was not thinking clearly when naming the middle girl. Pearl said that she chose an unusual name, Fiery, because her labour was so long and difficult with their second daughter that she pictured the baby as fiery and furious, kicking and clawing on her way to leave her mother and to enter the world.

Jamil and Pearl never broached the topic of marriage to Fiery because there were no suitors queueing up or dispatching their mothers or sisters to offer a dowry. Indeed, they were both relieved when Fiery failed to express an interest in marriage. It was best that they had no knowledge of their daughter's secret sadness, for she knew that she would disappoint her husband on his wedding night. She was a proud girl and strong, so she hid her unhappiness, putting on a bold face, telling all the older women in the neighbourhood who chided her for remaining single that she had no interest in a dead household brought about by the selfishness of most men in Yemen. Over time those feelings became real to Fiery, becoming part of her belief system, perhaps because she had expressed the idea so many times.

Fiery knew that her parents' marriage was unusual in Yemen, only because her father was an intelligent man who had grown to love a woman who, despite her lack of beauty, was worth his affection. Fiery had heard few women praise their marriages, most confiding that women must accept that they are on earth to devote their lives to serving their husbands and raising good children. Women had to forget about any passion they might have for work outside the home. Those passions, they said, were reserved for men, who had a natural inclination to be self-centred.

Fiery startled the women when she told them that she looked upon them as miserable wives stuck in mechanical marriages. After pausing with shock at Fiery's words, most chuckled, sincerely believing that her harsh words stemmed directly from her un-fulfilled life and her homely features, which they believed would never create excitement or offers of marriage. Every woman on earth wanted marriage and children, as they saw it.

And so the years passed. Fiery occupied her days with classes and filled her nights with studying, earning high marks and secur-ing four degrees before her father Jamil left a big hole in the heart of the family when he suddenly died from a heart attack while teaching one of his classes.

To support herself, and her mother, Fiery began teaching at a small university close to her mother's home, where she would always live. Poor Pearl was so lonely; she missed Jamil so much that she walked around in a grief-stricken daze for several years. Eventually, she managed to pull herself out of the cycle of sorrow and found some enjoyment spending time with her grandchildren from her two sons and other two daughters. She was industrious too, keeping house for Fiery, who soon found her passion as a revolutionary fighter for the rights of women, a fervour that had been building in her heart for years, for she knew that to be free is a human need, and Yemeni women were not free.

As an educated woman, she had been dismayed when she read that her beloved country of Yemen was considered the worst place in the world to be a woman.

All of these things I learned directly from Fiery.

*   *   *

Travel inside Yemen has always been unsafe. Very few of Yemen's roads are paved. Only major cities such as Sana'a, Aden and Taiz have paved roads. If one wants or needs to travel outside the main cities, one must take a four-wheel-drive vehicle or risk being stuck on the side of the road. Small buses are limited to a few regular routes. There are taxis, but the drivers are often unskilled and the vehicles in need of repair. Most perplexing, some people drive on the left side of the road, while others drive on the right side. There are no railroads in the country. There is sea travel from the ports, but it is challenging to obtain the necessary permits. All of these difficulties occur when there is no war. With war, the difficulties and dangers of travel increase dramatically.

But none of these travel inconveniences halted Italia's plans to bring Fiery to Saudi Arabia for a meeting with Sara. Dipping into her millions, Italia rented a secure and cosy sailing yacht from a Yemeni politician and bribed the same man to provide her with the necessary permits to leave the port of Aden and sail the eastern Red Sea to Jeddah. Italia had no problems entering Saudi Arabia, as Kareem's father had given her a long-term visa, along with a letter of permission to visit the kingdom whenever she liked.

One day, a month or so after our initial telephone call with Italia, Sara called me to tell me something I never expected to hear. 'Sultana!' she said, in an excited tone of voice. 'We must get to Jeddah. Italia is waiting for us there with that fearless woman.'

'What?'

'Believe my words or not, Italia has arrived in Jeddah. She sailed up the Red Sea! She is waiting for us there with the woman called Fiery.'

I caught Sara's excitement. 'Let us go. Now!'

Sara and I both had palaces on the Red Sea at Jeddah, so we kept plenty of clothes and other necessities there. Within a few hours, we had boarded Assad and Sara's private jet and were on our way. My daughter, Amani, chose to accompany us, for she had been one of the few Saudi royals who had been against the bombing of Yemen and now she wished to interview two women who were surviving under the bombs that Saudi Arabia and other countries in the region were dropping.

'Do not get into a political discussion or argument with these ladies,' I warned my daughter. 'Let us see what they have to say. Then you can argue with your father when we return to Riyadh.' Amani was wearing her stubborn face, so I pinched her arm. 'Do you hear me, daughter?'

'Ouch! Stop it, Mother,' she replied. 'I will not argue with them. I will listen, absorb their words and write an opinion piece for a newspaper when I return to Riyadh.'

'You will not do such a thing,' I advised her, although I knew that no Saudi newspapers would permit her writings to be published. None, I knew, would take a formal stance against our new royal leader, King Salman, to criticize his actions against the Houthis in Yemen. In fact, other than my daughter, all the royals I knew personally, as well as the vast majority of ordinary citizens, believed that King Salman was reacting correctly to the rebels on our border. Saudi newspapers reflected the positive sentiments and full support for King Salman expressed by most Saudis.

Amani then opened a book to read, one that recommended how to best raise Islamic children.

Sara had closed her eyes and was resting, for she had told me that she was up very late the previous evening, when she and Assad had kept one of their grandchildren, who had colic.

I sat and stared out of the aeroplane window. I felt a sense of anticipation growing, for I was enthralled to meet this woman named Fiery, knowing that she must be very brave if the spirited Italia was awestruck by her courage.

Later that afternoon Italia and Fiery were welcomed into Sara's palace on the Red Sea.

It was good to see Italia again. She looked no older than a young woman of thirty years, despite her true age, which I knew was much greater. Truly, I found her more beautiful because she was even more self-assured and obviously fulfilled by her crucial work on behalf of women, giving her smoky eyes extra sparkle.

Fiery was more than I had imagined. A more confident woman I have never met. Her passion was so strong that within moments I could see that she was not a woman who merely talked, she yelled. She was not a woman who ever walked, she ran. Everything about her was set at a high speed.

Yes, she was homely, but only for a moment. Her personality and character contradicted everything expected of conservative Muslim women, at least when applied to matters of politics and business. Fiery was one of those women whose colourful personalities increased their attractiveness. Within an hour of our meeting, I could tell that Fiery had easily achieved a certain female splendour.

The four of us shared a common bond that was immediately evident. Very quickly, Italia, Fiery, Sara and I were talking like we were sisters. Perhaps it was because all four of us had spent enormous amounts of time working against the discrimination of women.

For once, Amani was sitting quietly, thank goodness.

Sara posed an important question. 'Fiery, tell us what is happening to women under the Houthi rebels.'

Fiery spoke without editing words or emotions. 'Those dogs are like most of the men who rule over women. Their doctrines are even more conservative than what our society demands. They are now imposing their own interpretation of the Koran on how women should conduct themselves and go about daily life.'

'I was praying for the opposite,' Sara murmured.

'Yes. As were we. But these men are eroding what limited

freedoms we have gained. Although women in my country have never enjoyed trouble-free lives, the street harassments and threats against us are ballooning to a dangerous level. It is now impossible for any woman to go about her business without being followed and verbally abused.'

Fiery exhaled noisily. 'My students tell me that men linger outside the university gates to insult them, ordering them to wear black gloves and black socks, demanding that their hands and feet be covered. A few of the girls said that a gang of five men are there each morning and every afternoon when classes end. They are intimidating criminals, trying to grope the young girls when they pass to get through the gates.'

'Do the guards not intervene?' I asked.

Fiery's laugh sounded like a short bark. 'The guards are men. Most are against education for women. They think the girls are getting what they deserve.'

Italia spoke for the first time. 'Fiery has even gone to see Abdul-Malik.' She chuckled. 'He believed he could ignore her, because she is a woman, but after Fiery sat on the walkway leading to his home for a full day, refusing to leave, he agreed.'

Sara and I looked at one another. We both knew that Abdul-Malik Badreddin al-Houthi was the head of the movement, while two of his brothers were also leaders. Their older brother, Hussein, had organized the Houthis into what they are today. One family had been responsible for the success of the movement that had overthrown the Yemeni government and was now causing conflict between Saudi Arabia and Yemen. For sure, Fiery was brave to make herself known. The way to survive rebellions is to keep one's head down low, but this was not Fiery's policy!

'What did he say to you, Fiery?' Sara asked.

'Oh, he was like most men. When in a certain situation, they talk without really saying anything. He told me that he was going to ensure that women have a prominent role in the new government under the Houthis, and that women are respected from a religious point of view.'

Fiery chuckled. 'He even promised me a position in the government, but I told him no, that it was best that I remain on the outside, looking over the government. I would be his *insurance policy* by never letting him forget that girls and women are not to be deprived by this government too. I held my Koran to my heart and pledged that I would never stop pressing for the rights of women. I would be his human aide-memoire, I promised. And I was not exaggerating. I will never give in until the day I am put in the ground beside my father.'

I grimaced, knowing that life in Yemen was not going to go well for Fiery. Men who rule in our region of the world only accept small doses of criticism from men, and none from women.

'I left, and when I returned to the university the following day I was told that I was on probation; if I did not cease my activities against the Houthi government, I would be sacked.'

'She will not be sacked,' Italia told us. 'I will bribe a university official and they will do something to save her job.'

'No, no bribes,' Fiery said. 'No bribes, Italia.'

Italia laughed in such a way that we knew she would do what she had to do to protect Fiery.

'She did not stop, though,' Italia explained. 'Fiery has organized ten non-violent protests, calling for the end of guardianship laws, child marriages and discrimination in the workplace.'

'Of all the crimes committed against girls, none is more important than that which relates to the marriage of children to men,' Sara said in a grim tone, probably remembering her own youthful marriage and the sexual abuse she endured.

'Yes, Princess. Italia has told me of your work. I know this problem persists in Saudi Arabia just as in Yemen. But I believe it is more prevalent in Yemen. Fewer people are educated there. Most Saudis who are educated are turning their backs on this primitive practice, or so I have been told,' Fiery said.

'Child marriage still lurks here,' Sara said, 'but not so much as before. Of course, we do not know exact numbers because the shameful practice is often kept hidden in a dark corner.'

'For sure it is out in the open in Yemen,' Italia said. 'It is accepted by most Yemenis. They think little of an eight-year-old girl marrying a man of forty years or more. More than one girl has died after her wedding night. Then the family tries to conceal the death because they want to avoid the attention given from outside media.'

I had heard about the eight-year-old child to whom Italia was referring. The girl, called Rawan, had lived in the north-eastern province of Hajja. Her story was fairly common: a child from an impoverished background, living in the villages of Yemen. Most families in such villages live on just a few dollars a day and so money speaks to their needs; many families agree to sell their young daughters for financial gain.

This was the case with Rawan. After a fee was paid to her father, the poor child was pulled from school to be married to a forty-year-old man. Although the old grooms routinely promise not to have sex with the child until she reaches puberty, few of these promises are kept.

On the night of her marriage the terrified Rawan was raped to death.

When the media was alerted to the story, the family and the groom lied, saying that Rawan was alive and well. But everyone knew that she was dead. There were witnesses to her burial.

I felt that Fiery was reading my mind when she said, 'We once had a law that set the minimum age at fifteen for marriage for boys and girls. But clerics and other conservatives pushed the lawmakers until the law was repealed. So now there is no minimum age. The only protection offered is an article of the law that says the groom is prohibited to have sex with the child bride until puberty, but such a prohibition will not stop a man from having sex with a young girl. Unless the girl dies, there is no way to know what has happened behind closed doors. Young girls are raised to be too frightened to speak out, no matter what bestial acts men might perform on their young bodies.'

We ended the afternoon in tears. With the Houthis now in power in Yemen, the situation for girls and women had become even harder.

'We were at the bottom before, no higher than the dirt under our feet,' Fiery said. 'Now we are under the earth, scrambling to push up. We are back to the lowly position we once held.'

I gave a start. Fiery was right. Yemen had been named as the worst place in the world for women. With the few rights they'd previously had being reduced, what could be lower than the worst? My broken heart ached, for I have been fighting to end discrimination against women for my entire life. In too many countries, such as Yemen, Iraq and Syria, the plight of women had plummeted to a new low, deteriorating into an intolerable crisis.

Before Italia and Fiery left Sara's home, we offered financial support to help lead the women's movement in Yemen. Italia smiled and claimed that she would be responsible for the financial needs of women in Yemen, but Sara told her, 'When you are fighting such a cause, Italia, money vanishes quickly. Be sure and keep enough money so that you are not destitute in your old age.'

Ever positive, Italia laughed. 'I would just marry another prince, Sara.'

I said nothing to dispute Italia's plans, but, even though she was still beautiful, I knew that over time wrinkles would appear and her shoulders would stoop. No one can slow old age for ever.

Sara and I pushed until Fiery agreed for us to put a large sum of money into her bag. 'There is more when you need it, Fiery,' Sara promised. 'And, dear lady, our promises will not be broken.'

'Yes, Princess. I thank God every day that I am a woman and that there are women who share my passion, women like me who will never give in.'

'Never,' I said loudly. 'Never will we give in until every woman in the world has the right to freedom and dignity.'

Tears formed in the eyes of Sara and Italia, but Fiery and I were defiant, prepared to continue the battle that was coming, in Yemen and in Saudi Arabia.

Chapter Four

Maha's Secret

MY ELDEST DAUGHTER, MAHA, is a young woman with strong opinions and a brave heart. She does not allow anyone to alter her life's path, which is living as a female with full independence. Maha is out of favour with some family members who have witnessed her aggression in advancing her agenda. This, I believe, is because my culture reacts negatively to powerful women.

Despite Maha's distinguished trait of being honest with all, there are times when she feels that secret-keeping is best. For example, while many know of Maha's unbending character, no one outside our immediate family has knowledge of her unwavering endeavours to aid those in need. I have verbalized little of this aspect of my daughter's personality in the books written about my life. Instead I have divulged many of her teenage dilemmas, some more serious than others, which I have done with Maha's permission. My daughter smiled with nonchalance regarding the stories I disclosed of her youthful indiscretions. This is because she has confidence that all young people become stronger by challenging society, as she did when a teenager.

My daughter is different from most people in other ways, too.

She has never sought any accolades for anything she has done to better the lives of others, cautioning all who know her to maintain her anonymity when it comes to her good deeds.

But the recent rise of radical Muslims roused my daughter to a fury so great that I stood in dazed silence. Kareem told me later that he believed our daughter had been stricken by several penetrating emotions at once. After a few moments of silent thinking, I replied with certainty: 'Yes, rage and embarrassment.'

Maha's rage was layered with embarrassment when forced to face the unwanted reality that it is Muslims who are spreading violence and death across Arab lands. There is no one else to condemn at this point in history, though we both concur that European interference and occupation in Arab lands fractured from the dissolution of the Ottoman Empire during and after the First World War propelled Arabs down a volatile path nearly impossible to avoid.

Nearly one hundred years have passed since the European treaties were made that linked hostile tribes to one another to form nations, and after all this time the Middle East remains unstable.

Despite the meddling of foreign nations in the past, Maha and I both agree that the time has come for Arabs to pull together to solve the enormous problems that are devastating our entire region. We must look no further than our own shores to find solutions.

After her anger subsided slightly, Maha resolved to find a way to reduce the suffering of her Arab sisters and brothers. And so her anger-fuelled resolve led her on a secret adventure that she wished to keep hidden from her mother. But, in the end, she could not.

While Kareem will let a few weeks pass without close contact with Maha, I telephone each of my children several times a day, whether they are in Saudi Arabia, Europe, Asia or the United States.

Maha understood that she would never be able to keep a secret from her mother, although an assortment of deceptions on her part led to six days without communication. Just as I was set to fly to Europe to search for my daughter, who was supposedly touring Pompeii in Italy, I received a correspondence that revealed her secret travel.

Once Maha's clandestine travel was known to me, I was impelled to keep her whereabouts from my husband. Her secret was later exposed by her sister, Amani, who was afraid for her sister's physical safety.

And this is how Maha's secret mission came to enrage my husband, sending him into a mindless fury. Such rage I have not witnessed since the earliest days of our marriage, when he discovered me in the office of the doctor who had agreed to terminate my first pregnancy.

Thanks be to God that Kareem unearthed my harmful scheme in time to save the life of our most precious son, Abdullah. But that is another narrative from many years ago, and I must not stray from a most important story.

My daughter's secret mission was so unexpected, and incredibly complicated, I feel it best that Maha tells you about it in her own words, from her personal correspondence to me, now to be revealed for the first time.

A Letter from Maha

Dearest Mother,

My mind is seeing your face as I write this letter. I know you well, Mother, as you know me. You will be so bewildered to receive an unexpected courier packet from London that your face will turn white, your lips will pucker, and your forehead will crease. As you read the words I have written, you will moan, clasp your hands over your lips, and collapse into the nearest chair. Before you have finished reading my communication, you will shed tears and possibly rend at your clothes.

This I know as surely as if I am in Riyadh, positioned beside you.

But whatever you do, you must not tell Father about what I am to confide. My letter contains a secret that only you and Abdullah can know. I know exactly what Father would do, which is to follow me to force me to leave my current location, and to forget what it is I must do. With Father's enormous power and prestige, he would succeed in convincing the authorities of this land to expel me.

This must not happen! I would never forgive you!

I know that you promised Father that you would no longer keep important secrets from him, but this is not your secret, Mother, it is my secret. Therefore you can relax your mind and know that you are not keeping any secrets that belong to you from Father.

I am trusting you and my brother to fight the urge to violate my trust in you.

Mother, I know by now your eyes are rapidly moving over the page to discover exactly where I am and what it is I am doing that must be kept secret. I am sorry to bring this unpleasant surprise to you, but I am not touring Pompeii in Italy as you believe.

I apologize for my elaborate ruse. I am truly remorseful that you wasted many hours gathering information from travel agents on Pompeii. I felt most contrite when you sent me endless messages on what I must do if I heard Mount Vesuvius rumble. Mother, I could not stop laughing when you told me to keep wet towels in a bag and to put those towels over my face and head and to look for a huge boulder to cower behind in case the volcano blew. I blushed when you insisted that you must travel with me so that you could be my lookout for any smoke that might billow from the mouth of the volcano.

You were correct when you told me that Mount Vesuvius is the only active volcano in the region and that it has a tendency to erupt. I am so sorry that you have been carrying this worry in your mind since the day I misled you with my story of touring southern Italy and Pompeii.

You really are the most wonderful mother in the world, and when you said that you must be with me on this trip, and that you would throw your body over mine to perish with me if the volcano erupted, for you would die anyway when you heard that your daughter had choked to death on the hydrothermal pyroclastic flows, I felt so guilt-ridden for your worry that I almost told you the truth.

Mother, I will not torture you a moment longer. Here is my secret: I have made the trip safely to Turkey. Today I am on the southern border of Turkey, near to Syria. I am donating my time and my money to support the refugees most in need, those who have escaped the horror of the Islamic State fighters (ISIS) and other terrorist groups.

Before you scream and pull out your hair, know that I am not doing anything remotely foolish. Mother, I am here to follow your path in life, which is to relieve human pain and suffering wherever possible.

I am in Turkey for a simple reason. The Turkish people have very kindly opened their borders to poor Arabs and Kurds fleeing the radical Muslims who are trying to destroy all life in their path. If the Turkish people can open their hearts, minds and purses to help these poor refugees who have been forced to flee their homes to escape the violence of war, every Arab should do the same. I am an Arab woman without children. I am an Arab woman with financial resources. I am an Arab woman with the freedom to help.

If I do not help, who then?

Now, please stop weeping. I am safe. I am not alone. I am travelling with two friends who previously volunteered to work in the refugee camps. They are well established and know the 'ropes of volunteerism', as they call it.

One of my friends, Rabia, is from Turkey. Only a few months previous to now, she worked in the first of the refugee camps formed in her country for the Syrian refugees. Rabia is the reason authorities at the camp accepted us easily. My second friend, Hilda, is from Germany, someone who carries the guilt of her Nazi grandfather, who was an SS officer who was captured by the Russian army while stationed in Hungary and was subsequently worked to death in the coal mines. She travels the world helping others, trying to repay the debt she feels she owes due to her grandfather's activities.

I am so pleased that I chose to live in Europe, Mother. How else would a Saudi princess ever come to know and befriend such fascinating people from Turkey and Germany?

The important point is that, thanks to Rabia, both Hilda and I have the proper credentials as volunteers to enter the camp and to work with the psychologically war-scarred children. However, not all Syrian refugees live in the camps, some have chosen to live in small Turkish villages and towns hovering on the border with Syria. Therefore, I plan to expand my work to include some of these families, as they do not receive shelter, food and education from the Turkish government.

So you see, Mother, while I am a novice, both friends are well versed in this kind of work. Hilda, whom I mention above, has for three years volunteered with a small human-rights organization to work with women and children in Gaza. Hilda says it was a nightmare to enter Gaza through the Israeli Erez Military checkpoint. The nightmare did not come from the long hours of waiting but due to the actions and words of the Israeli guards who tried to intimidate her with suggestive remarks, telling Hilda that a pretty blonde girl should be worried about rape from the animals she was going to help. Hilda said that while she never once had fear of the men in Gaza, she was nervous about the Israeli soldiers who had a special hatred for Westerners who volunteered in Gaza or the West Bank, considering those who help the Arab children as personal enemies of Israel and Israelis.

This was a surprise for me. I have always believed that all Europeans and Israelis were the best of friends. This is not the case, Mother.

To her despair, Hilda was recently forced to discontinue her volunteer work in Gaza. She said that each time she left Gaza to visit her parents in Germany, Israeli authorities required her to endure long waiting periods for approval to renew her visa. After her fifth departure from Gaza, she never again received a visa to return, although the officials in Israel would never say a direct 'no' but instead reported that no decision regarding her visa had been yet made. The long delays were their special way of keeping people out of Gaza, even those who were offering free assistance to innocent women and children.

You can be comforted that I am not in Gaza, Mother. Hilda says that volunteering in Gaza was the most dangerous work of her life, while volunteering in Turkey holds little danger. Turkey is safe. So long as one does not cross over into Syria, there is nothing to fear. And, Mother, a trip to Syria is one I would never make. I am not dim-witted, Mother. There are radicals near to the Turkish border who yearn to kidnap Western reporters, or attack Syrian refugees on their way in to Turkey, or back in to Syria. Can you imagine how excited they would be to capture an Al Sa'ud princess? Never would I give those false followers of Islam an opportunity to cause you and Father one moment of anxiety, or to create a vexing problem for Uncle Salman.

So, put your troubled mind at ease. I will keep my distance from the Syrian border. You have my word.

Now, please remain calm as you read my letter.

There is much misery all around me, but I have concluded that I must use my time and resources to allay some of this misery. I am most eager to tell you how I am spending my days. To do this, I must describe the camp, the village, as well as the lives of the refugees, people who have had to 'run for their lives'.

First of all, please know that I am financing this trip and paying all expenses. My friends have little money to spare, as both are so generous that they give away nearly everything they have to those who have nothing, so it is only fair that the one with the expendable income pay the expenses. It is the best money I have ever spent in my life.

You will be relieved to know that my friends and I are not living in the camp, nor are we living in a dangerous neighbourhood. I have rented an acceptable apartment in a safe area in the village nearest to the camp. Knowing how you and Father worry about my safety, I have hired three men as security officers, and they have signed documents agreeing to be discreet and as inconspicuous as possible. I have also rented a car and have two drivers on call. Like the security officers, they have agreed to be as inconspicuous as possible, as we must not stand out in the area. (No one other than my two close friends knows that an Al Sa'ud princess is a volunteer. I am using the special passport Father paid to have issued several years ago in the event our family had to flee revolution in Saudi Arabia and, as you know, the document does not identify me as a princess.) Many volunteers mingle with the hired helpers in the camp; a large number live in the village, so it is not unusual to see men and women of other nationalities in the area.

I know you will want to know about my living arrangements, so I can reassure you that we are in a safe neighbourhood. Where we are staying is not a luxurious villa but a modest and simply furnished apartment with three small bedrooms and two bathrooms. There is a common living area and kitchen. There is a balcony, which is fairly spacious, so it is pleasant to enjoy our early morning coffee there and plan our work day. Yes, Mother, early morning!

I know this will surprise you, as I have always been a late sleeper. But now I am so motivated by what I am doing that I awaken by seven each morning and, after a simple breakfast, the three of us are driven to the camp.

Oh Mother, the camp! I would send photographs of the camp and of the people but since I am not an official photographer I do not want to create unease in the hearts of the refugees. I have witnessed how they become reluctant and even fearful when people insist on taking their photographs. I have been told that they are frightened that, if identified, their family members left behind in Syria will be targeted by the government or by other factions.

I will not cause them any unnecessary anguish by taking photographs.

Most of these people were once respected, hard-working middle-class people in Syria, but are now individuals without jobs, homes or schools. While lucky to have survived the war in Syria, and the subsequent flight through violent factions of gangs who are fighting each other, their lives are now incredibly bleak, marked by the repetitiveness of life when there is absolutely nothing to do but to talk, eat and sleep. These are people who once lived in good homes, enjoyed careers, and found joy in raising their children and visiting with their families and neighbours in a normal manner.

But such lives are now nothing more than hazy memories or even dreams. Their everyday lives today are like vivid nightmares that they must endure.

Mother, I will now describe for you the sights my eyes have seen, the odours my nose has smelled, and the sounds my ears have heard. I have a strong desire for my memories of the camp and of the refugees to become memories for others. Perhaps this will happen.

On that first day, when I was allowed entry and walked past the guarded entrance into the camp, I was pleased that there was no stench. In fact, the camp is kept as spotless as a camp can be that is inhabited by thousands of people. There was noise; my ears heard the clamour of a large city occupied with many large families. I heard the cries of babies, the shouts of children, and the sporadic chatter of adults. Because everyone is on foot, the camp lacks the sounds we generally hear from automobiles, buses, trains or aeroplanes; this is a city with few motorized vehicles, although occasionally you will see the delivery trucks carrying stoves, refrigerators and other heavy-duty goods.

My eyes saw endless white containers, the type of huge metal bins I have seen transporting goods on cargo ships. Thousands of these were placed in neat rows. Drying laundry was hanging on lines within a few steps of nearly every container. There were pathways between the containers. My imagination took me to the image of those pathways being a well-worn history of thousands of human feet going here and there.

I peered into a few of these – what I thought were empty – containers. Within, I saw neat stacks of blankets, clothing and other supplies to one side, while there were inexpensive carpets on the floor, and small kitchenettes on the other. Although I did not actually inspect any of these container homes too closely, I feel certain there are toilets or some kind of similar facility in every container.

I was a little overwhelmed by everything I saw that first day. As I continued passing by these 'homes', it suddenly dawned on me that up ahead people were spilling out of them and, in the early morning light, I could see they were beginning to queue for their food rations for the day. Some were mothers, tugging at their hijab with one hand and clutching their coupon books in the other as they walked rapidly down the path. This, it turned out, was part of the women's daily chore. There are just ten grocery outlets servicing all the families in the camp, and although I hear the food on offer is fairly bland it is plentiful. No one is going hungry. (All Arabs should thank the Turkish government for their generosity. No country has done more to help these people.)

I recall that some of the men had heard gossip that their families might be moved from the camp into a Turkish village (which is something all desire). I overheard their conversations with one another, searching to seek what truth lay behind the rumours; they were obviously concerned about the welfare of their families. Others, however, were hurriedly making their way to meet other men to play backgammon or other board games, a means of whittling away endless time in a camp where few have jobs. There were children of every age and size, so many that I thought of a disturbed beehive. The children captured my attention. I've become accustomed to joyful faces and spirited shouts from children at home, as they play and squabble, but this is not the situation for these camp children. Nearly every child's face was aged far beyond his or her years. I'd never before seen a small child with an old face and it touched me greatly.

The children break my heart, Mother.

Once we arrived at the container marked administration, specifying the meeting place for volunteers to receive assignments, the appearance of those children had so pained me that I specifically pushed for permission to work with them.

The attention to detail by the people who are running this camp is impressive. Although I had previously submitted to a number of meetings and interviews, I was again questioned and even given two tests to ensure that I have a suitable disposition to interrelate with children. You know more than anyone how I adore my niece and nephews. Obviously my relationship with them has prepared me a little for working with children and I was assigned to the special classes for the most troubled children, which is what I requested.

After two days of special instructions, I began my work.

There are specially trained paediatric medical doctors who work with these children. I am one of six volunteers whose only purpose is to make these children feel safe and secure. We attempt to entice them to play games. We hug them. We coax them to eat their meals. We indulge them in every way possible, for these are children who were caught in the

86

epicentre of one of the most brutal wars in the Middle East. These are children who have lost parents, grandparents and siblings. Their little lives have been shattered.

This is what I do every day. I play with children; I comfort them and make them feel the hand of human kindness. If only I can bring a smile to one of their faces, then I will ask nothing more of life.

There are twelve children in my group. Their ages range from four to six. Four are boys. Eight are girls.

All four boys are mute. Two of the girls are mute. All six of the mute children have lost a parent. Three of the boys lost their fathers during the war, although thankfully they did not witness their deaths.

One of the mute girls lost her mother in a particularly gruesome manner. The woman was shot in the head in front of her three children by a young fighter who was out to prove his bravery. I was told by another volunteer who makes the mental assessments of the traumatized children that the poor girl was splattered with her mother's brains, and a chunk of her mother's skull struck the girl's cheek so violently that the child's face was visibly marked by cuts and bruises. Mother, I could only think of the girl's mother and how she would have mourned to know that her fragmented skull would physically and mentally wound her baby. The medical staff who are in mental care and work with the traumatized children discover these details when questioning the children or the surviving adults who were with the children at the time.

Two other girls lost both parents in a Syrian government bombing attack. It is said that one of the two girls actually pulled out her mother's head and her father's leg while she was sifting through the rubble looking for them. It was from that moment that the girl lost her ability to speak, although we were told that she screamed for hours. Since her shrieks of anguish subsided, she has not made another sound. This small girl with large dark eyes and a lovely little face sits quietly with lips compressed for the entire day. She takes no notice of the toys and games we use to try to entertain her and lift her spirits. She does eat, but you can see that she takes no pleasure in the food. She usually drinks water, and only reluctantly sips apple juice when coaxed. There is no spark of life in her eyes. She is completely withdrawn and detached from everything around her.

The medical team is becoming apprehensive because they were informed by the surviving uncle, who assumed responsibility for his dead brother's children, that if the child does not recover her ability to speak, he will be forced to consent to give her in marriage to a rich Gulf Arab who noticed the beautiful child and offered a large sum of money for the pleasure of marrying her. The uncle claims that he is married with children of his own and cannot be responsible for a dumb girl. She is almost seven years old, and the uncle says that she will soon be old enough to learn the responsibilities of adulthood and marriage.

Does the uncle not care that the potential groom would be raping a child – a child already so psychologically tormented that she cannot speak? I am going mad with worry for this child. I must save her!

Such a plan would have been unthinkable for Syrian families prior to the civil war. These educated Arabs lived tranquil lives and would never have agreed to sell their daughters. But sadly the war has brought much misery and poverty, and today the unthinkable is now a real possibility for some desperate people.

At the end of the day the children go to the containers to join family members, or those family members who have survived the war and the journey from Syria to Turkey. What they do at night while home I do not know. Most likely they are left to their own resources, ignored by family members who consider them a burden.

Mother, this aspect of my culture greatly troubles me, for

I know from your work that if a child is vulnerable through disability or if she or he is traumatized in any way, the family turns away, saying that it must use its resources to raise the children who are mentally and physically fit – those who are able to work for the family.

At the end of each day I join my friends at the front gate, where our driver awaits. We sometimes stop along the way in the village to buy some food, and perhaps take a few minutes to pause at a café for a cup of tea and a sweet, for we too are tormented by the anguish we see and need a little relaxation. I feel physically and mentally drained from the emotional tugs at my heart and mind, yet nothing could pull me away from these people.

Although our Turkish neighbours speak and smile when we pass, there has been no time to become more familiar than this. It is said that many ordinary Turks are incensed that the Syrian refugees are receiving benefits that ordinary Turks are denied and in need of. But we have seen no bitterness thus far. We will be making efforts to befriend our neighbours, as well as other Syrian refugees who have managed to avoid living in the container camp. These are the refugees who held on to enough money or jewels to rent apartments in the village. However, we are also told that as the funds diminish, many of these families are marrying their daughters off to affluent suitors. Girls as young as eight years old are being used like a valuable commodity by many families, their little bodies bartered and exchanged for money, sometimes for marriage. Even more alarming, sometimes girls are provided for a weekend or a week for a wealthy man's pleasure. My friends and I are determined to save as many girls as possible from this odious situation. They should not be the solution to the financial dilemmas their families face.

Mother, I can barely write these words, as my body is still trembling from the memory of something I have just witnessed. I met a young woman named Yana who was captured, raped and tortured by the ISIS fighters. While attempting escape from Syria to Turkey, the caravan she was travelling with was attacked by a small group of fighters. Many of the fleeing Syrians escaped, including her parents. But Yana was grabbed out of the vehicle in which they were travelling and kidnapped, along with her two younger sisters, both of whom are still missing.

This is how this tragic story came to me. As I was clearing my work station at the end of the day, a woman came in to collect one of the mute boys for her neighbour. I instantly became aware of her because she was wearing a niqab, which exposed her eyes but nothing else. Few Syrian women wear the niqab, as you know. Everything about this woman suggested youth. Her shoulders were broad and her stride was sure. I listened as she spoke to the mute boy. Her voice was youthful, with a melodious cadence. When the boy refused her kindly gesture to walk from the classroom, the woman suddenly lost her composure and began wringing her hands, which I noticed were visibly scarred with angry raised red stripes.

I walked to her and placed my hand on her shoulder, as she was small compared to me. I asked, 'What can I do to help?'

I was completely stunned when she burst into sobs and collapsed into a chair.

I was concerned for the mute boy, but his expression never changed; he stood and stared, as he always does. I suppose that the poor child must hear the sounds of weeping women all hours of the day and night. Feeling that he was neither better nor worse from the situation, I turned my full attention to the veiled visitor. I stood beside her and rubbed her shoulders.

Our eyes met, and I believe she could sense that I truly cared about her circumstances. Without speaking, she removed her niqab.

My heart skipped several beats. Those raised red stripes I had seen on her hands were also streaked across her face. I knew then that someone had taken a sharp blade to a face that was, quite obviously, once delicate and lovely. I could tell by her small features, her large eyes and her full lips that she had been a very attractive girl. Finally, I stammered, 'What happened? Who did this to you?'

She bewildered me with her admission. 'Oh, I did it,' she said in a calm voice. Then she removed her abaya. Underneath she was wearing a plain navy dress with sleeves to her elbows. She pulled up her sleeves, showing me that the red bands went all the way up her arm. I assumed then that much of her body was covered in red stripes. And it was.

I will condense a very long story for you, Mother, but will tell you more when I see you. This poor Syrian girl has endured more terror and abuse over the past year than I can bear to contemplate. Yana and her two younger sisters were beaten by their captors even as they sped across the desert. All three pleaded to be returned to their parents, of course, but their pleas were a source of amusement for the brutal men who had captured them.

They were transported to a fighters' camp to be locked in a cramped room in a small house. They were taunted, told that they would be kept for the high-ranking fighters due to their youth and beauty. The only benefit was that gangs of men would not be free to rape them, at least until those high-ranking fighters tired of them.

Yana was only seventeen years old, but she was suddenly the guardian of her two young sisters. She knew that she must defend them at all costs. One sister was only ten and the other was twelve. When confronted by her rapist, Yana offered herself in place of her sisters. At first the fighter who had claimed her agreed. He raped her several times a day, but he kept his promise and did not assault her sisters. Then one day when Yana was sleeping, her rapist unlocked the door, rushed into the room and snatched the youngest of her sisters.

Yana leapt to her feet and tried desperately to rescue her sister, but her rapist was twice her size and punched her in the face. The force of the blow rendered Yana unconscious and she briefly passed out. It was only the horrific screeches coming from her little sister that brought her back to consciousness. Yana pleaded from behind locked doors for her rapist to leave her little sister alone, to return her, but of course he did not. He threw the grievously wounded little girl back into the room when he was finished with her. Two days later he repeated his brutality with Yana's second sister.

Although she knew she would be executed for killing an ISIS fighter, Yana plotted to murder their rapist. She waited for the opportunity to seize a weapon. One day after a particularly brutal attack, Yana realized that her captor had removed his dagger and placed it with his trousers between Yana and the wall. Yana seized the dagger and tried to plunge it into her rapist's stomach. But the man was strong and he knocked the dagger from her hand, laughed in her face and goaded her to keep the dagger and use it to kill herself and her sisters with it if she dared.

Not surprisingly, utterly beaten and distraught by her lack of power, Yana suffered a breakdown a short time later. She said she played with the dagger for a few days, before being possessed with a courage to self-inflict pain on her own body. She began cutting the flesh on her arm. Once she started cutting, she said, she could not stop. Slicing her flesh gave her an enormous sense of relief. The cutting also served to act as a self-inflicted punishment for her failure to protect her sisters.

Eventually, Yana began to cut her face – the face her mother and father had claimed to love. Looking back, she remembers thinking that mutilating herself was a useful act. The rapes would most likely stop because her pretty face would no longer be a magnet for her rapist, who had enjoyed lusting after her. Just as she was about to mutilate her little sisters for the same purpose, to free them from being raped, the rapist and several other men burst into the room. They'd heard the girls screaming, as if they were fearful for their lives. The men took *the dagger then dragged the distraught Yana from the room she shared with her sisters.*

She never saw her young sisters again, although she heard their cries of pain and terror through the concrete walls. It seemed that the high-ranking fighter was so enraged with Yana that he allowed the lower-ranking fighters to rape her young sisters at will.

Yana was right in her assumption that without beauty she had no value to her captors. She was freed from being raped, for her face and arms were scabbed and ugly. Sadly, the torture of hearing her sisters repeatedly raped was more painful than being raped herself, or so she said.

Then one day some of the fighters burst into her room and bound her hands before pushing her into a vehicle. She was driven for several hours before being released in an area not far from the Turkish border. The shouts of her tormentors still ring in her heart. 'Yana!' they bellowed. 'Tell the women you meet that someday they, too, will be ours!'

A kindly Syrian family found Yana wandering alone and rescued her, giving her a lift to Turkey, where she was taken in to live in the container camp.

And this, Mother, is the story of Yana.

I will not abandon her. I will do what she will allow me to do for her. To my surprise, she refuses to consider surgery to smooth the scars on her face and body, saying only that she prefers to be an undesirable woman, unwanted by all men. I volunteered to pay for the best European plastic surgeons, but she says an emphatic 'No.'

Tragically, I am told by others here that there are many other rape victims living in the container camp. No one will identify them exactly, for few refugees will open up like Yana. I am told that when a woman claims she has heard of a woman who was raped or has received a letter from someone in Syria with details of a friend who was raped, it is in reality actually this woman who is speaking of her own experiences.

As you know, our society finds a way to blame every female victim, so who can fault these women for keeping their history of rape and abuse a secret?

Mother, tonight I was looking in the mirror and contemplating the life I have lived, comparing my childhood, and now my adulthood, with the lives of the children and women who I encounter daily. Although I feel enormous sympathy and care, truthfully I feel like a war correspondent who sees all but can do nothing. This is not a good feeling.

Yet for the first time in my life I finally and fully understand why you have devoted your life to the cause of women. Now I know the significance of your work.

I want you to know that now your daughter is doing the most important work of her life.

I love you,
Maha

My daughter's communication marked the beginning of an episode that turned my close family upside down.

But, of course, I did not know that at the time.

Chapter Five

Infamy in Pakistan

S TILL CLUTCHING MAHA'S LETTER, I stumbled across the room and tumbled face forward on my bed. My mind was bubbling with a multitude of emotions. I felt elation even as I suffered sadness. I strained to smile, but my lips spread no further than a tremble. Ultimately the tears gushed and I wept. My heart was breaking for my daughter, and for the traumatized women and children she was seeking to serve.

I have always counselled my children that those who have great wealth – particularly those born into wealth without having worked for it, such as is the case in our own family, the Al Sa'uds – owe a debt to society. And while I have always envisaged the day my children came of age – an appropriate age to accept their responsibilities and undertake charity work – now that my daughter was in a place and situation I sensed might be risky for her, I underwent remorse that I had steered my child to true peril.

Indisputably, danger lurks for those who push societies to transform. Nearly all who gain power take offence when censured by their citizens or others, even if the criticism might provoke positive change for their own people. Many governments choose the regrettable approach of using the power they possess to imprison, torture and even put to death those who dare to condemn or call for progress. There are even famous cases in my own country where those who have dared to speak out have been arrested, imprisoned and sentenced to floggings and years in prison.

Societies tend to be equally less forgiving of dissenters, with too many people clinging stubbornly to the way things have always been, and reacting angrily when various segments of society demand change. When people are uneducated, or simply lack curiosity to seek knowledge, change appears as a frightening unknown. Such fear leads to aggression, even violence. This we have seen in countries such as India and Pakistan, where anyone not of the majority religion can easily be falsely accused of blasphemy, a favoured manner of harming one's enemies, and the state will too often execute these innocent people without a proper trial.

These factors combine to mean that there is a possibility of immense danger for one who pushes for reform.

Moreover, there is the potential for enormous personal pain. Many people walk the earth without recognizing the agony of the lives of so many, but for those people who do take note and truly care the misery they witness becomes their private sorrow.

I know this to be true, as there have been times in my life when I have felt that my eyes have seen only grief and my heart has felt only pain. I have lived with what I call the 'pain of compassion' for much of my adult life and know the toll the anguish takes. Now my child was to follow. Once the desire to help others settles in a heart, a hunger to assist flourishes. There was no doubt in my mind that my daughter, Maha Al Sa'ud, would now devote her life to serving others. Her endeavours would bring sorrow even as they brought joy.

To calm my nerves, I comforted myself with the knowledge that the joy of improving and changing lives would overshadow Maha's sorrow.

After some long moments had passed, I stood up and glanced into the mirror that hung over my dressing table. I noticed that my eyes were red and swollen, and I knew that I must put cold compresses upon them quickly, if I was to avoid Kareem's scrutiny. My husband becomes very inquisitive if he suspects that I am upset or if I am keeping a secret from him, and is always determined to get to the bottom of my troubles.

Just as I placed Maha's letter on my dressing table, Amani knocked lightly on the door. 'Mummy, may I come in?'

I smiled, pleased that my youngest child finally understood that it was best to knock before entering her mother's private quarters.

'Come in, darling,' I said with anticipation, forgetting moment-arily that my eyes were swollen from weeping. I was not expecting Amani, but whenever one of my children or grandchildren visit, I am anxious to see them without delay; my day brightens when I am in their company.

Amani burst into my quarters. Her head was lowered, as she was looking at some photographs, but I could see that her face was twisted with anxiety.

What now? I wondered.

Just then Amani looked up at me. She suddenly stopped and, staring into my face, she said, 'Mummy, have you been crying?'

Other than Kareem, Amani was the last person I wished to know of Maha's current mission. 'Darling,' I stammered, 'no, I am suffering from an allergy from the profusion of flowers that your father sent to me.'

It was true that our home smelled heavily of perfumed flowers. Kareem and I had had a minor squabble the previous week and the day before he had surprised me with many bouquets of yellow roses, one of my favourite flowers. But, as usual, my husband had overdone his gesture and I could not count the number of roses placed throughout our palace. Sara had visited that afternoon and she had suffered such a headache from the strong scents that wafted through the palace that she had departed earlier than planned.

'Mother?' Amani queried in a disbelieving tone.

'Yes, Amani. It is nothing.' I stared pointedly at the photographs in her hands and nodded. 'What is in your hands, daughter?'

Amani clearly did not believe my words. I am not a mother who seeks to worry my children, so there have been many times when I have attempted to keep a painful truth from one or all of them.

Amani's gaze shifted from side to side, searching my room for any evidence of what might have brought her mother to tears. Seeing nothing to question, she said, 'Let us have a cup of tea, Mummy. I am quite distressed and would like to relax a moment before I tell you a story that will bring back your tears.'

I sighed. I had been unsuccessful in my attempts to convince Amani that the scented roses had created a flower allergy. I would have to be on guard, for no one is a match for the passion of my daughter. In past years when attempting to burrow out the sins of her siblings and their friends, Amani had become as skilful as the finest private investigator.

But I hoped that such activities were behind her, as all in our family had strived mightily to encourage her to lose this most un-appealing trait.

'Yes, darling.' I glanced at the clock, guessing the time we had before Kareem would arrive. Believing that we had several hours, I said, 'But give me but a moment to repair my face and I will join you in the small sitting room.'

'Yes. I will wait for you there,' Amani promised.

I kissed my daughter's face before walking away, trusting that she would exit my quarters. Never did I suspect that she would do a hurried search of my room while I was in the powder room or that she would find her sister's communication from Turkey.

To my alarm, I would soon discover that Amani had read enough of Maha's letter to create a great upheaval in our family.

Half an hour later I joined Amani in the smallest of our sitting chambers. The room has an intimate feel and I always select that setting when there are no more than two or three individuals in attendance. My daughter and I had sat there on many occasions, discussing the joys and sorrows of our family life, and of the world.

An attractive display of tea, coffee and fruit juice, along with fresh fruit and small sandwiches, were waiting for me at the small dining table set up in the sitting room. Our tea was served by a dear girl named Dilipa from Sri Lanka who is part of our home life. Her name means one who gives and protects, and Kareem and I had observed that she lives up to her name, for Dilipa was the most kind-hearted of all our employees, and always consoled others when they were lonely or homesick.

Looking at sweet-faced Dilipa, I considered the millions of homesick foreign workers living and working in Saudi Arabia. Although Kareem and I employ hundreds of people in our homes and businesses, we are always fair and just to those who work for us. None have to worry about not receiving their salary, or being physically abused in any manner. I have always felt empathy with the foreign workers, as various problems plague so many of them. As a teenager I befriended one of our Filipina housemaids, who confided to me the tragedy of some of her friends who worked for other Saudi families. As a sensitive child, I was already aware that many foreign workers found it very difficult to leave their loved ones and take up employment far from home in order to support their families. I knew they would be lonely and more than a little lost, even if they were well treated by their employers.

People who have not lived in Saudi Arabia have little or no awareness of how completely Saudis depend upon their domestic employees. Nor would those people know that there are nearly ten million expatriate workers in the kingdom. This, in a country with only nineteen million native Saudis. I have been asked many times why there is such a necessity for foreign workers; although there are simple answers to this question, few will respond truthfully. However, I have no problem admitting the painful reality. Few Saudis will consider working in a service job, for most believe they would lose face if they took a position where they served others. Therefore, Saudis have no choice but to hire foreign workers for menial jobs in the commercial sector, as well as in the private sector, where millions work as housemaids, cooks and nannies. Since women are forbidden from driving, any Saudi family who can afford a driver has one – men originating from Indonesia, Egypt and the Philippines mainly.

A second reason for the high number of expatriate workers is the low number of Saudi females in the workforce. Although a high percentage of Saudi women obtain education, in the workplace many fiercely resist hiring them. Employing women creates many complications, and obstacles, for an organization since men and women are forbidden from face-to-face contact: gender segregation is an inflexible rule. Even the rooms in an office building must be rearranged, for it is imperative to keep male and female employees separated by walls or temporary partitions. Then there are unreasonable men who complain that simply knowing a sensual female is in the building is too distracting for them to work productively. These ignorant men truly believe that females cannot control their desires and are working only to seduce men. Such unenlightened men can, and do, create endless problems for the employer.

It is easy to understand why it is much less problematical to simply ban female workers. Due to this impediment, the percentage of females in the workforce is dismally low. I am sorry to say that my country is filled with educated women who are sitting at home, not allowed to use their skills productively.

I was born in Saudi Arabia. My family rules Saudi Arabia. I am a Saudi Arabian woman who loves her country. However, I cannot deny that we are behind the times in so many ways: transformation is long overdue.

I have tried to play a secret role in the change that must come to my country, for I have been an anonymous and rigorous voice for many years now, alerting the world to the abuse endured by so many Saudi women, even those of the royal family. I have succeeded in some ways, and failed in others.

Since I was a child I have overhead the powerful men in my

family – the very men who are able to bring improvement to the lives of so many – say that the Saudi journey to gender and democratic reform must be gradual, that great turmoil would result if the government moved more rapidly than the street, meaning moving faster than the citizens of Saudi Arabia.

I agreed with their assessment once, but no longer. I believe that the majority of Saudi men, even men in my family, truly like keeping women in a secondary position – although they will give many different reasons for being unable to elevate women to their rightful place in society – thus denying them the ability to live lives of dignity.

I also believe that most ordinary Saudi citizens desire more freedom for women, and more democratic reform for all residents living in the kingdom. In our case, 'the street' is ahead of the government and of the religious authorities, who would like nothing better than to keep all women imprisoned in their homes, just as it used to be in my grandfather's time, when women were not even allowed to walk from their homes or private garden to go to a shop, even if escorted by their male guardian.

I used to believe that before I departed this earth I would live in a land where women are free, and where the men who help those women are not punished. I now fear that this dream will not be realized. On the day of my death, I feel certain that I will still be criticizing the continued lowly status of females in my country.

My thoughts reverted to my daughter and I smiled and began to eat. After we shared a light lunch, Amani spoke. 'Mummy, you seem far away. What are your thoughts?'

I smiled. 'At that very moment I was thinking of the people who make our lives so easy, Amani. We are very fortunate that we can spend our time doing the things we wish to do, rather than be burdened with housework and the other time-consuming chores so many women in our world undertake.'

Amani shrugged. 'Mummy, they should be very happy to have a job to enable them to support their families.'

I gazed at my seemingly unfeeling daughter but did not react to her disappointing words, reluctant to spark an argument with this, my most complicated child. Instead, I asked, 'Tell me daughter, what are your thoughts? I am interested in knowing what is occupying your mind today.'

Her face inscrutable, Amani spoke in an unemotional tone. 'I was thinking that soon the Islamic State will celebrate a year's anniversary.' She paused. 'I have also been reflecting on the sad plight of the many thousands of people caught in their path.'

I looked intently into my daughter's eyes.

Amani stared at me without blinking.

When my eyes started to sting, I blinked.

How, I wondered, could it be that both my daughters were on to the same subject matter at the identical time? This had never happened in the history of our family. Maha and Amani are as different as two girls can be. While Maha had always been devoted to human rights, Amani had dedicated her life to animal rights, although over the past year she had awakened to the importance and the matchless personal satisfaction one experiences when helping other humans. She had taken particular interest in darling twin girls, Afaf and Abir, the daughters of a woman named Fatima, whose life had dramatically changed for the better when Kareem and I brought her into our home. Amani also took special notice of my educational charity work for girls in Palestine.

I sat speechless, speculating for a moment whether Maha had written a revealing note to her sister at the same time as she had communicated with me. But I instantly cleared that possibility from my mind; Maha did not trust her sister and would never divulge such an important secret to her. I could not blame Maha, as Amani's reactions in the past were enough to make anyone wary of trusting my youngest child.

'Mother? Are you still with me? The Islamic State? Do you have any idea what we might do to help the people being tortured by those men who claim to follow the Muslim path?'

I bit my lips and looked away, apprehensive that I would say the wrong thing.

Amani sighed deeply before expressing her strong opinion of the men behind the Islamic State. 'You know, Mother, from what I have read, those men seem to know nothing about the goodness and kindness of the Prophet and of his teachings.'

'You are right, daughter,' I murmured, as I nodded my head in agreement. 'From what I have seen reported in the news, these men are hiding behind our faith even as they behave in ways that would surely win the Prophet's condemnation.'

Amani's eyes were glistening. I wondered if my daughter was going to weep, something out of character for Amani, who generally keeps a check on her tears. Her voice breaking, she asked, 'What about the young girls and women who are being sold like camels at auction? Have you heard of these things?'

'Yes. I have learned many things. I pray that much of what I have heard is rumour, but I fear that it is not the case. From all reports, these ghastly men become very joyful, even excited, when given the opportunity to rape very young children.' I grimaced. 'It is a picture that I do not want settled in my mind, but once heard it is impossible to erase the image of what those innocent babies are enduring.'

My daughter was twisting her hands in despair, for she was a mother who loved her children dearly: if they stumbled while running, even without sustaining injury, Amani became visibly upset.

'Amani, try to be calm. It appears that the world is unwilling, or helpless, to stop these people. Indeed, the men in our family have learned that the governments of the United States and of Europe have no further interest in helping their friends in the Middle East. I believe that the latest debacle in Iraq convinced the Americans that they best leave the Middle East altogether, that there is nothing to be gained from intervention in this region.'

I paused, searching for words that might reassure my child. 'But, Amani, at least Uncle Salman is doing what he can to stop the rebels in Yemen.'

'Are those Houthi rebels a big threat to us?'

I paused a second time, gathering my thoughts. 'The situation is complicated and it is difficult to say with certainty what will happen if there is war, or if they are ignored altogether. Your father believes that they must be stopped, for the sake of the Yemeni people. As for me, although I do not believe that even if they take full charge they would be a huge threat to our country, I also believe that a wise man or woman would never wish for an enemy to be so close. If the Houthi are allowed to create a stronghold in Yemen, it would be very easy for them to slip across our border and create unrest in our own country.' I hesitated for a moment. 'Yet all our hearts break for the innocent civilians maimed or killed under our Saudi bombs.'

I looked into my daughter's eyes. 'Mistakes are made during such tense times. We will have to wait and see the outcome.'

'Why do we not bomb the Islamic State, rather than the rebels in Yemen?'

'Amani, while it is clear that the principal danger is coming from Syria and Iraq, the problem with the Islamic State is thorny. How can a country like our own, with a small population, fight so many men who have carefully perfected the tactics of war and terror taught to them by their own rulers?' By my words, I was speaking of the men who had served under Saddam Hussein, a most ruthless ruler who controlled Iraqis through fear of what would happen were they disloyal to him or the regime. The Syrian regime had been equally repressive. It seems that the most devoted fighters were from those two countries, although there were plenty of volunteers from other Arab lands.

When she reached for her cup of tea, I saw that Amani's delicate hands were trembling. Now I believed that Amani's questions about the Islamic State had nothing to do with Maha and her letter. My daughter was in despair due to the current crisis in our region.

I tried to reassure her that what was happening was not due to any blunders made by the Saudi government but had occurred due to forces we could not control. 'I can barely believe what is

happening across Arab lands. Although the Syrian government
has always been strong-armed with their citizens, from what I
know of the Syrian people, they are good.'

Amani's face turned the brightest pink as she considered my
words. 'And the women who join them? Women from Europe
who are making the journey to Turkey to join these men? Have
you heard of them?'

'I do not know much about them, Amani. I have read a little.
Truthfully, daughter, I am more interested in the victims, not the
women who bolster these loathsome men with their support.'

Obviously my daughter was keeping up with the men and
women who joined the Islamic State. She said, 'Mummy, these
women leave their countries in Europe to travel to Turkey then
cross the border to marry the fighters. Then they help to patrol the
regions that have been captured. The women who join the Islamic
State then attack those who are unwilling to join them. I have
always thought that men are too often drawn to the violence of
war, but it is a new thought for me that women enjoy such actions.'

For once my daughter knew much more than her mother about
an Arab crisis. I decided then that I would find out about these
women from Europe or other lands who were supporting men
who were rapists and murderers.

'Have you any first-hand knowledge, Mother?'

'Of the women who join the fighters?'

'No.'

I was confused. 'Knowledge of what aspect of this, Amani?'

'Of the refugees.'

'Oh, the refugees.' I paused, noting Maha's connection to the
refugees. I have never wanted to intentionally lie to any of my
children, but Maha had placed me in a position of trust, and I
could not disclose my eldest daughter's newfound passion of
volunteering in the refugee camp. 'Daughter, I can only tell you
what I have read, or heard. Nothing more.'

Amani appeared to be near tears, probing further, bombarding
me with several questions at once. 'Mummy, are we in danger

from the Islamic State? Do you and Father worry that these violent men will one day be in Riyadh?'

I remained silent, not knowing how to comfort my child.

Understanding by my silence that I could not offer reassurance, Amani's voice cracked in emotion. 'Are my children in danger?' she asked.

My youngest daughter is the mother to two young children. Little Prince Khalid is now three years old. Amani's second child, a little girl she named Princess Basinah, is only eight months old.

Kareem and I feel keen disappointment that our daughter cannot cut her ties with the animal world, even when naming her daughter. Basinah is a nice name, but it was chosen by my daughter only because the meaning is 'little kitten'. Amani rarely calls Basinah by her name, addressing her instead as 'my little kitten'. But there is nothing that I can do but support my child, despite the unconventional preferences in her personal life.

Hearing the fear in my daughter's voice, I began to feel very anxious and vulnerable. As a mother, it is almost unendurable to witness fear or pain when it comes to my children. But I reminded myself that Amani was no more fearful than the millions of other people living in the Middle East. Everyone in the region was occupied by the severity of the threat, with many enduring painful deaths at the hands of those who have no mercy in their hearts.

Few events in modern history have shaken the stability of the region more than the current movement headed by the Islamic State fighters, despite Saudi intelligence estimates that there are no more than 50,000 to 75,000 fighters. In their crusade to establish an Islamic state to be governed by their version of sharia law, these men have terrorized huge swaths of Syria and Iraq, with promises to leave no current Arab regime in place. Although their numbers are small in comparison to the size of the armies they attack, thus far their ferocity for war has immobilized most of those they have met on the battlefield. Much to the Arab world's chagrin, large numbers of those sent to defend their countries have fled rather than do battle with the Islamic State fighters. This, even though they have ample soldiers and the latest weapons to defeat their enemy. Only the Kurdish fighters are uncompromising on the battlefield, matching and defeating the Islamic State fighters in battle after battle; but there are not enough Kurds to protect all the Arab lands.

'Darling, no, your children are not in danger. Do not forget that Saudi Arabia is a huge land, and there is a vast desert between Riyadh and the Islamic State fighters. Our king is a man who believes in protecting Saudi citizens and the holy sites. Uncle Salman has led our close friends and neighbours in the region to attack rebels in Yemen. This showed great courage and wisdom. Do you believe that our uncle Salman will sit calmly on his throne if our country is threatened by the Islamic State? Never will that happen,' I said with certainty.

Amani continued to sob, despite my reassurances.

I leaned towards my daughter, holding her small frame in my arms. 'Amani, you have your mother's word that your father and I will never allow anything to happen to you or your children. Now, stop weeping, darling, or I will weep with you!'

Amani's tear-filled eyes stared back at me and she eventually became calm. I took this opportunity to change the subject. The pictures that I had seen in Amani's hands were now lying face-down on a small table next to where we were sitting. 'Amani, darling, brush away your tears and tell me why you came to see your mother. I want to know about the photographs I saw in your hands.'

'Oh, yes, the pictures.' Amani shifted her position to reach out for the photographs. 'Well, first of all, Mother, the pictures I am about to show you have nothing to do with the victims of the Islamic State. These pictures have to do with women in Pakistan, women who have been cruelly and intentionally injured by Pakistani men.'

This was an unanticipated matter. To the best of my memory, I had never heard Amani express concern about the human rights of Pakistani women.

'Pakistan?' I asked, reflecting on a time some years before when my sisters and I had gathered in a circle to protect a young Pakistani girl named Veena from further sexual attacks inflicted by three of my nephews.

That was on the occasion when my husband and I, along with our three children, joined my siblings and their children in the Saudi desert at Wadi al Jafi.

All Saudis I know carry a deep and lasting affection for the desert. Although I will not provide a full history of my family for this story, it is good for readers to know that the rulers of Saudi Arabia were settled village Arabs, rather than Bedouin, who roam the lands. Still, we remained solidly attached to the desert, as our country is mainly desert, with only a few large cities and some villages located in liveable areas that are scattered throughout our vast country. Even village Arabs feel at home in the desert, for so much of our country's history is entwined with the desert, a history that pulls us to the vast empty sands.

So it was a happy time when our family retreated to the desert to reminisce how our ancestors had lived so simply long before the oil was discovered. Having said this, I will admit that our holiday in the desert was a luxurious occasion, for as much as we like hearing the tales of our ancestors, we have no desire to do without the indulgences of royal life while revelling in the memories.

The event began most joyously, but soon became sour after various upsetting episodes concerning some of the more difficult men in our family.

First of all, my brother Ali was bitten by a snake. At the first telling, it was believed that the snake was a poisonous yaym, and that Ali was doomed. Later the snake was captured and it was found to be a much less poisonous hayyah. Although Ali suffered pain from the bite, he did not die; during his suffering, he stunned and irritated me with his request that I apologize for all the wrongs I had committed against him over the years. I was so dumbfounded I could barely speak, for I had gone to what I thought was my brother's deathbed to hear his apology and confession for his sins against me. The episode left a bitter taste; my family was very relieved that Ali did not die but no one seemed to notice his continued arrogance and bad behaviour towards me.

The second, and most serious, situation occurred when the screams of a woman brought me from my bed to my feet. My sisters, Nura and Sara, joined me in investigating the screams. We discovered a horrifying crime. Three of our nephews were raping a young Pakistani woman, who we later came to know as Veena, whom we thought worked in our sister Dunia's home.

The poor victim *was* from Pakistan, but she did not work for Dunia. Rather, Dunia's son had travelled to Pakistan to purchase a young woman to serve as his sex slave. The young woman had been sold to our nephew for a pittance, but it was a good sum of money for the parents of the girl involved. Before the evening was over, we had saved Veena from a terrible fate.

Tragically, my nephews were never charged with the crime, since other members of our family protected them; however, there were a few restrictions put on them by the eldest male in the family. In my country, the plight of a young female worker is virtually ignored, by society and by the government. Rarely have I known of punishment given for a Saudi assault upon a foreign worker.

But due to the actions of the females in our family, Veena's life changed dramatically, and for the good. The girl lived and worked for Sara for years before she requested to return to Pakistan. That is when Sara and I financed a business for Veena, a small sewing factory, so that she might help her family.

Following that experience, my son Abdullah has travelled to Pakistan at least once a year and has made good on his promise to help other women achieve economic independence.

However, Pakistan is the business of my son, not Amani. I had never heard Amani and Abdullah discuss his good deeds in that land.

While I know that Pakistan is like so many countries that practise extreme gender discrimination nationwide, I had never heard Amani express an interest in helping women from Pakistan. As for me, while I have read many tragic stories, my charity work is mainly limited to girls and women who live in Arab lands.

'What woman do you know from Pakistan?' I asked.

'I have no friends from that country, but I have recently discovered the most troubling tales of abuse, Mummy. I want you to do something about it.'

I stared at my daughter's face, in which was reflected a special kind of pain that I recognized; it is the pain of knowing another's agony but being helpless to bring an end to it.

Amani then placed one particular photograph beside my hand. I clutched at my throat as I shrieked – only to be silenced at that very moment by the arrival of Kareem, accompanied by our son Abdullah and his small daughter, Little Sultana. With arms out-stretched, the darling little girl ran straight to me.

When I came to my senses and realized that Little Sultana was examining the picture in my hand, I flipped the photograph on its face.

'Jaddatee, was that a picture of the bad jinn that comes in the night?' Sultana quizzed.

I turned to see my son and my husband standing side by side. Abdullah looked at me with curiosity on his face, while Kareem appeared confused, never having seen a photograph of a woman so grievously wounded she resembled a monster, or at least that is what Little Sultana had mistaken the poor woman for.

I quickly regained my composure to make light of the photo-graph. 'No, darling. That was a cartoon picture, a surprise for someone special.'

Little Sultana's voice rose in pitch, anticipating something very nice. 'A surprise for me, Jaddatee?'

By this time both Kareem and Abdullah knew that they had interrupted an important meeting. Abdullah wisely shifted Little Sultana's interest. 'Sultana, you came to see Jaddatee's new aquarium with the beautiful blue and pink fish. Come with me now, and Jaddatee will join us later.'

He increased Little Sultana's desire to examine our new aquarium that Kareem had recently filled with exotic tropical fish by suggesting, 'We will ask for some peach ice cream, too.'

'Ice cream!' Little Sultana ran to her father, holding his hand and walking with him out of the room.

My darling granddaughter could be very mature at times, but still, she was only a child at heart and ice cream was a certain magnet; she had loved ice cream since she was old enough to taste it, and peach was her favourite.

Kareem asked, 'Is everything all right?'

I sighed in relief, while Amani raised her eyebrows but said nothing.

'I will return later,' Kareem said finally, as he gave a little wave, then followed his son and Little Sultana.

As soon as I was alone with Amani, I gestured for the photographs, looking carefully at each sheet. Each sheet had two images, photographs that were obviously before and after pictures. One photograph showed a healthy, beautiful woman. The second photograph was evidently of the same woman, dreadfully disfigured after a horrendous assault.

I saw a lovely young Pakistani woman with unblemished skin appearing jovial and untroubled, for she was smiling broadly. The second photograph was of the same young woman, but her jaws and chin were now fused to her neck. Her lips were gone, and her mouth was fixed permanently in a large circle, exposing her teeth fully. I groaned, realizing that most likely this was the woman's expression as she was attacked and that she would probably be permanently scarred in this manner. The agony she was enduring was clear from the helpless look expressed in her dark eyes.

I saw a young girl who could have been no older than thirteen or fourteen, with bright eyes filled with gaiety and fun. In the second photograph, those eyes were gone, replaced by two blackened holes. The skin on her face was hideously scarred.

I saw a young mother with two precious daughters, all three smiling with anticipation, most likely eager to see the resulting photograph. I saw the same young mother with one of her daughters, both showing grievous wounds. The mother's chin no longer existed. There was a gaping wound, as though her chin bone had been eaten away. The child's nose had disappeared, replaced by two small holes. Her ears had been eaten away. One eye was gone and the other appeared sightless.

There were more than ten photographs of attractive girls and women before a great tragedy struck, and a second photograph showing the effects of the catastrophe.

Although I believed I knew what had happened to these women, I asked my daughter. 'Amani, darling, what has happened to these poor girls and unfortunate women?'

Amani was visibly upset, as though she had heard of these poor women for the first time. 'Mother, these women are all victims of acid attacks. Almost all the attacks were made by their husbands, or by a rejected suitor, although a few of the women were falsely accused of blasphemy, and villagers attacked them. Some of the children were victims because they were standing near their mothers when their father threw acid at the mother. One of the young girls was attacked because her parents rejected a suitor, a man old enough to be her father. He hired some young thugs to follow her when she left the house with her grandmother. They threw acid on them both. The grandmother died, and the young girl was left with the traumatic injuries you saw.'

'Oh, Amani. I was afraid this was the story.'

Distraught by the images I had seen, powerful images that conveyed joy, followed by images that shrieked of tremendous agony, grief and loss, I buried my head in my hands. I knew something of the history of acid attacks throughout the world, but I have always found the subject so painful that I had intentionally avoided becoming involved. Besides, one person can only do so much, for there are only so many hours in a person's life. I had devoted my adult life to the education of girls because I believe that only when all women are economically independent can they rule their own lives, and teach their daughters the value of education and the ability to fend for themselves, if necessary. While crucial to success the world over, I have discovered in life that education is most important for women who live in the developing world. When an impoverished family realizes that a woman has the means to work and make a contribution to the family's income, that is when she gains respect. Often, the 'respect' is purely a cynical attempt to use the woman as a method of working for the good of the family; in such circumstances, the money a woman is able to earn brings her some form of protection from attack.

Although Saudi Arabia has known some cases of acid attacks upon women by their husbands or family members, this was a crime that seemed to be more common in Pakistan, India, Bangladesh, Cambodia, Yemen and Afghanistan, although it does occur around the world, even in the United Kingdom. I also knew that the hideously scarred girls and women rarely received support from the government or their communities. Like most crimes against women, the victim is generally blamed. If a woman is divorcing an abusive husband, the community feels great sympathy for him, and makes excuses for his criminal behaviour, saying that the woman should not have left her husband.

'Tell me from the beginning. How did you learn of these stories?' I hesitated, but only for a moment, adding, 'What is it that you would like to do to help these women, Amani?'

For certain, if my daughter wished to become involved and create a charity for victims of acid attacks, I would help her as much as possible, although I know my personal limits. I am not ashamed to say that I do not possess the emotional stamina necessary to meet with the women of acid attacks and do the 'on the ground' work that is essential to help and protect them. While I could provide funds, and individual support to Amani, I do have a point where I break. Should I find myself around a child or young woman who had instantly been taken from a lighthearted and cheerful life, becoming a shell of a human who has no physical ability to turn her head, or chew her food, or see, or hear, I know that I would make the victim's situation worse with my cries of agony and tears.

So over the next hour I heard from Amani exactly how she had become drawn in to the lives of acid victims from Pakistan.

Amani's cousin, Princess Sabrina, had recently approached Amani about the plight of Pakistani women who were the victims of acid attacks.

Sabrina is a princess several years younger than Amani. The two became close friends after meeting at a cousin's wedding. The couple were the parents of three boys and three girls, all of whom have good reputations. Sabrina had lived a sheltered life, as she was the youngest child of her father and mother. While her parents are very wealthy, the father is not in line to the throne, so they are considered to be one of the more minor royal families and do not become involved in decision-making in the kingdom.

Still, the family is well respected because it has never been involved in a scandal, something unusual in a country where there are many royals who have more money than they can spend. The combination of too much money and plenty of free time brings out the worst in many people.

Sabrina's father met his Lebanese wife when attending school in Lebanon. Their marriage was not arranged, and was based on genuine affection, a love that has endured many years of living in restrictive Saudi Arabia. Since they live half the year in Beirut and the other half in Jeddah, the wife's life was less constricting than most women who are married to a Saudi prince.

After Sabrina graduated from college as an honours student, her proud parents asked what she might like as a special gift. To their astonishment, she asked that they give her the gift of travel. Sabrina wanted to experience the adventure that she believed might be found if she could only tour the world, to be away for a year or more, to explore on her own. She had taken a number of courses in photography and was told by her professors that she had a gift. Sabrina had a dream that one day her images, and possibility even articles written by her, would feature in *National Geographic* magazine.

Although the family is enlightened, the parents would never allow a young, unmarried woman in her family to travel the world alone. Anything might happen, and their scandal-free reputation might end.

Sabrina was told by her parents that the gift of travel was hers to claim, but that two of her brothers must accompany her for the entire trip. The world can be a dangerous place for the naive, they said, and their lives would be ruined should anything damaging happen to their youngest child.

Sabrina reluctantly agreed, hoping that her brothers would learn to trust her judgement and allow her to wander off on her own to find the adventure that she knew was waiting. While Sabrina had no desire to meet any man, she was high on the idea of adventure, or finding her passion in life.

Sabrina's first stop on her world tour was Egypt, a country she knew quite well, so there was nothing new to attract her interest, despite the wondrous history of the country. Her second stop was India, which was tantalizing for Sabrina, because it is a multifaceted country, colourful in every way. There's something for everyone in India, and Sabrina came away with some amazing photographs to share with friends. Yet there was no exceptional story that created unique enthusiasm in the young princess.

But then Sabrina arrived in Lahore, Pakistan.

Lahore is a city of the arts and is considered the cultural heart of Pakistan. Much of the city is beautifully maintained because the citizens are proud of their flowers and green gardens. There are many art festivals, and music is celebrated. Film-makers have made the city their home. The Pakistani intelligentsia thrive there.

An artist at heart, Sabrina felt at home in Lahore and eagerly roamed the city, accompanied by her protective brothers, of course. Just when Sabrina felt that she had found her spiritual home, she saw a veiled lady stumbling on the sidewalk. A compassionate girl, Sabrina rushed to assist, but the veiled woman pushed Sabrina away. Sabrina was lugging several cameras in her hand, and while attempting to keep a grip on her cameras, she lost her footing. As she fell, Sabrina instinctively grabbed at the woman, whose veil came loose and flapped in the breeze.

Sabrina saw the woman's face, which was scarred from severe burns, but she curbed her horror and helped the woman refasten her veil. The woman scurried away, but Sabrina followed; she felt she had no choice but to discover what horrible tragedy had created the disfigured face she had seen, and to offer assistance if needed. Her parents had given her more money than she could spend, saying that she should have no economic pressure during her trip, and she knew that, if needed, there was plenty to share.

At first, Sabrina believed that the woman must have been burned in a house fire, but she soon learned that the truth of her injuries was more perturbing than an accident.

Sabrina, followed by her perplexed brothers, tracked the woman into an open courtyard after the woman accidentally left a metal gate ajar. There, Sabrina saw a sight she could never forget even if she lived for a thousand years. There were more than ten women sitting in the garden. Some women were wearing veils, others were wearing sunglasses, while others sat quietly with their mutilated faces exposed.

Sabrina had stumbled upon a house of horrors.

When the women saw Sabrina with her cameras, no one moved. They believed that she had been sent to photograph their injuries for the courts, as most had court cases moving slowly through the Pakistani legal system. But when they noticed Sabrina's brothers, men they did not know, all the women shouted in terror before scattering into the building adjacent to the garden.

Sabrina used her verbal skills to persuade the administrators of the women's home that she had not come to do harm to the women, or to the establishment. She convinced them of her truth, that she had the ability to help by making a substantial financial donation to the home. All she wanted in return was an opportunity to help the women, to make a record of the women's injuries. She promised not to release any information to the public, unless the women specifically requested her to do so.

Prior to travelling to Lahore, Sabrina had little knowledge of the country. Although at first sight she had loved Lahore, she was devastated to learn that such a beautiful country is not a safe place for women. She soon discovered that Pakistan is one of the worst countries in the world for women, and that the government, the police and the legal system fight *against* women, rather than for women. She was not aware that acid-throwing by men on women who are their wives, or children, or simply a woman they admire, is at epidemic level – and, sadly, is growing and becoming more common. She did not know that the Pakistani courts have only convicted one man out of many hundreds who have committed the crime.

Once Sabrina learned the extent of the problem, discovering that many Pakistani men believe it their right to destroy women's lives in the most harmful manner possible, causing the greatest physical agony, lifelong bodily disfigurement that brings severe psychological damage, she made the decision to make the acid women her life-long project.

Knowing that she would need help from others, she contacted Amani, telling her the stories and sharing the photographs that I had seen.

Princess Sabrina had found her passion.

Now it seemed that my daughter and I would be sharing it.

'There is so much more to tell you, Mummy,' Amani said. 'I have stories that will chill your heart and bring tears that you cannot control.'

I shivered, knowing that such stories were going to render me sleepless for many nights.

'Amani, I will help you if you like,' I assured my daughter, 'but I cannot promise that I will travel to Pakistan and help you and Sabrina there.'

My daughter's expression was one of extreme disappointment.

I am weak when it comes to my children, and so I quickly added, 'This is something I have to think about, Amani. I am not getting any younger. I must guard my health, and, my darling, this is the most troubling topic in the world. Already I am shivering in despair at the sight of those women in the photographs.'

That is when Kareem walked into the room. 'Little Sultana is becoming restless. Is it possible for you two to continue your conversation later, after Abdullah has taken her home?'

'Yes, of course,' I replied. 'We will come now.'

'Amani, gather your photographs so that Little Sultana does not see any other pictures of these poor women,' I reminded my daughter. 'We will discuss this further tomorrow. I have many questions about these women, and what the Pakistani government is doing to stop these crimes.'

'Yes, Mummy,' Amani said in a voice so sweet that I could believe for a moment that she was still a little girl.

To my horror and surprise, that is when Amani looked at her father and asked, in the same innocent voice, 'Father, did you know that Maha is in Turkey, volunteering at one of the refugee camps there?'

I gasped. Clearly, Maha was right not to trust her sister with her secret.

Kareem froze. 'What?' he said.

Amani replied before I could speak. 'Maha is in Turkey, Father. She sneaked there so as to work with the refugees. I fear that she is in danger.'

My husband gave me an angry look, one that nearly stopped the blood flowing through my veins.

'Sultana! What is this? Another secret?'

Amani glided out of the room, as if the conversation was no more important than the flavour of ice cream we might enjoy later. But Kareem was set to fight, and I knew that the night would be a long and difficult one.

Chapter Six

Maha: Where the Heart Goes

KNOWING THERE WAS WISDOM in avoiding a confrontation with Kareem, I raced past him and out of the room to find Abdullah, the only person in our family who I knew would join me in supporting Maha's decision to help the Syrian refugees, and who might have a chance of softening his father's wrath over my secret-keeping.

Kareem can be aroused to a great anger against me and our two daughters, all of whom have great passions for various causes. Rarely, though, does Kareem have reason to disapprove of our son, which I believe is due to Abdullah's calm, self-possessed personality and his soothing manner.

Abdullah had no indication that Amani had discovered Maha's secret, so he was startled when I called his name in a screech of despair as I dashed into the area of our palace that houses our new aquarium.

'Abdullah, where are you, son?'

As I sped into the room, I quickly saw that Abdullah was sitting next to Little Sultana at one of the five tables placed in the middle of the room. This angelic girl was eating a small bowl of peach ice cream illustrating the dainty manners she had recently learned while taking a charm and etiquette class from a pleasant British lady who was currently popular with the royals as a teacher of valuable social graces.

I had interrupted my son as he was observing the various rare tropical fish that slowly swayed as they swam, giving every indication that they were contented and tranquil in their outsized environment.

The year before Kareem had hired a professional to build an impeccable home for fish, an aquarium that circled the room from floor to ceiling. Spectators felt as though they were drifting in the blue waters with the tropical fish. Upon completion, a marine expert had stocked the aquarium with sea life, mainly from the reefs and coastal mangroves of the Red Sea. There were fifty different species of fish and other sea creatures, all carefully selected for their flamboyant and multicoloured beauty, including clown fish, jellyfish and even sawfish. I glanced over and saw that a school of clown fish had gathered in a low corner of the aquarium and appeared to be examining Little Sultana and Abdullah with a great intensity. But who could know the mind of a fish?

Even Amani approved of our aquarium, one of the few she agreed was large enough to keep fish from being psychologically damaged. I have never heard of a fish needing therapy, although Amani believes that such attention is valuable for those poor fish kept in small aquariums or in tiny bowls sitting atop tables and desks, where fish tend to swim round and round, indeed appearing rather hysterical to be in such a confined space, which even I admit is cruel.

There had been several unpleasant incidents when our daughter had demanded that the owners of fish kept in such conditions release their pets from agony and instead give them to her to keep in spacious water containers. Each time this had occurred, the proprietor of the fish was so befuddled that it was agreed that my daughter could take possession of the little creature.

Due to Amani's obsession with the well-being of all animal life, whether those living on land or swimming in the sea, no one in our family has experienced a moment of boredom.

While Little Sultana expressed no anxiety about my dramatic entry, Abdullah discerned that something was amiss, for I was panting and had clearly been running through the palace.

'What is happening, Mother?'

I was about to explain the trigger that had created the drama when Kareem burst into the room, his anger expressed on his rosy-coloured face. My husband was ready to fight. I knew the signs.

To my vast relief, when Kareem realized that Little Sultana would be a witness to any row we might have, he loudly inhaled, pulled up a chair and sat. I marvelled at his self-control as I observed his expression slowly transform from immense anger to a studied calm. My husband sat quietly, smiling at his son and granddaughter as though there was nothing of importance on his mind.

I joined the table, and almost miraculously, as though we were on video and the kitchen staff was watching closely to see when Kareem and I entered the room, two more bowls of ice cream were served.

I assumed that Abdullah had alerted the staff we would soon join them, and ice cream was already dipped and put into the bowls to be kept cold in a small freezer in the room next to the aquarium, ready to be served the moment we settled in our chairs.

Abdullah looked warily at me, and then to his father, but Kareem said nothing of importance, as he chatted with Little Sultana. The two of them raved about the delectable taste of the ice cream. Abdullah joined in the senseless chatter. I was not unhappy about it because their mindless prattle gave me time to think. My thoughts zipped through various scenarios, as I worked out how I might convince my husband not to react without thinking first. Knowing Kareem, I felt certain that as quickly as possible, he would depart on our private jet from Saudi Arabia for Turkey to force his daughter to leave the volunteer work so important to her, and to abandon the refugee children she was helping.

Just then Amani came into the room to tell us that she must return home, but not before saying that she would call me in the morning to further deliberate about the women of Pakistan we had discussed. I was exceedingly annoyed with my daughter and for once did not reply with the sweetness she is accustomed to hearing. Despite this, I saw that Amani was not in the slightest concerned that her mother was furious at her misbehaviour.

I had reason for my anger. There was no doubt in my mind that Amani had invaded my privacy to search through my quarters, finding her sister's confidential letter to her mother. I was so eager to reprimand my youngest child that I dared not open my mouth to speak a single word. That is why I feigned a mouth full with ice cream and nodded rather than respond verbally.

Amani was irritatingly cheerful as she smiled at me to bid a final farewell.

I love my children dearly and have often been accused of being an overindulgent parent; if they are sometimes insensitive and badly behaved, I feel I must take the blame.

I would tend to my daughter later, but for now I believed that Abdullah and I must make a collaborative effort to prevent Kareem from behaving rashly. Maha was of an age that she could live as she pleased, despite parental dissatisfaction. Knowing Maha had combined her strong character with a great passion for volunteering, I suspected that Kareem might regret trying to dissuade her from following her chosen path.

Several years before, Kareem and I had bestowed great wealth on our three adult children. We had also made generous legal trusts for our grandchildren, which would be available to them at the age of twenty-five. Maha, Amani and Abdullah had all reached the age of economic independence; they enjoyed life without financial worry and could still devote much of their wealth to charitable causes.

After Little Sultana finished her ice-cream treat, she very politely dabbed her mouth with her napkin before carefully folding and laying it beside her bowl.

My adorable granddaughter was practising her etiquette lessons, I thought to myself.

Smiling, she leaned forward to kiss me, then her grandfather, before saying, 'Thank you for the delicious treat.' She paused, 'I would like to see the beautiful fish now. Would you care to join me?'

Kareem and I melted in pleasure, for we are both devoted grandparents and nothing gives us more joy than the cuteness of our young grandchildren. Long ago I heard from an elderly auntie that the only perfect relationship between human beings is that of grandparent and grandchild. I now know that to be a certainty. While parent and child relationships are often marked by disputes, for a parent is wholly responsible for that child's welfare, grandparents are kept at a comfortable distance from daily responsibilities.

The grandparent and grandchild relationship is a most rewarding one – for all concerned.

I watched as Little Sultana entertained herself by pressing her face against the aquarium walls while staring raptly at the varieties of fish.

With Little Sultana out of hearing range, Kareem could not restrain himself a moment longer. He looked at his son and, in a low tone, voiced an urgent appeal. 'Abdullah, did you know that Maha was in Turkey? Volunteering at a refugee camp?'

Abdullah paled, instantly trapped in the middle of a dilemma. If he said yes, he would be breaking a promise to his sister to keep an important secret. If he said no, he would be lying to his father.

'Abdullah, do not follow your mother's path by keeping secrets from me,' Kareem said in a soft voice that was nevertheless stern, as he shot me a dark look.

Abdullah glanced at me. Seeing my son's misery, as he was caught between his sister and his father, I intervened. 'Husband,' I whispered, 'I will tell you what I know, but in private. Let us see our son and granddaughter to the door, and we will settle this between us.'

Kareem looked in my direction. 'I am sorry, Sultana, but you will stretch the truth first one way and then another. I will have to put the puzzle together from many broken pieces.'

I stiffened. I had volunteered to discuss Maha and her mission with Kareem, and now he was insulting me.

I decided to ignore my rude husband. 'Abdullah, when is Zain expecting you and Little Sultana?' Zain, Abdullah's wife, was a perfect wife, in my opinion, but she did like to know her husband's schedule. I wished to give my son an excuse to leave, forcing Kareem to discuss the problematic set of circumstances with me, whether he wanted this dialogue or not.

But Abdullah has always been wise, and his wisdom is topped by a strong character. These two characteristics mean that he generally makes good decisions. Therefore, I was not surprised when he responded to his father's question with an important Islamic teaching from Prophet Muhammad.

'Father, from the time I was a child, you and Mother have always told me that every Muslim must give in charity.'

'That is true, son. Do you think I have a problem if Maha gives many millions to the refugees in Turkey, Jordan and Iraq? No, I do not know, nor care, what she does with her inheritance. But I am concerned for her safety. Abdullah, I cannot have my daughter there, single and without protection in a camp filled with many thousands of desperate people.'

Abdullah pushed aside his ice-cream bowl. 'Father, you once told me a particular story when on a specific Eid holiday you caught me taking the fruit and candy from the baskets that were filled by our family to give to the poor in charity. I would like to now remind you of that story.'

Abdullah was always such a good child, and I did not recall such an incident. I like to know everything that has affected my children in life, so I leaned in to hear this story.

Kareem quietened and nodded. 'Go ahead, son. I am listening.'

'You told me this story, "The Prophet Muhammad said, 'Every Muslim must give in charity.' The people around him asked, 'But what if someone has nothing to give, what should he do?' The Prophet replied, 'He should work with his hands and benefit himself and also give in charity from what he earns.' The people then asked, 'If he cannot even find that?' The Prophet replied, 'He should help the needy who appeal for help.' Then the people asked, 'If he cannot do even that?' The Prophet finally said, 'Then he should perform good deeds and keep away from evil deeds, and that will be regarded as charity.'"'

'Father, you and Mother pressed the importance of charity to your children all through our early years and you told me that although I was too young to work and give my earnings to charity, I should stay away from evil deeds, such as stealing candy and fruit that was meant for the poor; you said my good behaviour would be considered charity.'

Abdullah paused before making the most important point: 'Father, it is very easy for our family members to give money, for we have more than we need, but when we give of ourselves, and give of our time, and feel with our hearts what the unfortunate endure, then that is true charity. Maha is living up to what is expected of all Muslims. My sister, your daughter, is one of the few who gives completely, with her money, her time and her heart.'

Abdullah observed his father for a moment, then said, 'Father, Maha has gone where her heart has taken her.'

I saw that my husband was thinking seriously about what Abdullah had said because he was biting his lower lip, a habit of his that shows when he has a lot on his mind.

'Son, I will consider what you have said. I will speak with you again in the morning and tell you my decision. Although you are right that as Muslims we have to give, I still feel that I cannot allow my daughter to be in physical danger.'

Abdullah then replied, 'Well, Father, it is said that nothing great has ever been achieved without danger. Maha is doing a great thing, and it is even greater because she can easily live a life of idleness and luxury and send money for others to carry out this arduous work. But nothing is greater than being on the ground where the need exists, to help physically, psychologically and financially.'

Kareem said nothing in reply, but pulled his son to him for a brief hug.

Abdullah gazed at his precious young daughter, who had momentarily forgotten her etiquette lessons as she was skipping with delight to leap into her father's arms. She squealed with pleasure, 'I saw a fish as big as Little Faisal! The fish was blue and green!'

Little Faisal, the brother of Little Sultana, was just a toddler, and his sister adored him, although he was much too small and young for true companionship for an eight-year-old girl. But I was happy that Little Sultana was dazzled by the fish. I looked at Kareem in gratitude for all the unusual projects he arranges for our children and grandchildren to enjoy, such as the giant aquarium.

My husband felt my stare and looked at me too, but with a scowl.

I shook my head and looked at Kareem in disappointment. Although my initial reaction was alarm at the thought of Maha being in a refugee camp, I was quickly soothed by her reassurances of safety, and the knowledge that my eldest daughter was accomplishing something very important, assisting those in great need as well as furthering her own passion for goodness.

Abdullah turned his attention from Little Sultana to his father and said, 'Father, there are children as loved, as precious as my child. These children have been abused most mercilessly. Try to think of your granddaughter and know that there are thousands like her who have endured the most horrendous harm. It is people like Maha who have also gone with their hearts, and are working to try and bring those children back to a normal place in life. What would the world do without such people, Father?'

I had to fight back my tears, remembering the little girls my daughter had described in her letter, knowing that those little girls were as precious as our own.

When I squeezed my granddaughter goodnight, I praised God that she was not in danger of violence, rape or murder. Those innocent children Maha was helping had once had parents and grandparents who loved their babies just as we love ours.

I then embraced my son with great feeling, wondering how it was that I had given birth to someone so strong and so wise.

As Abdullah walked away with Little Sultana in his arms, I wiped away a tear, and when I glanced at Kareem, I saw that he, too, was fighting back emotional feelings.

I gently touched my husband's arm, to remind him that I was there, but he pulled back from me and resumed his cranky mood, telling me, 'Sultana, we will discuss this in the morning. Meanwhile, I am going to have our aeroplane readied for a trip to Turkey. Tomorrow I will see my daughter.'

I stood in shock as Kareem rushed away.

Then I knew that despite the wisdom of Abdullah's words, Kareem was going to take his daughter from Turkey.

My husband locked the door to his private quarters and refused to hear my plea to enter. Thus, he blocked my plan of disclosing Maha's letter, and my strategy to encourage him into accepting the fact that his daughter has the right and the wisdom to make her own decisions. I also believed that my husband should be aware of the precise security safeguards Maha had already taken. She was not living alone. She had found a safe apartment. She had hired twenty-four-hour security. She had arranged to have drivers and a vehicle at her disposal. Maha had taken every precaution she could and I desperately wanted Kareem to know these things so that they might allay his fears a little.

I, too, of course, was desperately worried about Maha's safety, but Kareem's over-reaction had somehow changed my own mind about wanting her to leave Turkey. Initially, I longed for nothing more than to command my daughter either back home to Saudi Arabia or to her other home in Europe. My only concern was that she was out of any kind of danger as soon as possible. But my husband nudged my sense of right and wrong, reminding me that Maha was a well-travelled, strong-minded and independent woman who has seen much of the world. She is a woman who has been making her own decisions for many years now. If any woman on earth can take care of herself, Maha bint Kareem Al Sa'ud is that woman.

*   *   *

Early the following morning I received unwelcome news from Abdullah. He telephoned to tell me that his father and his uncle Assad were airborne, flying to Turkey even as we spoke. Abdullah had tried to contact Maha to warn her, but he told me, 'She is not answering her cell phone.'

I glanced at the clock. 'She will be in the camp by now,' I said. 'For certain, she cuts off her phone. Knowing Maha, she will avoid any interruptions that might distract her from her work with the children.'

'Should I fly there too?' Abdullah asked.

After a moment's hesitation, I said, 'No, son. Maha can handle this. However, we must both attempt to reach her so that she is not shocked to see her father storm through the camp.'

I hesitated, then added, 'And she should know that neither you, nor I, leaked her secret.'

'Yes. You are right, Mother. Maha will be unhappy with us until she knows the source for Father's discovery of her secret. As far as Father is concerned, I doubt they will let him in the camp. He has no credentials. From Maha's letter, they run a tight and very secure camp. The Turkish government is handling all these things in a very professional manner.'

I gave a resigned laugh. 'Son, you know that your father will do what he must do to see Maha. He will be impatient, unwilling to wait until she leaves the camp later today.' I repeated my words: 'You know what your father will do.'

I heard my son exhale loudly. 'I wish he would not give bribes, Mother. That is the sort of behaviour that creates true loathing of Saudi royals. Until the rule of law is accepted and this kind of behaviour stops, we will never receive proper respect in the world community.'

My son was correct. Yet I've never known a Saudi royal who saw the harm in offering money to get what he or she wanted. Although bribing has been perfected in the Middle East, I know that it happens all the time, and in most corners of the world, anywhere two entities meet, those who desire a specific thing that cannot be had without a financial disbursement, and those who desire wealth and are eager to acquire money by exchanging something of significance for cash.

Since I was a young woman there have been a number of highly publicized bribery scandals regarding Saudi military equipment contracts with Western nations. While the media in the West chases a story like this and publishes scathing reports of those who benefit, Saudi officials shrug. Bribery is a way of life in Saudi Arabia. It has many faces. Nearly every Saudi feels they are entitled to use their own money to obtain whatever it is they want. Nearly every Saudi sees nothing wrong if a person is enriched when taking a percentage of a business deal.

'I agree, son, but when it comes to his three children, Kareem is not a man who listens – not to anyone. He has most likely already spoken to someone high in authority and has offered a large sum of money. I have yet to know of a person who has said no to the sums Kareem is willing to give to get his way, and most particularly when it comes to his family. Once in Turkey, he will be like a powerful sandstorm, covering the entire area until he finds Maha.'

'Father is making a grave mistake,' Abdullah said in a disappointed tone. 'I know my sister, and when I read her letter I knew in my own heart that she has found a great passion in this cause. I only hope that Father's actions do not create a permanent schism between himself and his daughter.'

With those fear-provoking words ringing in my ears, Abdullah said his goodbyes, but not before saying that he was going to bed for a much needed nap. He had barely slept the night before, worrying about Kareem and Maha.

I felt deep concern, for I had never known Abdullah to take a nap since the days he was a toddler and was forced to do so by his mother. I gritted my teeth in anguish, knowing that Kareem had made a poor decision, which threatened to adversely affect all our lives.

That night I was so disheartened I could barely sleep. My rest was interrupted by nightmarish dreams filled with visions of an angry Maha evading her father by fleeing from the camp and falling into the hands of dangerous men, never again to be found by those who love her so much.

The following morning I spent some time attempting to ring Maha, but without success. Abdullah was also trying to reach her, but similarly with no luck. We could do little more than fret about Kareem's strategy and feel anxious about Maha's reaction.

The morning's endeavours and frustrations had put me in a foul mood even before Amani visited later in the day to resume our discussion about her cousin, Princess Sabrina, and the project to help Pakistani women who had been savaged by acid by their fathers, brothers, husbands or potential suitors.

Amani was smiling broadly, happy to see me, she claimed.

I vowed not to raise my voice, and spoke lowly but without dithering. 'Daughter, we must discuss your sneakiness,' I declared.

'Sneakiness?' Amani giggled. 'Is there such a word, Mother, or have you invented a new word that I will soon see recognized in the dictionary.'

'You are not amusing me, daughter.'

'All right, Mother. Tell me, what sneakiness?'

'Sit,' I commanded, gesturing with my hand to the chair beside me.

Amani sat, but still showed no sign of concern. She even smiled and struggled to clasp my hand as I spoke, though I refused it.

'Amani, I am truly upset. Daughter, you searched my private quarters. You discovered a confidential letter your sister had written to me and you chose to reveal the secret Maha asked that I keep from everyone.'

Amani retained her friendly expression, boldly exclaiming, 'Yes, Mother. I do not deny what you are saying.'

Pleased that my daughter was not trying to cover her deeds with a lie, I still would not retreat from my anger. 'Why, daughter? Why did you do it? Why did you do *exactly* what your sister requested me *not* to do?'

Amani squeezed my arm in affection and said, 'Mother, when I saw your tears, I understood that something very bad was upsetting you. When you refused to share your troubles, my love for you compelled me to try to discover what this serious problem was. I was afraid that you or Father had been diagnosed with a serious illness. I had to know your secret, or I would have gone crazy with worry.'

Amani smiled sweetly. 'I did not really do a search, Mother. Maha's letter was lying openly on your make-up table. It was there like an invitation for me to read. I was not so bad to do that. It is not the same as a thief who breaks into a locked safe, a closed door or a drawer. The letter was there. I had to know what was disturbing the mother I love with all my heart.'

While my anger slightly dissipated following this declaration of love and devotion, it had not completely evaporated and I pressed on; Amani needed to be aware of the consequences of her actions.

'But, Amani, your father is on his way to force Maha to leave Turkey, to give up her work at the refugee camp. Maha will be furious with me, wrongly believing that I did not keep the secret she shared and that I disapprove of her work, which I do not!'

'But, Mother, I agree with Father. Maha should not be there. I am certain that danger lurks for anyone so close to the Syrian border. The men and women of the Islamic State are capable of luring the innocent across that meandering border. Anyone who looks upon Maha will know that she is a woman of means. She carries herself with such confidence and authority. Someone will try to discover the identity of the tall, beautiful Arab woman who has the funds to hire drivers and security. She will be set up. I am convinced of this. They might send someone to entice Maha away with stories of suffering children. Maha, you know, would investigate. Mother, she may be a world traveller, but this is an unsafe region and Maha is not familiar with the area. She might be lured into an automobile, or across the border. Once caught, she would be helpless.'

My throat tightened in fear and tears came to my daughter's eyes. 'Anything could happen to her; these are desperate men, Mother.'

I held up my hand, 'Please, daughter, please do not remind me.'

Although most Muslims believe in punishment by death for certain heinous crimes, most believe in executions that are quick and merciful, praying to Allah for a 'merciful dagger' or a 'merciful sword' or a 'merciful knife'. In recent times, very sadly, some of the more merciful acts relating to punishment have been ignored and abandoned by those who favour more sensational and brutal treatment.

'Mother, we must think of these things. We must think of what we might do to stop this most violent movement. In this region we are all in danger.' Amani paused momentarily. 'Maha should not be so near to them. Those men despise the Arab regimes in power, and their families. As a Saudi princess, Maha would be made a special example.'

'STOP, AMANI! STOP!' I shrieked, the unbearable image of my daughter being executed imprinted on my mind. 'I will not hear this kind of talk.'

'Mother, you should thank me for alerting Father. I am very glad that he has flown to Turkey to bring her home.'

After enduring the images Amani put into my mind, I felt a twinge of relief that Maha might soon return home. Though I reminded Amani, 'This is your sister's passion. Would you be so glad if your father pulled strings to keep you from ever again helping an animal in need, daughter?'

Amani turned her eyes away from my own, unwilling to put herself in a similar situation, for she was passionate about her animal-rights work.

'No, daughter, do not turn away. Think of what I am saying. What would you do if your father ordered you to never again work for the relief of animal suffering? Would you stop?'

'I would not put myself in extreme danger to save an animal. I am just not brave enough, or foolish enough, Mother.'

'But daughter, we are skipping over the important matter. You revealed your sister's secret. That was wrong, Amani. Wrong!'

'I disagree, Mother, and I do not regret what I have done.'

It was a stalemate. Amani would always believe she was correct to expose Maha's secret, whereas I defend the right of anyone to conceal secrets of a personal nature, so long as no one else was harmed.

I sighed and turned away. I was thinking about ordering a cup of tea when the shrill ring of our home telephone shattered the silence. A grim-voiced Abdullah advised me that he had heard from Maha, who was, as we feared, enraged that her father had been informed of her whereabouts and of her mission.

'Where is she?' I asked, suddenly struck with the strongest desire for my daughter to be with her father and on her way home to Saudi Arabia.

'She is with Father on the plane. I believe she has been officially relieved of her volunteer post at the refugee camp.'

I slumped forward, happiness and sadness mingling in my mind. My daughter was physically safe. On the other hand, I knew that she would surely be miserable to be leaving her mission of compassion.

'Do you know when they will arrive?'

'It is around 1,300 nautical miles from Istanbul to Riyadh, Mother. I estimate that it will take Father's aeroplane between six and seven hours of flight time. They are only an hour into the flight.'

I was astounded that my son knew the exact distance but,

knowing Abdullah, he would have done proper research the moment he knew his father was in the air.

'Thank you, my son. Please do come and be with me when Kareem and Maha arrive. Maha needs to understand that it was Amani's concern for her well-being that created your father's plan to bring her out of Turkey and the refugee camp. Maha will be so angry she will not absorb the words I speak, but she will hear you.'

'I will come within the next four hours, Mother. Tell Amani to remain there, too. All the family needs to be in attendance.'

After ending the call, I spoke to Amani. 'Your brother insists that you stay. We will all face Maha together, so that she is aware of our true concern for her safety.'

Amani appeared displeased and uneasy. 'Oh, Mother, I do not agree. You know how Maha will be.' She twisted her fingers nervously. 'She might strike me.'

While my daughters have been known to be violent to one another, such a thing was rare since they had become adults. 'Your father and Abdullah will be with us. Neither will allow violence.'

Amani squirmed. My youngest child has always had a tendency to create chaos and then disappear for a time, giving anger room to deflate. For once, she would 'face the music', as I have heard my Western friends say.

I insisted that Amani walk with me to my quarters, so we might refresh ourselves.

'What about Princess Sabrina, and the poor wounded women in Pakistan?' she asked. 'When will we decide what action to take on their behalf?'

'This has been a trying morning, Amani. I cannot think clearly. Let us refresh ourselves, take a brief rest, and then discuss the issue before Abdullah arrives.' I looked at Amani, touching her lips with my fingertips. 'The agony those poor women are enduring will make us forget our minor problems, daughter.'

Amani startled me by bursting into tears, sobbing loudly while grasping at me. 'Thank you, Mother,' she gasped. 'I cannot stop thinking of those poor women.'

Enfolding my daughter's small body in my arms, I stumbled into my quarters, leaving several alarmed servants standing open-mouthed in the long hallway.

*　　*　　*

While expecting Abdullah to join us in waiting to submit to Maha's wrath, I spent a tense hour with Amani watching a documentary she had brought to the palace for me to see. For certain, the searing documentary took our feelings away from personal family problems. The film was entitled *Saving Face* and featured the humane works of a British plastic surgeon named Dr Mohammad Jawad. After learning of the horrific nature of the suffering endured by acid victims, Dr Jawad began frequent travels from England to his ancestral country of Pakistan to perform plastic surgery on the women and girls who were casualties.

While I had known something of male-on-female acid attacks prior to Amani's interest in the violation, I had not realized how common acid attacks had become in various countries. It is a distressingly easy method of destroying a woman's life because acid is readily available in Pakistan, and in many other countries. Indeed, battery acid is a favourite liquid for many, since the acid is used by nearly all households for one thing or another.

The women are left in great pain; their looks are destroyed and they become isolated and alone as they are too ashamed to appear in public. It's a particularly vicious kind of an attack that cannot be overcome.

The documentary film was like no other I had ever seen. While poignant and disturbing, it was so perfectly filmed that I was drawn into the lives of the women. There were moments when I felt as if I was sitting in the examination rooms with the victims who were marked with horrifically scarred faces, arms and bodies. As Dr Jawad explained the procedures he might have to do to save their sight, or to spare them from the ridicule of thoughtless people who so cruelly mocked them for their disfigured appearance, I really felt myself a victim too, with my emotions igniting in anguish, fear and anger.

Even prior to Amani's revelations, I knew that violence against women in Pakistan was on the increase; statistically, only Yemen has more incidences of this terrible crime. Thousands of women in the country are kidnapped, raped and murdered on an annual basis, according to the Aurat Foundation, an organization that monitors news reports regarding violence against women. Surprisingly, there is not a law in Pakistan that criminalizes domestic violence. No man in Pakistan fears arrest and imprisonment for violence against a woman, although a few men have been arrested and charged as examples when specific outrage garners the attention of the Western media.

One such case was the shooting of the bold and fearless teenager Malala Yousafzai, the young woman who was supported by her intelligent and brave father to obtain an education. After Malala wrote a blog on the BBC about her life in the Swat Valley under the ruthless Taliban, and spoke to the media about the importance of education for girls, she was ambushed and shot while riding a school bus. Malala survived and after recovering spoke out even more strongly for education for girls. Her book, *I am Malala*, brought worldwide attention to her story; and she was one of two winners of the 2014 Nobel Peace Prize.

How pleased I am that one young woman has made a huge difference and has increased attention on the plight of females in her country.

British newspapers, for some reason, are the best at following the stories of abuse against women in Pakistan. For this I offer my respect to them on behalf of women worldwide who desperately need such media attention.

Pakistani women are mostly in dire need of honest public officials who can bring about laws that will support women in their attempt to access the legal system. Yet this has not happened.

This puzzling negligence continues, despite the fact that there have been powerful women in Pakistan. Benazir Bhutto was elected Prime Minister of Pakistan, serving from 1988 to 1990, and then again from 1993 to 1996. She was always formidable in the political arena, first as the eldest daughter of Zulfikar Ali Bhutto, who was a prime minister too, and then as a Prime Minister herself. After her first victory to win the office of Prime Minister, she spoke to a large crowd and the words I best remember are: 'We gather together to celebrate freedom, to celebrate democracy, to celebrate the three most beautiful words in the English language: "We the People!"'

I was personally ecstatic, believing that she meant men *and* women of Pakistan, yet I never read or heard of Benazir Bhutto making women a priority. From all my research, I have failed to find a single law Bhutto supported to change the status of ordinary Pakistani women. I had followed her campaign promises with great fervour and knew that she had vowed to repeal various laws that were controversial, laws that curtailed the rights of women in her land. But when no reforms were made during her first rule, women's rights organizations in Pakistan turned away from their female Prime Minister, making it easy enough for Bhutto to forget about half the population in the country.

Her careless neglect of women was a mystery to all, since she was a woman living in a land where women are routinely victims of abuse. I saw Bhutto at a distance once when she was travelling with her father, who was the Pakistani prime minister at the time. I met her once when she was Prime Minister. I will never forget the occasion. That date was 11 January 1989, after she had travelled to Saudi Arabia to meet with my uncle, King Fahd, on 10 January. Her trip to Saudi was her first official visit abroad after assuming office in Pakistan.

While the men of my family were uneasy with a female ruling a Muslim nation, King Fahd had always had a special affection and respect for women, even admitting to an innocent crush on the British Prime Minister, Margaret Thatcher. Therefore, he was pleased to welcome Bhutto to the kingdom, despite the fact Saudi women at that time were not allowed to participate in any public forums or meetings, although the situation is not much improved even today.

From what we were told, the meeting was friendly and plans were made to solve certain problems, such as the three million refugees from Afghanistan that Pakistan was struggling to maintain (the war with Russia had created a huge exodus from that country into Pakistan). Our King Fahd generously offered to assist Pakistan with financial aid.

I recall my father saying that Bhutto had promised King Fahd to make Pakistan as prosperous as Japan. This did not happen, as we all now know, but with her knowledge of economics, there appeared to be much hope in her heart to bring economic change to the country she loved.

There was one function where twelve Saudi princesses were invited with their husbands to meet Bhutto, and I was one of the token twelve, as we lightheartedly called ourselves. Before the social function ended, though, I felt bitter disappointment.

Despite the fact we were both women living in countries that discriminated against females, I felt her scorn for me as a Saudi woman of the royal family. This, I believe, is because Saudi women have never been allowed in any ruling position, while she was respected and encouraged by her intelligent and influential father from the time she was a young girl. During the function, when I gained an opportunity to speak to Bhutto, I attempted to discuss the special problems faced by women in our countries, but I was brushed off with some superficial small talk and she soon turned away from me to address a powerful man from my family.

I walked away, feeling the rejection keenly. I will always marvel that most powerful women do not make the lives of other women a priority in all things. Until this happens women will forever remain in secondary positions in many countries.

I always wished that Bhutto had made the plight of Pakistani women a cornerstone of her government when she had the power to do so. When she was assassinated on 27 December 2007, I felt true grief that she was dead and sorrow that while alive a wonderful opportunity had been missed by that intelligent and capable woman. I had always hoped that she would return to power and realize her mistake in not supporting the women of her land, a country that is so important in the world of nations.

Women must support other women; we must stand as one in the fight for equality, whether our background is high or low on the economic scale. Without this support from all sides, women will always be fighting for the right to live with dignity.

Amani nudged me, 'Are you watching, Mummy?'

My thoughts had strayed to what might have been, but I had seen enough of the documentary to know that Amani and I would offer our support to Princess Sabrina. While I could not travel to Pakistan and play an active role in the care of the acid-scarred girls and women, there would be funds made available. I knew that this would bring great relief to Amani and Sabrina, and hopefully would pave the way for the disfigured victims to regain some semblance of normal life.

Despite the fact that I will not meet these women face to face, I shall never forget those featured in the documentary with Dr Jawad.

One victim, named Zakia, lives in my heart. As a woman who suffered abuse for many years, she felt she had no option but to seek a divorce from her brutal husband. Courageously she pursued her case through the courts, and on the day she appeared for the hearing she faced her furious husband, who was incensed that she had dared to seek a divorce; according to him, she was his property, he owned her.

As Zakia left the courtroom her husband leapt up and threw the corrosive battery acid directly at her face. Her left eye and cheek and her nose melted under the burning chemical. She felt unimaginable pain as her scars tightened, making it nearly impossible for her to eat, drink or even smile.

Another woman named Rukhsana is the saddest case of all. The memory of her story will be with me as long as I am on this earth. In fact, I have posted her photograph in my quarters lest I let a day pass without praying for her well-being. As horrific as Zakia's story is, Rukhsana's is even more harrowing. Her husband and his entire family plotted to kill her in the most gruesome manner possible because she dared to leave the house with her children without permission. She returned after her visit but that mattered little. Three monsters were in waiting.

The husband threw the acid, his sister poured petrol and her mother-in-law lit the match. Rukhsana rolled on the floor, writhing in agony, burned nearly to death. She survived, but with the gravest of injuries. She remains in the home where she was attacked, hoping for the opportunity to see her daughter, who the family keeps from her. Isolated and in pain, Rukhsana is living behind a brick wall.

This lonely tragic woman's life is too wretched to imagine.

At the end of the film, when the screen turned to black, my daughter and I sat silently, for such a film causes emotional shock. But before I could recover to think Amani said that she had much more to tell. My daughter walked to the corner of the room and retrieved a large folder holding many more photographs of women whose lives had been ruined for ever.

I looked at an image that Amani warned was supposed to be a woman, yet I saw no face. Eyes and nose and lips were gone. There were two large blackened holes where eyes had once been, and two smaller holes where once there was a nose. The former mouth was now nothing more than an open gap showing pro-truding teeth without lips.

There are many others like this poor unfortunate being, girls and women whose lives have been utterly ruined by men who believe that such attacks are justified if a wife makes a decision to leave an abusive marriage, or if a girl refuses a proposal, or even if a young woman dares to attend school. Or, like Rukhsana, she leaves her home without permission. While some surgeries can be performed to alleviate pain, it is impossible to replace eyes that have been burned to nothing. Indeed, most of the women who are victims of acid attacks are left blinded. In all my years of working with abused women, nothing feels crueller to me than this kind of assault.

My daughter was waiting for my response.

'Amani, darling, why does the government of Pakistan not make this brutal crime a top priority?'

Amani quickly answered my question. 'Sabrina was told that government officials believe that acid attacks tarnish the image of their country, and so they prefer that the crime be ignored. They do not want Pakistan to attract this kind of attention. Even the families of the victims are pressured to keep quiet due to the social stigma.'

Suddenly, I felt very weary. Without the firm leadership of government, how would such crimes be stopped? Truly, I felt all the life drain from my body. What cruelty! What agony! What pain! My heart felt shattered to think of the women who were personally afflicted with indescribable pain, heartbreak, loneliness and shame.

Such cruelty has the ability to tear hearts into little pieces.

And that is what I felt when I heard the roar of my daughter, Maha. Her shouts alerted the household that all was not well.

Kareem was early! Abdullah was late!

I clutched Amani, as she leapt to her feet to flee the room. 'No, daughter, we shall face this together. This will pass and all will be well.'

As I gazed at my youngest child, with her smooth skin, her beautiful eyes, I felt my strength return. The faces of my children and grandchildren were undamaged – they were safe.

From that moment, I knew that every personal problem I encountered would be judged against the extreme challenges faced by so many Pakistani women.

Somehow I found strength to look upon Maha when she rushed into the room with the most indignant expression. When Maha saw her sister, she made straight for Amani's face, with hands outstretched and long nails reaching to attack.

I screeched so loudly that Maha temporarily halted.

I pleaded, 'Maha, daughter! Save your strength to fight the men who rape women, or throw acid upon them. Save your strength, daughter!'

Maha lunged past me to her sister.

I had seen the flash of lightning. Now I awaited the sound of thunder.

Chapter Seven

Dr Meena

As Maha loomed menacingly over us, I was suddenly re-minded that my eldest daughter is very tall, many inches taller than her mother and sister. The truth is that most Saudi princesses are tall. We surprise those unfamiliar with our family, as most expect delicate women of a short stature. Saudi men are the reason for this, as they have various requirements that they press their mothers and sisters to pursue when looking for a suit-able bride, and one of the most important is that any future wife be large and strong.

Saudi men long for beautiful brides, as do most men in every culture. Of course there are other requisites besides beauty and height when 'bride searching' in my country: money and power are also desired. There is no more coveted bride in my country than one who is beautiful, tall, wealthy and of a powerful family.

But while most will understand the desire for power, wealth and beauty, seeking women who have unusually sizeable statures is met with disbelief by those who come to know the little secrets of our society and culture. The reason for this obsession with height is that our men covet big and strong sons who will tower over other men. Do not forget that the country of Saudi Arabia was formed from various areas within a huge land; my grandfather, who was a fierce warrior king, felt an urgent need for many large, strong sons to gain an advantage on the battlefield. These sons he had with his many wives. Therefore, Saudi men have always sought tall wives who will produce tall sons. Due to the habit of tall men marrying tall women, many Al Sa'ud men are well over six feet, while women in the royal family often rival their husbands in height. The genes that determine a tall body flourish in my family.

Despite the large physical size of many of the Al Sa'ud females, most women in our family spend their days and nights relaxing while visiting with other family members or sampling delicious foods prepared by world-famous chefs. We are a family who believes that pampering is beneficial for one's health. While some royals do move about while dancing at weddings, most prefer the physically sedentary life. You will rarely see a Saudi princess exercising or exerting herself in any way. Perhaps that is why so many of my royal cousins have fought obesity and diabetes as the years of life have passed.

But Maha is strikingly different from most royal women in our family. While she is similar in height to many of her cousins, she is also very strong. She was always an active girl, enjoying sports with her brother. Since becoming an adult, she has increased her physical strength through weight training, bodybuilding and cycling. Perhaps living in Europe has encouraged her to embrace the exercise craze. But at least she is not an exercise extremist. Thanks be to Allah she has not developed huge muscles such as the ones I have seen on females on some television shows in the United States and in Europe. Such female muscles are looked upon with admiration in the Western world – as I know that such activity takes enormous time and devotion. But truthfully, that kind of muscle strength in a woman perturbs and even frightens people from the East. We are not accustomed to women who enjoy flexing their muscles while wearing a bikini. Just as our veiled women draw unwanted stares and attention in the West, bikini-clad muscle builders induce an identical reaction in Saudi Arabia.

The lack of physical activity of Saudi women stems from deeply entrenched traditions of discrimination against females. A shocking fact is that girls and women are not allowed to participate in sports activities without written permission from their male guardian. Saudi men follow the culture, government and religious clerics, all of whom have always frowned upon the athletic endeavours of women. The religious clerics have denounced the move for physical education as a 'Western innovation' and claim that such activities will end in infidelity and even prostitution.

Such statements cause my blood to reach a point of boiling. I sometimes feel that the religious clerics in my land detest the fact that women are living, breathing creatures who might enjoy activities other than serving a man.

Therefore, until 2014, physical education classes for females were forbidden in state-run schools in Saudi Arabia. This is a country where one will never witness groups of girls enjoying sports. However, this situation is beginning to change, mainly due to the International Olympic Committee (IOC), which has lately encouraged various Muslim countries, including Saudi Arabia, to allow women to participate in the Olympic Games.

Saudi Arabia had never before sent a female athlete to any Olympic Games, but in 2010 for the Summer Youth Olympics in Singapore, we entered our first female competitor, a young woman by the name of Dalma Rushdi Malhas. Dalma successfully competed in the equestrian challenge, winning our country's only medal, a bronze. It, of course, lifted my heart to a soaring height and I leapt with joy that our only medal winner was the lone woman.

Despite this breakthrough, our struggles continued when it was discovered that Saudi Arabia had no plans to send female athletes to the 2012 Summer Games in London. There was panic in our royal family when there was talk of Saudi Arabia being forbidden from participating in that Olympics. Such a thing would cause our people to lose face. Over the loud objections of the religious clerics, the men of my family buckled, reluctantly agreeing to allow two women to represent us. This ground-breaking decision was a big victory for Saudi women.

The two females who were chosen to attend were sixteen-year-old Wojdan Shahrkani, who was entered into the judo competition, and nineteen-year-old Sarah Attar, who ran the 800 metres. There was a big debate over the headscarf my government required Wojdan to wear. But after some negotiation she was allowed to wear a swim cap rather than a loose head-covering that might get tangled during the judo competition. Although Wojdan lost to Melissa Mojica of Puerto Rico, most Saudi women keenly enjoyed the symbolic victory of her presence.

While Sarah did not impress the crowd with her speed, she was soundly cheered, for all there knew the challenges she had overcome to represent our male-dominated nation.

I know from what my husband has told me that both of these young women were warned to avoid speaking about the issues of gender discrimination that grips our land so tightly; that is why no one saw the girls giving lengthy interviews. They were required to behave modestly, and that is what they did, before they returned home.

Although there was no physical education allowed in schools when Maha was young, she has always dedicated time and attention to health issues. Now in her late twenties, she can claim the spot of being in the best physical condition of anyone in our immediate family. On the other hand, her sister Amani is petite and delicate; she shuns anything to do with exercise, although a few years ago she did employ an aerobics trainer. The entire situation was most amusing to her brother Abdullah because rather than do any exercise Amani spent the allotted time trying to convert her instructor to Islam. Amani did not succeed, as the trainer was a devout Christian. Thankfully, the two women remained affable, her aerobics teacher being very tolerant of my religiously assertive daughter.

I now admit that my daughters' personalities align with their body types, as Maha defends herself physically, if necessary, while

Amani psychologically manipulates all situations in order to get her way.

I have never sought to gain physical strength, but now I was regretting this choice, as Maha was on us in a flash. Although my daughter exhibited no violence towards her mother, merely pushing me aside as easily as if I were a child, she showed her sister little mercy. When I saw that Maha had gripped Amani in a headlock, I gasped, 'Maha, no!'

As Maha began to twist Amani's head, I felt terror in my heart. That kind of forceful rotation could cause severe injury, so I leapt into the fray. Although I am not large or strong, it was my duty to rescue my child. To my despair, I quickly realized that I could do nothing to save Amani from Maha's grip. My youngest daughter was pulling at her own head with her hands, but she simply wasn't strong enough. All she could do was scream. Thanks be to Allah that Kareem remains youthful and is still fast on his feet. He very carefully separated our daughters, pulling Maha's hands and arms slowly from Amani's head and neck as though he was unwinding an octopus from its prey. I said a small prayer of thanks that Maha only has two arms rather than eight!

Hearing the commotion from the hallway, Abdullah ran in at that moment and aided his father, yanking Amani away to a safe distance from Maha, whose flashing dark eyes and angry facial expression conveyed absolute fury.

I heaved a sigh of relief that Amani appeared to have escaped physical harm. I glanced at Kareem. My husband's expression was unreadable although he appeared physically spent and very weary. I yearned to speak, to console my daughters, but I startled myself when I impulsively burst into tears. I am not a woman who easily weeps. My usual response to such family spats is to separate and protect my children, but for some reason I felt a great loss, tremendous sadness, and an undefined grief that overpowered me.

While Kareem and Abdullah consoled me with kindly looks and soothing words, Maha was too angry to notice my despair. Amani remained silent.

I further surprised myself when my weeping intensified into loud cries. I lost control. I fell into a chair. I held my head in my hands and wailed. I really do not know what came over me, but the family squabble ended as quickly as it had begun when Maha tore away from her father and came to me. 'Mother. Please stop crying. Please.'

Amani found her voice, shouting, 'Father, help Mother. She is losing her mind!'

Kareem came close, touching my head and stroking my shoulder. 'Sultana. All is well. Please, darling, do not cry. Control yourself, please.'

Still holding Amani in his grip to protect her should Maha's calm behaviour turn out to be a clever ploy whereby he would lose his focus and give Maha the opportunity to renew her attack upon her sister, Abdullah moved near to me, whispering, 'Mother, please. You are frightening the servants.'

I did not know until later that more than thirty-five people who worked for us in our palace and on our grounds had gathered in a large group near to us, believing that a great tragedy had occurred. This, because my screams reminded all of hysterical women who have unexpectedly lost all those whom they love. Such cries typically imply death.

I have been through many serious and even terrifying moments in my life, but never have I lost command of my thoughts or my actions. I was in the early stages of a minor breakdown, although I did not know it at the time.

Maha was becoming more frightened. She assured us all. 'Mother. Father. Abdullah. Do not worry. I will do no damage to my sister.' She paused, and when she spoke again her voice was suddenly stern again. 'Although Amani deserves a proper thrashing.'

Amani whimpered like a baby, a state to which she sometimes reverts when events she has created have taken a disagreeable turn.

I regained my ability to speak, shouting through my sobs, 'I am ashamed of my family. For the first time in my life, I am ashamed of you, Maha, and of you, Amani, and of you, Kareem.' As usual, Abdullah had done nothing to gain a reprimand.

'Me?' Kareem said in loud disbelief.

'Yes, YOU, my husband.'

Once again my tears flowed and my cries sounded loudly. A few days later my son laughingly told me that the bizarre noises I was making reminded him of our palace alarm system, which everyone claims is eerie.

By this time Kareem was openly alarmed, for he has known me since I was sixteen years old and we have lived through many emotional moments, yet he had never seen me lose control of my senses – unless I include the time he stupidly announced that he was going to take a second wife. My reaction at his declaration was so fiercely tempestuous that he never again approached that taboo topic. And that is why our roof continued to cover a palace holding one man and one wife and their children.

Pushing the chair away, I stood up and glared at Kareem. Without thinking, I spoke my mind, saying, 'Husband, you created this fight by forcibly removing Maha from her charity work. You could have handled this situation in an astute manner, with words rather than actions. Think of our grandfather! What would he have done in such a situation?'

Kareem was silent, encouraging me to further make my point. 'Kareem, you and I both know that he would have used wise reasoning to gain what was needed. Please, my husband, gain from the astuteness our grandfather demonstrated!'

Kareem blanched. From the time we were toddlers, as grandchildren of Saudi Arabia's first king we had been told endless stories of the wisdom Abdul Aziz, our grandfather, displayed in every crisis, whether personal, tribal or national.

One particular story showed his wisdom and restraint because it focused on the primal instincts of all tribal men to protect and control their women. When our grandfather was in exile with his father in Kuwait after suffering defeat and loss in the Nejd, in middle Arabia, by the Al Rasheed clan, most cousins joined the Al Sa'ud, showing their loyalty, except for one set of unfaithful, rebellious cousins. When our grandfather returned to the Nejd to renew the battle with the Al Rasheeds, the same cousins joined him in battle. Once again the unfaithful cousins remained noticeably remote. But our grandfather healed the family friction when he welcomed those fickle cousins with open arms, even marrying three of his own sisters to the most wayward of the cousins. Grandfather knew that intermarriage had the power to heal ruptures in tribal families.

One of the three brides given in marriage to the most defiant cousin was our grandfather's closest and dearest sister, Nura, whom he held in the highest esteem.

Sometime later, the rebellious cousin became disgruntled; he began asking for favours that our grandfather refused, and so once again the cousin revolted and began raiding parties against his brother-in-law.

But there was one major problem for the defiant cousin – he was very much in love with his wife. He could not bear to be away from Nura and could not resist her charms. While on a raid, he lost his willpower and came to his beloved wife, sneaking in to see her, and then sneaking away in the middle of the night like a thief.

When Nura became pregnant, Abdul Aziz was in a quandary, thinking that his sister had broken the most stringent of religious and desert codes. It was only when our grandfather learned of the deception – that his disloyal brother-in-law was the father of Nura's child – that his heart softened. He tucked his anger away into a pocket and welcomed his brother-in-law back into the family.

This goodwill gesture meant that there was no danger of war within the family and, as a result, many lives were saved. Although our grandfather was a fierce warrior, he had the wisdom to recognize that there are times when a man must accept circumstances he cannot alter, and should not try to change.

None of Abdul Aziz's sons or grandsons can compare to the great man; but nevertheless, all male offspring desire nothing more than to be likened to King Abdul Aziz. All the male cousins I have known, Kareem included, imagine themselves as wise men who at the very least meet the high expectations laid down by their grandfather.

As I was reflecting on the great man, I could not help but remain focused on Maha's sense of outrage and anger, and I turned to her. 'Daughter,' I said, 'I know you are upset. You have the right. Although Abdullah and I kept your confidence, I was careless with your letter, and I am sorry. But, Maha, you are old enough now to know that violence, even when you are at your most angry, is never an acceptable way to handle a problem.' I trembled. 'You are very strong, Maha. You could have seriously injured Amani. You were twisting her neck and head with tremendous force. What if your sister, the mother of your nephew and niece, ended up with serious injuries which left her disabled for life? What if your sister had never again spoken, or moved, or even had the ability to think? What then, Maha?'

Maha's head dropped. She slowly nodded, thinking for the first time of how the evening might have ended.

Amani, obviously shaken by the image I had described, pulled away when I moved to touch her arm. 'Amani, your sneaky ways must end. How can you reconcile your life as a devout Muslim and yet behave in a way that causes so much damage to others by uncovering secrets that are not yours to know, daughter. This kind of treachery must stop, and it must stop now!'

I made no effort to wipe away the tears that were streaming down my cheeks.

'There is one other thing. All of us speak grand words; we profess to caring for those less fortunate than ourselves and say that we must help others. But just think of the energy and time we waste on such squabbles – time and energy that could be put to good use elsewhere.' My voice rose in tone with my emotion. 'As you, my girls, are fighting over a secret revealed, women in

Pakistan and across this region are facing a lifetime of pain and agony. As you, my husband, are squandering large sums of money removing our adult daughter away from the important work she loves, young girls are being captured and raped by treacherous soldiers. Who will help them if not Maha and other brave souls who cannot endure the injustice of the situation?' I shook my fist as though I was an actor on a stage inspiring an audience, but I was speaking of life and death, matters that meant so much to me. 'We cannot fight against each other! We must help these helpless people!'

I had stunned my husband and children. They stared at me with mouths open.

'Kareem, you ask why I am ashamed of you. Husband, it is a sin if any of us waste one moment of our lives doing anything but saving or at least helping those who are being tortured or raped or disfigured.'

I gestured my disgust by raising my hands into the air, as I darted from the room. My family hurried behind me. Excited servants scattered when I burst through the crowded hallways. Kareem nearly caught up with me, but I succeeded in entering my quarters and bolting the door, refusing to acknowledge his frantic knocks and pleas.

Declarations of love and devotion from those I most love were encircling me as I fell into an uneasy and exhausted sleep.

*   *   *

After sleeping heavily, I mercifully awoke without immediately re-calling the previous night's family drama. As I lay quietly, wishing to prolong my rest, a telephone rang.

I am old-fashioned when it comes to communication. I only see social media when my children and grandchildren assist me. I do have several expensive cell telephones, and use them when I am travelling, but I am most happy with a sturdy landline telephone in my hand when I am having lengthy conversations.

Thus, I have three private telephone lines set up in my quarters. To keep organized and to know who is calling, the telephones are coloured red, black and beige. They are positioned side by side on a special table, with ample room for pens and writing paper. The red telephone is used only to speak with close family members, such as my husband Kareem, my sister Sara, and my children and grandchildren. I always answer that telephone quickly. The black telephone is limited to those with whom I work at various charities. The beige telephone is for good friends and associates.

I saw the light blinking on the beige telephone. I groaned, then rolled over to get out of bed, answering the phone on the fourth ring.

My special friend, a medical doctor named Dr Meena, was calling. Never one to waste words, the serious-minded woman greeted me with a rapid good morning and I hope you and your family are well, without pausing for me to return the same polite and customary greetings.

'Princess, I am upset on this day. I would like to ask for a meeting with you. At your convenience, of course.'

I have known Dr Meena for more than three years now and, although she has my private telephone number, I have never received a call from her that was not prompted by an important issue. Dr Meena is one of the most diligent, hard-working women I have ever known; she spends nearly every waking moment caring for the lives of others. She does not have leisure time to chat socially with me, despite my princess status. This is one of the many reasons I so respect Dr Meena. She is not a person who will seek insincere attention from anyone, even from those with a royal rank.

For those who have not read *Princess: More Tears to Cry*, one of the five books written about my life, Dr Meena was introduced to the world in that tome.

I first met Dr Meena in 2012 at an educational seminar held at one of the royal hospitals in my country. Dr Meena was a distinguished presenter. She is not a dramatic beauty, but is attractive, and has the kind of distinct personality that ensures she will be someone never forgotten.

Dr Meena was not ashamed to describe her brutish childhood. She was born in Saudi Arabia in a poor hamlet known as Al-Kharj. She was the fourth child, and fourth daughter. Her birth, in fact, brought about the divorce of her parents, for her father, like many Saudi men, was an ignorant man who was unacquainted with the scientific fact that it is the man, not the woman, who determines the sex of a child. Thus, he berated his innocent wife for bringing four daughters into his life as though it was a plan put in place to harm him because the most uninformed men in my country scorn daughters and adore sons! He divorced her as quickly as he could say the words 'I divorce you' three times. He then forced her to return to her parental home, where she was not welcome. In fact Dr Meena's maternal grandparents tried to lock their daughter and four granddaughters out of their home, but they did not succeed due to the quick thinking of the eldest daughter, who wrapped her little body around her grandmother's legs and refused to release her grip.

As horrible as it was, it could have been much worse because Dr Meena's father had earlier snatched her from her mother's arms and declared that he was going to bury her alive in the desert. This would have been Dr Meena's fate, and Saudi Arabia would have lost one of their better physicians, had not an uncle intervened. This uncle reminded her father that our Prophet Muhammad famously said, 'If anyone has a female child and does not bury her alive, or slight her, or prefer his children [i.e. the males ones] to her, God will bring him to Paradise.'

With the Prophet Muhammad's wise words ringing in his ears, Dr Meena's father returned the infant to her mother, saving her from an early grave.

However, the maternal grandparents were so poor that Dr Meena confessed to growing up without once feeling satisfied after eating a meal. Tragically, she was always hungry, which might have been the reason for her unusually petite size. Despite many family challenges, Dr Meena was allowed to attend school, and she was so focused on education that she became a star student, winning her teachers' help to access higher learning, ultimately succeeding in obtaining a medical degree. This is an incredible achievement for any Saudi woman, let alone one from a humble background.

Dr Meena is a very remarkable woman and soon I was considering a possible friendship, for I not only admired this young woman but was struck by the thought that she was someone who was in a perfect position to help me to attain my own goals of helping as many Saudi girls as possible to achieve an education, just as she had.

We were instantly drawn into each other's world. After meeting privately, I respected her even more and asked her to assist me in finding worthy girls and women who lacked the funds or family help to obtain a full education. There are many young girls with the same aspirations as Dr Meena, but too often family members push for them to marry young, to leave the family and join their husband's family, so that the bride's family might be the beneficiary of a huge dowry. When I learn of girls in such dire situations through Dr Meena, I often relieve the family of financial worries so that their daughter can continue her education rather than marrying young to bring in extra funds to the family.

Dr Meena had asked for a meeting, and I readily agreed, even though my family was still in turmoil over this latest incident between Maha and Amani. I plucked my work calendar from my desk and, after a quick look, suggested that we meet in three days.

When I questioned what the meeting was about, she paused, finally saying, 'Worthy Saudi men, Princess, worthy Saudi men.'

I was so aback that I could find no words, although I wondered which Saudi men had won Dr Meena's 'worthy' award. Many were the times I had heard her crown a Saudi female as 'worthy' of world attention due to fearlessness, or for enthusiastically working to help free Saudi women from the gender bondage that has been their fate for thousands of years.

I was suddenly so eager for the meeting that I was sorry that I had not scheduled it sooner.

I remained lethargic in bed until noon but then felt ready to face the day ahead. An hour later, I strolled leisurely from my quarters and up the long hallway to the front of our palace to visit with my sweet mother. Little has given me more pleasure in this life than looking upon her portrait at the beginning of each day. I had thought about moving my mother's picture into my quarters so that I might gaze at her prior to sleeping each night, but such a move would be inconvenient for the rest of the family, including my sisters and their children, as they too enjoy seeing the image of Mother when they walk into my home.

I enjoy several visits daily with Mother, as I strongly believe that we keep those we love alive by looking upon them, speaking with them and remembering them in all things we do.

'Good morning, Mummy,' I said as I gazed into my mother's beautiful eyes. 'You have been gone too long. I was only a child when you died, and now I am a grown woman reaching the age you were when you left us. I want you to know, Mother, that your baby daughter Sultana has missed you every day since the day you left us.'

I took great pleasure in sitting with Mother and remembering some of our most memorable moments, such as the evenings when she would sit with her daughters and share stories of her own childhood. Although she was a girl at a time when daughters were mainly scorned, that was not Mother's experience in her family home. She was one of three daughters and two sons. Although the sons were the more valued of the five children, my mother felt the love of her gentle mother, my grandmother. And, she told us, there were occasions when her father bestowed some attention upon his daughters. Mother always believed that he loved her best of all his daughters because he would sometimes sing for her, and in those days singing was forbidden. She used to sing for us one of the tunes she remembered and how we loved hearing her low, very unique singing voice. Now I am devastated not to recall the words, the tune or the tempo of that song. I made a mental note to speak with one of my older sisters to enquire whether the song was still in her mind and heart and, if so, I would memorize that song and sing it to my grandchildren. Little Sultana, I know, would love to hear a song with so much love attached to it.

I sighed heavily, thinking of how life would have been so much sweeter had my mother not left this earth when I was only a young girl. As a Muslim, I am not supposed to question God's wisdom when those we love pass from this earth, but it is impossible to fight back the feelings of love and yearning for her. So long as I am on this earth, I will mourn and miss my mother.

After I left my mother, I walked to the small private area where my family takes the noon-time meal. I was surprised but pleased to see my three children sitting with Kareem, all seemingly in the best of humour. Even Maha and Amani were exchanging smiles.

'What is this?' I asked, with a tinge of shock in my voice.

'Darling,' Kareem said, 'I was about to come for you. Last evening the children and I agreed to meet for lunch. When we arrived, we all wanted to wait so that we might eat our meal with you.'

I nodded, glancing at my children, all of whom had broad smiles on their faces and were looking at me with extreme affection.

'Sit, darling.' Kareem caressed my arm and hand, as he led me to a comfortable chair. 'We are having your favourite lunch today. There will be chicken salad with grapes and that special French bread you crave from your favourite French restaurant, Paul, on Tahlia Street.'

My mouth watered. There is no better place to have freshly baked croissants and French breads in all of Saudi Arabia.

'Abdullah was in the area and he thought to pick up a few things for you there.'

I flashed a smile to my son. He is the most thoughtful of all my children.

'Then, darling, we will have Lebanese honeyed pastries – some of your favourite, in fact, from the Set Al Sham. I sent my driver to Sulimaniyyah for the sweets and made sure that they were made fresh today.'

'That is so nice, Kareem.' I was very curious to ask how it was that my warring family was now behaving so lovingly, reminding me of the sweet pair of love-birds that we had recently given to Little Sultana to keep on her balcony. But I made a promise to myself to let my family talk this out. I generally take the lead in family discussions, but I was ready to sit back to see what everyone had to say for themselves.

Maha motioned for me to give her my hand, but just at that moment one of our new female servers from Sri Lanka brought tea and we were quiet until she was out of earshot, although I am certain that our servants hear much of what we say because they live in our home and it is necessary for them to be near to the people to whom they provide services.

Maha glanced around me to ensure that we were alone before reaching for my hand a second time. I placed my small hand in Maha's much larger hand, wondering for a moment about birth and how it is very small women can give birth to such large, healthy and strong children, but I brushed that thought aside when Maha began to speak.

'Mother, I believe that Amani, Father and I owe apologies. I know that you and Abdullah are the innocent parties in this matter. Amani has told me that you did not share my secret but instead she waited for you to go to your dressing room before searching your bedroom. That is where she found the letter I sent to you. From what Amani tells me, you had obviously just read my letter because you were in anguish when she walked in to visit. Her curiosity was aroused and when you did not tell her the problem she decided to find out on her own.

'That is when she discovered my secret.'

Maha gazed at Amani, who nodded her head and had the decency to look ashamed, as she should. 'I will try to stop my sneaky ways, Mother,' she faintly muttered.

I laughed, but not loudly. It would be the same to ask a leopard to remove its spots as it would be to stop Amani from nosing around in other people's affairs. But I held my tongue and said nothing.

Maha continued. 'Amani told me that she had just read some materials on the Islamic State, and knew their location and how close the Syrian men of ISIS were to Turkey. She had read that they do not respect borders and that it is routine for them to attempt to kidnap those who are working with the Syrians in the refugee camps.' Maha squeezed my hand. 'My sister's fear drove her to reveal my secret to Father. She did not know what would happen but never dreamed that there would be such a commotion.'

'This is all true, sister,' Amani said softly.

'Father has apologized as well. He now knows that he should have asked me to come home and discuss my charity work rather than arrive in Turkey like a dictator, spouting out orders and handing out cash. All of this just to keep his own child from the camp, despite the fact many young and innocent people have died, and others are in dire need of help.'

Maha looked at her father. 'My life is no more important than any other life on this earth. Those people in the camp deserve the chance to live, too, and most particularly the children. Every adult should be willing to give his or her life to save a child who has had so little time to experience this world.'

Kareem squirmed in his chair. He didn't speak, but he blinked his eyes in recognition of the truth of what his daughter was saying. And it was good for him to hear her speak so honestly and so directly.

I gave Kareem a slight smile, remembering the young man he used to be. In the early years of our marriage, my husband relished talking for long hours about all sorts of important issues. As the years have passed, he has become more private and keeps most of his thoughts and ideas to himself. Truthfully, I miss the young Kareem, who was idealistic and vocal about his ideas. I now hoped this luncheon might encourage him to realize that his communication skills have suffered over the years and that his family would welcome his thoughts and reflections.

Maha paused, giving Amani a meaningful look.

Thus prompted, Amani said, 'Oh, yes. Mummy, I agree with all that Maha has said. I should have found the goodness and strength not to be sneaking around and, of course, I know that some secrets are meant to remain secret and that I should not have looked through your personal things. This was an important secret, and I should have controlled my inquisitiveness. I was wrong, Mummy.'

It is so rare for Amani to apologize and to acknowledge guilt for her actions that in my astonishment I could find nothing to say, although I did lean in and give both daughters a kiss on their faces. When one is a mother, there is no way not to love your children, despite their disagreeable actions.

Quite obviously, the apology line-up had been decided upon prior to my arrival. All three of my children looked at Kareem with expectation.

'Sultana, you are sometimes more wise than your husband. And certainly when it comes to our children and our reactions to the problems that arise in families, you seem always to know what is the right thing to do or say. From this time onward, I will seek your advice before taking action. All decisions about family matters will be made jointly. I am sorry for my hasty trip to Turkey and for the chaos I caused.' Turning to the children, Kareem then said, 'I hope this is a lesson we can all learn.'

Abdullah was not there to right any wrongs, but he did speak. 'Mother, we were worried about you last evening. I have never seen you so upset. Everyone in the family has agreed to be more careful with their behaviour.'

I smiled. 'With all these apologies I hardly know what to say, except thank you.'

I could see that Kareem was relieved his words meant a great deal to me and so he continued to talk. 'Sultana, I believed you were on the edge of a nervous collapse and we were all so frightened. We want you to be well, happy and enjoying your family.'

Maha agreed. 'We really believed that you would need to see a doctor last night, Mother, to check your mental state. We were all panicked beyond belief. None of us left until Father slipped in to make sure that you were sleeping. Only then did we retire to our beds.'

'Your father slipped in? Is that correct, Kareem?' I asked in disbelief.

Kareem once again looked uncomfortable. Several years before I had put a special lock on my quarters so that when I wanted to have complete peace and relief from my dramatic family I could feel that no one could enter my most private sanctum. I had told Kareem that even he should not have a key. I must have a retreat where I felt myself totally private.

'You have a key?'

'Just one.'

'And how did you get the key, husband?'

I believe that Kareem considered telling me a lie. He opened his mouth. Then he shut his mouth. Then he opened it again.

'Kareem?'

Maha realized she had given up her father's secret. She blushed.

'The truth, husband. How did you get a key?'

His words rushed out. 'I paid the contractor a small bonus. I felt that we both need access to every room in our home, Sultana. What if you became ill behind locked doors? I cannot allow such a potential danger.'

I swallowed my anger, as I did not wish to fight with my husband in front of my children.

'Husband, let us discuss this later.'

'Yes. I agree.'

My poor husband was trapped and he knew it. He squirmed a bit more and then reached in his briefcase, which is always nearby, opened it and took out a velvet jewellery box from one of the most expensive stores in Riyadh. 'This is for you, darling. I love you very much, Sultana, and want you to be happy.'

Kareem knows that I no longer collect jewellery and that I have already given most of my jewels to my daughters. Maha had sold her collection, but Amani was keeping hers for her daughter.

I reluctantly opened the case, as I did not wish to feign pleasure over something as cold and impersonal as jewels.

The diamond and emerald set was breathtaking and clearly very expensive. An excited Amani counted twenty diamonds and ten emeralds in the necklace, and there were more large stones in the bracelet and the earrings.

I thanked my husband as sincerely as possible, as I knew he had given me the present with very good intentions. Every Saudi prince I know spends enormous sums of money on jewellery for the women in his family, but I am one of the few princesses who truly does not care to collect jewels. I lost the desire to accumulate such valuable baubles many years ago.

I closed the velvet box and leaned over to hug my husband. He enjoys buying presents for all in his family, and most particularly for me. Jewels are an easy gift for someone who is wealthy. I knew that I would probably never wear them, but I would save the jewels for Little Sultana, thinking that she might like to wear them at her wedding or for some other grand occasion.

As if on cue, Little Sultana ran into the room wearing a new electric-blue jogging suit, as she had decided to join her auntie Maha in the exercise room that day. She was so cute that she brought smiles to all our faces, and the difficulties and problems of the previous evening seemed forgotten once and for all.

Hopefully, though, some members of my family had been reminded of the importance of keeping secrets for the ones they love.

Within a short twenty-four-hour period, I had known despair and joy. I felt fortunate that all my children were safe and were making an attempt to have a more easy relationship with each other.

I would speak with each of them individually later, for I was unclear as to Maha's choice, whether to return to Turkey or go back to Europe. And I wished to know for sure that Amani had learned a valuable lesson and would stop her lifelong habit of sneaking around to discover the secrets of others.

I gazed at the ones I loved. Abdullah was laughing with his small daughter, while Kareem looked on proudly. Amani and Maha were discussing the women in Pakistan, and Maha was asking to see the photographs.

For the first time, I felt the years of my life gaining on me and felt myself the matriarch of my young family. Furthermore, for the moment, I could find nothing to fret about, and that was a wonderful feeling.

Little did I know that when I heard again from Dr Meena the dear woman would present a rash of problems for me to consider and inform me of an unexpected but important project that needed my attention. The undertaking would cause the most serious argument in years with my husband, leading to talk of divorce for the first time since we were a young couple with elevated emotions regarding nearly every issue of our lives.

Chapter Eight

Worthy Saudi Men

I WAS EAGERLY ANTICIPATING my meeting with Dr Meena, but the day before Little Sultana was stricken by an unexplained and extremely high fever. Abdullah first telephoned his father and a concerned Kareem rushed home from his offices. Amani heard the news from Zain, Abdullah's wife, and insisted she leave her children for the day and be with us. I barred her from visiting since we were uncertain if Little Sultana had contracted a contagious disease.

'No, darling,' I answered to Amani's pleas. 'May Allah forbid that all four of our beloved grandchildren become ill at once, possibly with a perilous disease. Stay with your children and protect them from a potential infection.'

These days when any Saudi is struck with a sudden fever, most tremble in terror of the disease originally known as severe acute respiratory syndrome, or SARS, which killed nearly a thousand people in a global outbreak in 2003.

This is because we have our own version of SARS in this region. Known as MERS (short for Middle East respiratory syndrome), it is a virus that is related to the common cold, but it can also cause a high fever and pneumonia. In the most serious cases, kidney failure or even death is a concern.

Much to the alarm of the men in my family, the Al Sa'ud rulers, the virus erupted in our own country in 2012 and has infected a confirmed 1,034 persons since that time. Of this number, 457 have died. It has since spread from the Persian Gulf to France, Great Britain, Tunisia, Italy and Germany. The outbreak is still ongoing, although it is not as rampant as before.

A worried Abdullah and Zain transported their small daughter the short distance from their palace to our own, where she would be treated in our palace medical clinic, which has all the latest equipment and is as well appointed as a private medical facility can be.

Kareem had had the clinic built some years ago so there would be no unnecessary time spent driving to hospitals in Riyadh should any in our family require medical attention. The trigger for his action occurred the same year that Abdullah obtained his driving licence. Kareem fretted endlessly about the horrific traffic we endure in Riyadh and was highly fearful that one of the many inexperienced drivers on our roads might crash into our son's vehicle. Thankfully, such an accident did not occur, but the clinic was hailed as a great addition to our palace regardless, in the event one of our children or grandchildren might sustain an injury or become ill with a contagious disease. We quickly realized the grand convenience of such a facility and so the project grew from a small clinic to a larger one. Kareem increased the medical staff so that our huge workforce of several hundred domestic and office employees had quick, easy and excellent medical care. In the beginning Kareem had employed only one physician, but he soon saw the need for a total of four European employees: those who come to live and work in the kingdom take on very long hours and, in return, ask that their contracts include a generous amount of leave time to enable them to return to their home countries each year, sometimes for as long as three months, for total rest and relaxation.

The four physicians, two males and two females, who are all

internists, rotate their working schedules so that three physicians remain in their quarters on the palace grounds at all times, while the fourth takes his or her scheduled leave to visit family, go on an annual holiday or attend a conference. The medical staff quarters are just five minutes' walking distance from the clinic.

Nothing is more satisfying for me personally than to know that the best care is available for my children and grandchildren, as well as for the people who work so hard to keep our household running smoothly.

Although our children and grandchildren have all suffered the usual childhood diseases, nothing had been serious to this point. As for Little Sultana, I was hopeful that she was suffering from nothing more than a common childhood fever. With this in my mind, Kareem and I were waiting together, albeit impatiently, at the clinic to see Little Sultana with our own eyes.

Finally, the family arrived. My heart plunged in true terror when Abdullah very gently and tenderly lifted Little Sultana from the back seat of his automobile. Her face was flushed a very bright red and she was covered in tiny droplets of perspiration. I knew instantly that her fever was extremely high. Our precious child refused to open her eyes even when her mother and father spoke her name, nudged her shoulder and asked her to respond. Abdullah placed her on a portable hospital bed that was rolled to the clinic terrace by two of the female aides. Kareem and I, much alarmed by the sight of the child, followed behind.

Just then I heard a loud clanking clamour and there was Maha, roller-skating on the pavement towards us! She had been exercising when one of the servants located her whereabouts and informed her of the emergency. Maha gave us a grim look but said nothing. Without exchanging a word, we all went into the clinic. Maha did not even bother to release her skates. Normally I would have expressed amusement, watching Maha deftly walk on the grass in her skates, but at that moment nothing could have entertained me.

When we entered the sitting room of the clinic, I saw a male physician standing over Little Sultana, a German doctor who was both serious and solemn in his manner. I studied his face very carefully as he assessed the child. I am a great admirer of German people and the fine work they do in the kingdom, but I find that they are not the sort of people one can easily 'read'.

The physician paid no notice to any of the women in our family, as most expatriate men who work in the kingdom feel that the slightest attention given to a Saudi woman might be mis-interpreted and cause offence. That is why they interact only with male family members and act as though the females are invisible. (Although my daughters and I could request a male physician for any illnesses we might have, it is our routine to be examined by one of the two female doctors. But since Little Sultana is only a child it was entirely appropriate for whoever might be on call to tend to her.)

I understand this cautious attitude, as so many Saudi men would fly into a rage if a man from another country looked or talked to their women. Indeed, I have heard of cases where Saudi men have attacked foreign men living and working in our land if they have been so bold as to open a conversation with their women, even if they are physicians and merely doing their duty as such.

The doctor spoke briefly and softly to Kareem and Abdullah, advising them that only they should be in the examination room. Zain refused to accept that she would be banned from her child and she firmly spoke up: 'Abdullah, I will go in too. No one can stop me.'

Abdullah nodded in agreement, telling the doctor, 'Little Sultana's mother must be with her at all times.' I felt the pull to insist upon staying too but knew in my heart that it was the place of my son and his wife to be with their child.

I pulled Kareem by his arm and said, 'Come, husband. Let's sit here,' then gestured towards the comfortable red sofas in the wait-ing room.

Kareem understood my point and he acquiesced, but before sitting he had a brief conference with the doctor. What he said, I do not know, but most likely he was telling the physician that he would receive a huge bonus should all be well. The doctor was obviously offended because he spoke up. 'I thank you, but I am paid well for what I do. Nothing more is necessary.'

I felt even more respect for the doctor – and was slightly embarrassed, as Kareem feels it is necessary to offer money for everything he wants. I do not agree with this tactic. In reality, I felt an urge to speak sharply to my husband, but I bit my tongue and turned away. Although I will speak my full mind in our home, and in front of our children and other relatives, I am too respectful of him, and of our relationship, to disagree with him in public.

Despite Kareem's heavy-handed approach, I knew that all would be well because my husband has always had a good relationship with all four of our doctors. He was especially familiar with the head physician, as both have a love of astronomy and sometimes the two of them share an evening staring at the stars using Kareem's super-powerful telescope, which had won the physician's notice. My husband also expressed his admiration that no one could order this man about, not even he himself – his boss and the man who paid his salary and the clinical bills. The German was known to be an outstanding physician, and he commanded respect. Kareem valued his attitude, as he has never cared for 'yes' men and likes to fill the jobs available with people he knows will perform at the very top level and, ironically, who will not be swayed by offers of bonuses relating to their work. For these reasons, we both had the utmost confidence in the medical staff operating our clinic.

Maha finally thought to release the various mechanisms that kept her skates on her feet and sat in her socks, which I saw had three holes in one, two in the other. My eldest daughter has never cared about 'things' and will wear clothes long after they are best suited for a dustbin. I knew that Kareem was displeased with her attire because she was wearing tight, stretchy leggings and a sleeveless top, but I had glared at him when I saw his expression of displeasure, whispering, 'Stop, Kareem. It does not matter.'

And it did not. We were on our own palace grounds and no one was there but our family and the people who worked for us. My daughter should be allowed to wear appropriate exercise attire when working out. Never had Maha worn shorts or revealing tops, and I knew that baggy trousers would be a threat to her safety while skating.

Looking at Maha, I remembered one instance when she had persuaded her sister into attempting to learn to skate. Amani had appeared more than ridiculous skating around with her abaya flying and her veil loosening from her face. These moments re-inforce my wonder that I could have borne two such different daughters.

On that day I had overheard the laughter of our servants but reprimanded none because they had a valid reason for their mirth. Although I am a Saudi woman who also wears the veil when I am in my country, I feel just as amused when incidents such as this occur, where the many metres of fabric we are obliged to wear hamper our leisure pursuits. When our family visits our palace in Jeddah, we often sit on our balcony and observe foreign beach-goers as they scrutinize Saudi women flailing about while trying to swim in the sea with their abaya ballooning with water and trailing behind them like a black octopus in the blue sea.

Such preposterous sights usually depress me because women should not be forced to swim in a long black costume. It makes them look foolish and it is dangerous. I have heard of two cases where young mothers have drowned while trying to swim in the full Saudi abaya. Such a thing should not be allowed to happen.

As a result of these cultural constraints, I rarely swim in the Red Sea, saving my swimming activities for when we are in Europe or other countries where women wear swimming costumes without concern that they will be attacked by religious clerics. This does not mean that I wear a bikini. I am a woman born and raised in conservative Saudi Arabia, and I would feel uncomfortable dressed in one, but I do not frown upon those who choose to wear such swimming attire.

My thoughts returned to the seriousness of the moment. The three of us waited for an hour that felt like a year. Kareem sat and stared straight ahead without speaking. Genetically, Maha is her father's child, and she has so many of his qualities, so she sat without speaking as well. I fidgeted, needing to talk to someone, but I was wedged between Kareem and Maha, both of whom have the bizarre ability to stare into infinity for several hours at a time while remaining voiceless. I was alone with my fear.

Finally, the German physician came to Kareem. 'You can put your mind at rest,' I heard him say. 'Your granddaughter will be fine. But she does have a virus.'

I gasped, thinking only of MERS.

Kareem reassuringly laid his left hand upon my right hand, preparing us both for bad news.

'Your granddaughter has somehow or another contracted a virus called respiratory syncytial,' the physician reported. 'Generally, children contract it from other children. Perhaps one of her playmates is sick and that is the source.

'But do not worry, this is not a fatal virus. Only rarely does it require hospitalization. But, in this case, and to put all minds at ease, I suggest that you take your granddaughter to one of the royal hospitals in the country so that there will be a large staff tending to her.' He paused. 'Is that possible?'

'Yes, of course,' Kareem answered. 'Anything is possible.'

Of course, Little Sultana could be admitted to any hospital that our family felt was best for her. As a high-ranking prince in the Saudi royal family, Kareem often submits requests for non-royal Saudi citizens who appeal to him for medical care and to be admitted into this hospital or that hospital. I knew that with one telephone call Kareem would have Little Sultana admitted to the King Faisal Specialist Hospital and Research Centre in Riyadh, as that is where most of the royals go when they need medical attention in the kingdom.

We are all very familiar and pleased with the hospital that was the dream of my uncle Faisal, who was also king, before being assassinated by his own nephew on 25 March 1975, one of the saddest days in Saudi Arabia's history; for us, this rivals the grief felt in the United States when President John F. Kennedy was assassinated.

The German physician was pleased. 'Good, good,' he said.

Kareem asked, 'Tell me more about this virus, Doctor, if you will.'

'This is the virus mainly responsible for bronchiolitis and pneumonia in children. Most are well after a few watchful days with appropriate medication and care. This is not a virus that calls for antibodies. Bringing down the fever and keeping Little Sultana hydrated is the best course to take. If she becomes dehydrated, the hospital can provide intravenous fluids, and even humidified oxygen. I've only known a few children, perhaps 3 per cent, who had complications.

'Her fever was highly elevated, so I have given her an acetaminophen tablet to bring it down. Only if there is a complication, such as bacterial pneumonia, will the physician at the hospital put her on an antibiotic. Otherwise, they will keep her as comfortable as possible, and will provide plenty of fluids. I predict that your granddaughter will be home and will be happily playing within the week.'

I breathed easily for the first time since I had heard of Little Sultana's sickness. I felt emotionally drained. Mothers and grandmothers worldwide will understand my extreme worry. There is nothing more upsetting than for a beloved child to be stricken with a potentially serious illness.

Maha and I hugged each other tightly. Maha volunteered to call her sister, to give her the good news. I rushed into the emergency area and saw my son comforting his wife, who was weeping tears of joy and relief.

Little Sultana was sleeping and it looked like her fever was not so high, as her cheeks were less flushed and she was not nearly so damp. I overheard Kareem calling one of his assistants and advising them to prepare the documents for our granddaughter to be admitted into the royal hospital in Riyadh.

Within moments I saw the medical staff preparing Little Sultana to be moved and I was unintentionally pushed to the side by the bed, as staff wheeled my granddaughter out of the emergency area and into a long, white van that had ample space to hold a hospital bed.

My heart contracted in fear watching Abdullah and Zain join Little Sultana in the vehicle. Kareem rushed away, shouting without turning back to look at me that he was accompanying Abdullah and Zain. I soon heard the roar of his automobile, as he raced his engine.

Maha calmly and methodically put on her skates and skated away. 'I will see you soon, Mother,' she called out. My daughter then paused, turned around, looked at me with some emotion and walked my way. She hugged me, kissed me and whispered, 'Mother, I want you to know that I think that you are the best mother, and the best grandmother, in the world.'

I was stunned and could not speak, although I felt my eyes become wet. Maha hugged me again before adjusting her skates and then skating away, as though there were no troubles in all the world.

With Maha's departure, I suddenly felt terribly forlorn and alone. As the excitement died down and life returned to normal for most, I stood quietly for a moment to collect my thoughts and then walked slowly back into our palace. I was determined to pick up the pieces of my everyday life for I knew that if I was not fully occupied, I would burst into tears – and once I began crying, I might never stop.

Given the situation with my little granddaughter and the fact that I felt emotionally exhausted, I ticked off in my mind several important social engagements that must be cancelled, none of which I regretted missing. That's when I felt the plunge of disappointment, for I remembered my much anticipated appointment with Dr Meena. She would be the first person I telephoned.

*   *   *

I slept fitfully, as Kareem decided to stay at the hospital, very much in command, as though it was a war room. Yet, I understood his decision. I decided to go to see my granddaughter the following day for I was also eager to know how she was faring and I felt impatient for the little darling to return home and resume her normal life. Anything can happen when one is ill, as I had discovered when a royal cousin travelled abroad to have what was believed to be a minor plastic surgery procedure in Europe, but nearly died from an unexpected complication when one of the nursing staff accidentally gave the princess cousin a medicine that belonged to another patient who was only three doors away.

After my cousin nearly perished from human error, I asked several of my office assistants to investigate the problem my cousin had endured. I was curious to know just how many people die from preventable medical errors and was quite shocked at the information one of my assistants uncovered after her research. According to the prestigious *Journal of Patient Safety*, as many as 440,000 people each year in the United States die from medical errors.

Such an astoundingly high figure of preventable deaths was enough to get my full attention.

The journal also reported that medical mistakes in America claim the third spot as the leading cause of death in that country! There were many errors that were made routinely, such as instruments left inside a patient during surgery, wrong dosages of medication, or infections from contaminated medical equipment.

There are also high numbers of preventatable medical blunders made in hospitals in the United Kingdom. All of this information was very troubling and I vowed to avoid elective medical care that would require a hospital visit, even though three of my sisters had travelled to Los Angeles, California, to have various procedures done to try to keep them youthful in appearance. Thankfully, those surgeries were successful and all returned looking refreshed and younger.

Although I have creases around my eyes, and a little pouch under my chin, once I had knowledge of preventable medical errors I decided to retain my facial features rather than risk mistakes that might cost me my life, and precious time with my children and grandchildren. Rather a live, ageing mother and grandmother than a youthful corpse, I teased my children when they asked if I might consider beautifying surgery, as had their aunties.

There is a second reason I have not embraced plastic surgery. I enjoy looking older than my children. I have a number of royal cousins who cannot be identified as mothers, as they look much younger than some of their adult children. This is not a world I would embrace. I am proud to be older, and to look older, than the ones I birthed.

Tired and emotional, I began imagining all manner of awful possibilities, including the chance of Little Sultana being given the wrong medication. Before I could think this through I telephoned my husband as quickly as my fingers could move. When Kareem answered, I was impolite, for I gave him no opportunity to speak. 'Husband!' I shouted. 'Demand two of each medicine for Little Sultana. You take one first, and if it is safe, then allow the doctors to give her the second tablet.'

Kareem was silenced by my bewildering instruction, but finally spoke. 'Sultana, calm down! You are talking like a crazy person. Who, exactly, do you believe I am? A food taster?'

My husband and I are familiar with food tasters, for the leaders of our Al Sa'ud family frequently hire food tasters when they are attending functions where food is prepared by those they do not know personally. Food tasters risk their lives, eating food prepared by others to confirm that it is safe for the one they are paid to endanger their own lives to protect.

Indeed, my own father had hired several food tasters for years. This habit began after my father became violently ill after eating food at a diplomatic event when Colonel Muammar Gaddafi, the leader of Libya, was the host.

Prince Abdullah and Colonel Gaddafi always had a stormy relationship: Abdullah is a man of his word and has always carried an aversion to known liars. During an Arab summit before the war in Iraq, the two men argued in front of others, which is not something usual in our culture. Crown Prince Abdullah failed to conceal his revulsion during the argument, telling the Colonel, 'Your lies precede you and your grave is in front of you.'

Colonel Gaddafi never forgot or forgave what he felt was a grave insult, and in 2004 a conspiracy to murder Crown Prince Abdullah was uncovered when American Abdurahman Alamoudi, and Colonel Mohamed Ismael, a Libyan intelligence officer, gave credible testimony under questioning regarding two meetings with Colonel Gaddafi during 2003. At those meetings, they had accepted money to assassinate Crown Prince Abdullah.

I was secretly delighted that Kareem was given copies of the secret documents detailing the meetings, for I was curious to know exactly what had transpired. Kareem secretly told me that Colonel Gaddafi was raving mad because Crown Prince Abdullah had not been assassinated as planned. Under oath, Alamoudi had sworn that Gaddafi shouted, 'I want the Crown Prince killed either through assassination or through a coup!' A second plan was to deliver funds to a group of Saudi militants who were plotting to attack the Crown Prince's motorcade with shoulder-held missiles. Thanks be to Allah that this mission failed, for some reason or another.

In a meeting held two months later, Colonel Gaddafi screeched the question as to why he had not seen 'heads flying' in the Saudi royal family.

All things considered, the men in my family are wise to hire food tasters, even though, on this occasion, my husband Kareem had no desire to be a taster, not even for our little granddaughter.

I could not let the matter rest. 'Well, why not? You are big and strong and nothing will harm you. Take her medicines first. Please, Kareem!'

'Sultana, you have finally lost your mind,' my husband retorted in a low voice. He told me, 'If you feel so strongly about the matter, then you should come immediately to the hospital. I will give instructions that you take Little Sultana's medicine. If you become ill, darling, we will not allow her to take the same medicines.'

I heard him give a big gasp of total irritation. He then disconnected my call.

I telephoned Abdullah and asked his opinion. Abdullah told me not to be paranoid, that they were watching everything given to Little Sultana and thus far she had received nothing but intravenous fluids.

Since no one else in the family was worried by the possibility of medical mistakes, I could do nothing but fret the night away, which was the reason I slept so poorly.

*   *   *

My health was quite obviously affected by the trauma of Little Sultana's illness, for I awoke the following morning with a sore throat and an aching head. Knowing that my granddaughter's progress might be further compromised should she be in the presence of anyone with an infection of some kind, I reluctantly called my husband and explained that I would be unable to be by Little Sultana's side.

I felt a tinge of anger when Kareem's tone of voice signalled relief; it seemed our conversation the previous evening had stacked my husband's feelings against me.

'Do not worry, Sultana,' he said in a happy voice. 'Your granddaughter is coming back to life! Her temperature is almost normal. She is smiling at me now, in fact. Stay in bed, rest and know that I will be home soon. The doctors here have told us that at the rate she is improving they expect to discharge her tomorrow morning.'

'Do tell her that I love her, Kareem. And that I am sorry I cannot be by her side.'

'She is surrounded on all sides, darling. Abdullah is on her right side. Zain is on her left side and Amani is at her feet. I am standing tall over all,' he chuckled.

While I do not particularly like going into hospitals, for they hold many sick and distressed people, if one of my children or grandchildren is a patient, then that is where I need to be. Each time I had business to attend to at the royal hospital, built by Uncle Faisal, I left in awe of what his once simple dream has become. There is no hospital in the world so beautifully appointed. Everything within the King Faisal Specialist Hospital and Research Centre is regal, even majestic, just like the great man himself. What joy it would be to see Uncle Faisal's face examining what his dream had accomplished – he would be incredibly pleased and proud of what the royal hospital had become, which is the most modern medical facility in the kingdom.

*   *   *

Although plagued with a cold and cough that prevented me from doing what I really wanted, which was to visit Little Sultana, I settled at my desk and began making calls. My original plan was to see Dr Meena the following day, but, with Little Sultana's illness and now my own unpleasant head cold and painful sore throat, I needed to rest and isolate myself from others.

When we spoke, Dr Meena fully appreciated my predicament and, although she was disappointed that we would not meet, she was very understanding. She mentioned that she would soon be leaving the kingdom for a medical conference in Switzerland, then added, 'Dear Princess, I know you cannot talk for long, but what I have to tell you cannot wait. I believe that a life is in danger. What would you think if I wrote you the details of the case which concerns me? Would that be acceptable?'

'Of course, Dr Meena, please do feel free to communicate with me in any manner you feel is best for the circumstances. Shall I send my driver to pick up the communication?'

'That would be lovely, Princess. The letter will be ready for collection first thing tomorrow morning. And I wanted you to know too, Princess, that the automobile and driver you so graciously provided for me is being used to transport more than twenty young women who would have no way to reach school, work or the shops to purchase necessities, or whatever else their needs might be.' She laughed lightly. 'I am pleased to report that these twenty women keep the driver and the automobile on the highway many hours each day.'

I felt very happy that something I had done was helping to make the lives of young women easier. People around the world believe that all Saudi Arabians are wealthy. This is not the case. The population of my country is very diverse, and in fact most people are not wealthy. There are many advantages to being a Saudi citizen – the government does help with interest-free loans, free education and even free healthcare, and, without taxes in Saudi Arabia, what a person earns stays with them; however, despite the many aspects of government assistance, there are poor people who struggle. There are many women who have no access to transportation, and to have a driver and automobile at their disposal is like the gift of freedom.

Without saying anything to Dr Meena, I decided at that moment that I would make a fleet of three cars and six drivers available to Dr Meena to be used in any way that would help Saudi female students and young Saudi wives. When one is dealing with Dr Meena, one knows that any efforts made to help others will go directly to those people in need. Dr Meena is the most honest person it is been my pleasure to know.

We closed the call with best wishes, although Dr Meena surprised me at the end when she said, 'And, Princess, I do hope that my communication will not harm your feelings. I have some things to say that you may not like hearing. If so, I pray for your forgiveness, because you are a good woman and you help many people. But there is someone who needs your help now, although I am aware that this particular project might well be difficult for you.'

My curiosity spiked. What unusual problem was coming my way? I considered Dr Meena's words for a long time, wondering how anything could be more difficult than some of the problems we had already faced together. Then I recalled her perplexing words: 'worthy Saudi men'. Truly, I could not concentrate on the work at hand for pondering over the puzzle.

Finally, I sighed heavily and pulled out some files that needed my attention, one of which related to a successful charity responsible for educating more than two thousand girls each year.

*　　*　　*

The next day, after Little Sultana had been released from the hospital and was recuperating at home, I was sitting at my desk when my office assistant delivered a sealed envelope from Dr Meena. Earlier that morning I had sent my driver to her hospital offices to pick up the communication.

I finished the business at hand before clasping the envelope to my chest. Most Saudis enjoy using personalized stationery, with their names and titles announced boldly for all to see, but Dr Meena was a simple woman who led a simple life. The envelope was of the least expensive paper, rough to the touch. I smiled, for I could tell that Dr Meena was not a frivolous woman and would never spend money on anything of luxury, particularly something such as stationery, which is in essence a person's calling card. Neither had Dr Meena addressed it personally to me, or put her own name as the sender. Instead, the word 'WORTHY' was boldly written across the envelope. I knew then that whatever the project might be that she wished me to be involved with, I would refer to it by this title.

I sipped my morning tea, then settled in a comfortable chair to read the correspondence that had been preying on my mind since Dr Meena's call.

Dear Princess,

I will not spend time complimenting you on the work you have been doing, as I know full well that you spend most of your waking hours slaying the negative things in our country that promote one tragedy after another. After knowing you but a few short years, I have seen that while your riches are ample, time is the one commodity that you lack. But, Princess, I will tell you that you have radically changed the lives of so many people. Unlike you, I am but a simple woman, but I know the importance of the work you and I are doing.

Over the past few years we have concentrated solely on Saudi girls and women because their need is the greatest of all those in our young country – a country formed on an ancient land, and bound into one nation founded by your own great-grandfather, only eighty years ago.

Finally our world is changing and, I believe, for the better, for the first time in our modern history.

What we have longed for since we were children is now happening. The windows of opportunity for Saudi women are beginning to open; they are now slightly ajar. But there are those who fight our every step. Then there are those who are beginning to help us. For the first time there are Saudi men who have seen the injustices of our culture, society and government. There are Saudi men who are standing by women and calling for change. There are Saudi men who are languishing in prison for doing nothing more than defending women's rights. Indeed, there are ten specific Saudi men who stand out as champions – men who are prepared to fight for equality.

While I would like nothing better than to address the severity of the problems each of these ten men are facing for

*doing nothing more than being truthful, I must concentrate
on one particular man who is a symbol of all that is good in
a human being. He is the Nelson Mandela of Saudi Arabia.
He is the Mohandas Gandhi of Saudi Arabia. He is the Oskar
Schindler of Saudi Arabia. He is the Dalai Lama of Saudi
Arabia. And he is the Aung San Suu Kyi of Saudi Arabia.*

*Who is this man, you say? This man is a young husband
and father named Raif Badawi. This young man has been
torn from his life of peace, and from his wife and children,
for the 'crime' of blogging and discussing human rights and
the wrongs that all thinking Saudi Arabians acknowledge in
their hearts, even if they do not have the courage to shout their
thoughts from the flat rooftops of our cities and villages.*

*But, Princess, Saudi Arabians are fortunate that this young
man has enough courage for all.*

*Although you and I have never spoken about Raif Badawi,
I know that you are a woman who misses nothing when it
comes to every major occurrence in our country, every major
change. Therefore I have no doubt that you know much about
this young man who is by chance creating waves of outrage
around the world by doing nothing more than refusing to give
in to tyranny.*

Yes, Princess, tyranny!

*I believe that Raif Badawi is the person who will create
change by simply being himself, a young man who cannot be
intimidated into silence. As I have said, I understand that you
can discover much about Raif Badawi on your own, but I have
a full heart when I think of this young man and I cannot stop
my words. Here is what I know of him.*

*Raif was born on 13 January 1984 into a conservative Saudi
family. He was born with a distinct character and could not
be swayed from doing what he believed was the right thing.
He has a desire to seek the truth. He takes the initiative. He is
very energetic. He prefers action. He looks for the good but
will confront the bad. He was born the man that he is today,*

although he could do little to express his ideas until he became an adult.

Raif met Ensaf Haidar, the woman who matched him with a strong personality and a feel for justice, through a friend, who happened to be his future wife's brother. You know the problems young people have meeting in Saudi Arabia. Raif and Ensaf's relationship began innocently, through conversations over a cell telephone. They did not meet and have illicit sex. They talked. This happened after Ensaf borrowed her brother's phone and found herself speaking to her brother's good friend, Raif. They were doing what is considered by many in our country to be a punishable crime: two young people having a conversation. TALKING! Once their families discovered that the two were chatting over the phone, they made every effort to stop it, but it was too late. Love had flowered during their long conversations and they were married in 2002.

Raif proved to be a dream of a husband by any woman's standards. He is a man who respects women, and he treated his wife as an equal in every way. How many Saudi women can claim such a husband? Pitifully few, Princess, pitifully few.

The couple lived quietly and happily, and started their family.

But a black sandstorm was forming, and it was set on a path that would separate the young couple.

The sandstorm started lightly, as most do. After Raif witnessed many wrongs committed in Saudi Arabia by those who should be protecting us, he began to write his blog and discussed the issues which troubled him. He never called for the downfall of our government. He never promoted violence. He TALKED about issues, using his vast knowledge of our land, and applying common sense to the social problems he personally witnessed.

Raif is a man who cannot keep quiet about injustices, whether against women or men, whether gender discrimination or whether personal freedom discrimination.

After the religious police gained his attention by their evil acts of targeting, harassing and arresting women who were doing nothing more than going about their daily business, Raif spoke out against them in his blog. He sees no need for religious police. He believes that Saudi Arabians deserve better than having a throng of men who can see no good in human nature running amok, arresting and terrorizing good people.

Princess, I have heard his words coming from your own tongue – that the religious police and conservative clerics are the first in line committing injustice against all Saudis. You share these feelings with Raif Badawi. The difference is that he spoke his mind on a public forum, on a blogging website named Free Saudi Liberals, which, of course, is now closed by our government.

The rest is history. Our government has moved against this young man as tenaciously as if he were a terrorist who had plans to murder thousands. His family has been torn apart – he has been ripped away from his wife and their three children. He has been sentenced to ten years in prison and one thousand lashes, for doing nothing more than speaking his mind.

As you and I have discussed on several occasions, ALL human beings must have the right to speak their minds.

This young man is locked in a small cell.

This man cannot see his growing children.

This man is being threatened with a death sentence.

This man is a thinker, not a man built to endure physical abuse.

This man has many health issues which may hasten his death.

This man has already endured fifty lashes.

I thank Allah that few of us know the pain endured by being on the receiving end of the lash. As a medical doctor who has treated two women admitted into the hospital after being flogged thirty times each for the crime of sitting in a car and having a conversation with a man who was not their relative, I can tell you that flogging causes unbearable pain, tremendous damage to the skin, as well as injury to the internal organs if the lash falls anywhere but the upper back, which it often does. I can also tell you that the 'Koranian rule' is rarely applied, where the one doing the flogging is supposed to hold a Koran under his arm so that the lashes do not come full force from the entire body but only from the elbow, thus with less force.

Princess, according to the women I treated, the lashes do not cause intolerable pain. At first. But after ten lashes, the pain is like a fire that inflames the entire body. The pain is so severe that victims search for words to describe it.

Some victims grit their teeth and make no noise.

Some victims scream in agony.

Some victims pray to Allah, asking for mercy.

Some victims faint from the pain.

Raif Badawi did not make a sound. Raif Badawi did not faint. He stood defiantly against his aggressors.

After a flogging, the victims are left so physically weak and in such pain that it is rare for them to be able to walk and it takes many days, even weeks, for the flesh to heal. The moment the wounds are sealed and the fluids of inflammation cease flowing, the next set of floggings begin.

Princess, there is talk that Raif Badawi will soon be tried for the crime of apostasy, the crime of abandoning his faith, as you know. With this will come the death sentence and a deep shame that we in Saudi Arabia will never forget.

Should our government murder this young man who is a bright beacon of light, the world will never forgive our government – or Saudi Arabians – for letting it happen.

It is in our hands, princess, to step in and stop this crime.

Numerous people and the representatives of many countries in the world are standing up to be counted. All are calling for the freedom of a young man who can change the world, just as Mandela and Gandhi brought change that will forever live in peoples' hearts.

Shall we remain silent? Shall we stand by and let this happen?

It is rare that such young men as Raif Badawi are born.

Can we allow his life to be snuffed out?

If he is allowed to live, he will represent a unification of all good things in our country.

Princess, I have never asked you to criticize our government, because our government is your family. Such a thing would be difficult for anyone.

But Princess, this is a case that needs your help.

It is my hope that you will shine the light of compassion into your husband's heart and ask him to pass that light to the men who rule over us all.

Find some way to convince them that there will be no threat to the government if ordinary Saudi citizens are allowed to TALK, to SPEAK OUT, to DISCUSS the issues that are in all our hearts.

Princess, as you know, I am devoted to Islam. Since the day Raif Badawi was arrested, I have been praying to Allah. I have been thinking about our revered Prophet Muhammad. I have never felt more strongly about anything, Princess. I believe with my whole heart that Prophet Muhammad would free Raif Badawi, and even become his friend and mentor. I believe that Prophet Muhammad would see the light in this young man's heart. I believe that Prophet Muhammad would show mercy to this young man, his wife and three young children. I believe that Prophet Muhammad would embrace the goodness that is in Raif Badawi and forbid others to harm him.

I believe, most of all, that Prophet Muhammad was a good man who would recognize a WORTHY MAN.

Raif Badawi is a worthy man, princess.

I have nothing more to say, as I believe that Raif Badawi says all there is to say for each one of us.

Talking should not be a crime.

Please read some of his blog posts, Princess. Although

forbidden, they are in the world of the internet and his words will be quoted for many years to come.

Raif Badawi is the best that Saudi Arabia has to offer the world.

He is a treasure that should be protected.

If not protected by us, then by whom?

I bid you farewell. You will be in my prayers, and in my heart. I know you will do the right thing.

My heart fluttered with dread. I knew the full story of Raif Badawi, and I had suffered too, wishing that he would be freed. But it was a subject I had not discussed with Kareem.

But knowing my husband, and the other men in my family, those who are at the top and who rule with power and strength, none would ever make an allowance for any criticism of the ruling family, or of the clerics, or of the social system.

I sat quietly and gathered my thoughts, wondering how my husband would react when I approached the topic of Raif Badawi.

When Kareem arrived home an hour later, he had a big smile upon his face and joy in his heart over Little Sultana's recovery. He was also pleased about a business deal that had prospered greatly. I did not get my hopes up, for I know that my husband's temper can spark and flare in a moment if the forbidden subject of the elderly rulers in our family is broached by anyone, even his wife.

I braced myself, as I am a wife who well knows the man she married, and I knew that there was little hope that Kareem would agree that Raif Badawi should be saved from his tortured existence.

I also knew that I could not mention Dr Meena's name or she would surely be severely punished for 'disobedience' against the royal family. The poor woman might end up in a cell near to Badawi himself!

I would have to accept the full responsibility for Dr Meena's thoughts and ideas.

Soon I was combating a full-flown firestorm, and the dread settled in my heart that I would never know the joy of declaring victory over an antiquated government system that appeared to be set in stone.

Chapter Nine

A Middle Woman

I AM NO LONGER a young woman. I am not yet an old woman. I am a middle woman.

I freely admit that I have borrowed this concept. I heard this expression from the American woman who has written five books, including this one, revealing various stories of my life as a princess in Saudi Arabia. She is older than me, but we are sisters at heart, and so our difference in years has never been noticed. When I asked her age a few years ago, she courteously responded: 'I am pleased to acknowledge that I am no longer a young woman. But I am not yet an old woman. I am a middle woman. Despite my middling status, my thoughts still revolve around the future, and what I might do to serve womankind, to bring better times to all people of the world. So I am a youthful-minded middle woman.

'I have gathered some wisdom along the way, and hopefully have become more intelligent. Think of me as a field whose harvest has come in, nevertheless vibrant and strong with leaves stretching to the sky seeking the sun, not yet familiar with withering and dying. I believe that to be a middle woman is to be the best woman of all, still filled with passion for all of humankind, wealthy with promise, and steeped in wisdom.'

Her words gave me a certain joy. I smiled at the idea that I am fast approaching my best time in life. For now, I will refer to myself as a middle woman until the day comes when I will take the lovely character and starring role of being an older woman.

Therefore, as a middle woman, I was wise enough to shut my mouth and better prepare myself for the storm that I knew was coming when I said to my husband, 'Kareem, I have something to discuss that you will not like.'

'Then silence your tongue, Sultana,' he replied, 'because I am happy today and do not wish to know anything of your latest passionate idea that will put me in a foul mood.'

I felt a smile grow from my heart to my face, for I know my husband too well. 'Yes, husband, my tongue will remain at rest, at least until after a new sunrise and sunset. But remember, tomorrow evening I will expect you to listen without speaking while I share something of utmost importance with you.'

'Tomorrow is a new day, wife, and I promise to listen to your words, even if I disagree with those words. But today? No, today is a celebration. Our granddaughter is home, safe from harm, and no longer in distress. I closed a deal earlier that will ensure the continuing prosperity of my business in the islands, a business that provides many job opportunities for the poor.'

He waited for a compliment or thanks from me regarding his business skills, but I said nothing, already planning my strategy for the following evening.

'Does my news please you, Sultana?'

'Indeed, husband. I am happy for all of us that Little Sultana's health scare was nothing too serious and that she is fully recovered. We are luckier than most to have three healthy children and four healthy grandchildren.'

Kareem gazed at me in expectation.

'Oh, and I am always pleased when your businesses prosper – particularly when help is given to those in need.'

And so the evening passed in a most pleasant manner, with cheerful talk over dinner about our grandchildren and Kareem's news that he was making even more money, despite the reality that if we were lucky enough to live one thousand years, we would be hard-pressed to spend the money now in our possession. Kareem makes money, and I give it away. Thus far he has not complained because we have felt no pinch of need.

He was so obsessed with his talk of money that I teased him: 'You are the maker. I am the taker. But what I take, I give away, so I pray to Allah that He has no complaint with me on this point.'

I am glad that my husband has developed his business acumen so well over the years that he is now a highly talented man in that world. His education was in law, but he discovered soon enough that his talents lie in the field of deal-making in the commercial sector. This is good news for all the family, for when Kareem and I first married my wealth was more than double his own. Undeniably, Kareem Al Sa'ud is a good and mainly fair man, but in our society, regardless of class or status, men are deemed to be the head of the home, and in educated circles they are, at the very least, one step ahead of the women in their lives when it comes to business matters; it is the creation of wealth and business concepts that appeal to male sensitivities. In my land, family concerns occupy most women and can empower them.

I have very little care as to who it is that counts the most money in their bank account, whether it is my husband or me. I spend much less on myself these days than I did in the past, for I only need so many expensive gowns, and no longer desire jewels; my six homes are all just as I need them to be, beautifully furnished and scattered around Saudi Arabia and in other countries in the world so that we always have a roof over our heads. I am aware that I live in a world of opulence, but in truth, other than food and shelter, I only need enough to ensure the safety of my children and grandchildren, and the peace of mind to know that I am not depriving my family when I spend my many millions on the charities that are close to my heart. Education is my top charitable priority, as I truly feel that only education can change the status of women in the world. But over the years other needs have been presented to me, and I am thankful to have ample funds to help those in genuine need, whether they be little children in refugee camps or women who are walking about with faces so disfigured that their lives are radically changed and their mere survival is uncertain.

After an evening of pleasantries, Kareem retired to his quarters to telephone his business managers, located in America and other places that are eight or more hours behind Saudi Arabia. Kareem now has so many interests in so many different countries that any hour of the day is a workday somewhere.

I retired to my own quarters and, once prepared for bed, I took out Dr Meena's letter about the worthy man Raif Badawi, re-reading her heartfelt words and trying to remember all that I know about the young human-rights activist. I made a note to have my assistants conduct in-depth research on Badawi and his wife Ensaf Haidar as a top priority the following morning, so that when I discussed his case with Kareem I would have full knowledge of the man, his activities, and the subsequent reactions from the Saudi legal system and government.

I was fighting a sinking feeling because I knew in my heart that the men of my family must be heavily involved in Badawi's case because his cause had reached epic proportions. Governments and people of many nationalities were demanding his freedom. Anytime the eyes of the entire world are focused on Saudi Arabia, the men of my family take an active interest in whatever the nucleus of the problem might be, which in this case was the young man Raif Badawi.

For the entire free world to condemn our government is a serious humiliation for the Al Sa'ud men. While I know that Kareem is not one of the few third-generation princes who will ever be in line to the throne – for too many reasons to explain here – and that such important decisions are not his to make, my husband has close friendships with those who are currently ruling. Hopefully they would hear Kareem's words, take them seriously and bring about a reversal in their decision to make an example of Raif Badawi.

*　　　*　　　*

I awoke from my restless sleep with worry on my mind. I was relieved to discover that Kareem had left the palace earlier in the day. His absence would give me the opportunity to work openly with my assistants, compiling a file on Raif Badawi. If Kareem were roaming about the palace, popping in and out of my private quarters, he would certainly discover my interest in the case which had fuelled a great deal of international interest. I felt it was essential that I was fully prepared to debate the issue in a wise manner based on facts and sound information. Although my grandfather, King Abdul Aziz, at no time had female descendants in mind when he was attempting to teach his offspring the wisdom that came so naturally to him, I feel confident he would be pleased to know that some of his granddaughters take pride in modelling themselves on his actions and taking an interest in vital issues related to the betterment of our country. Most female royals are nice enough, but they are notoriously frivolous because they are taught not to bother with important issues affecting public life in Saudi Arabia. Instead, they focus on what I believe are the shallow things of life, such as fashion and personal appearance. But there is great promise in the new generation of royals. I am seeing many more princesses who relate to the serious issues that affect most human beings. I am proud to say that I count my two daughters among these enlightened and wise young women. Each, in their own unique way, tries hard to make a positive contribution to society.

No matter what I did or said, there was no question that my understanding of Raif Badawi's position was certain to create a predicament in our palace. Over the years Kareem has suffered quietly as I have focused my work on gender discrimination in Saudi Arabia and other lands. And I understand his struggle with my passionate stance. Truly, until very recent times hardly any citizens of my country would have supported my passion to help change the world for women. My actions on behalf of Saudi females would have been considered by most as nothing more than that of a mischief-maker. Nowadays, though, there are many more Saudi Arabians who believe in equality and that women should live more freely.

Just as the Saudi public used to be against anyone heralding women's rights, the Saudi public is now against young people who are focusing on freedom of speech, such as Raif Badawi. Many believe that despite the daily irritations most Saudis endure at the hands of members of the Committee for the Promotion of Virtue and the Prevention of Vice (CPVPV), it is best to try to deal with the current mode of rule rather than to exchange what we have for a more aggressive form of militancy. Saudi Arabians know that the governments in Libya, Syria, Iraq and other Middle Eastern countries have been overthrown by those who support change, but in some instances those citizens are now ruled by a government much more toxic than the previous one.

Mainly Kareem acknowledged my activities because he is a man who agrees that gender discrimination against women in Saudi Arabia, or anywhere in the world for that matter, should end instantly. Perhaps this is because he is a man who loves his daughters and granddaughters; he does not wish for any of the four to suffer from intolerance and prejudice.

Now, if I entered the political realm and pushed for a prisoner to be pardoned, he would be sure to react negatively, for the political arena is very dangerous ground to walk upon in Saudi Arabia, whether one is a royal or not.

And so I began my day's work: my objective being to discover the world of Raif Badawi, an advocate of non-violence, finding out what he stands for, the actions he had taken and the Saudi government's subsequent legal prosecution of him.

By the late afternoon I felt I better knew and understood this worthy young man and his equally worthy wife. I held them both in high regard. Rather than punish such a man, I believed he should be rewarded. Saudi Arabia needs thousands of like-minded citizens. Both Badawi and Haidar are non-violent and are passionate advocates for basic human rights for all. To my dismay, my government is increasing its efforts to control the 'thoughts' of its citizens; such repression has never succeeded for very long in modern history.

I feel enormous disappointment and frustration that the men of my own family do not realize that non-violent activists are precisely what our country needs in order to move to the next step, to take our rightful place beside enlightened governments who are working on behalf of their citizens, rather than working against them. Why? Because both our social system and our legal system defy common sense. If there is anything that I have learned in life, it is that when change is needed, change *will* come, one way or another. It is wise at this time in our history to seek non-violent examples and encourage the fair-minded activists to help create gradual change rather than leave a space in the hearts of our citizens which may welcome violent militants who swoop down like angry raptors and destroy all in their path. We have witnessed all around the Middle East the tragedies that occur when citizens of repressive governments become so frustrated that they turn to those who preach violence. Millions of people have become refugees and beggars when violent extremists have overthrown governments. Should this happen in Saudi Arabia, the first action taken would be to behead or burn to death every Saudi royal. Then they would turn on the citizens of our land, creating scores of refugees such as we have seen in Iraq, Syria and Libya. It is much better to work with non-violent activists, who take the time to set up appropriate organizations to work with citizens, rather than create violence in the hearts of men by refusing to allow them to participate in decision-making and government.

No! Saudi Arabia does *not* belong to the Al Sa'ud family. Saudi Arabia belongs to *all* its citizens. Never have I felt so strongly on this point than after coming to 'know' the activist Raif Badawi.

For example, here are the most pressing concerns that demand change for most Saudis who are educated, intelligent, fair-minded and possessed of common sense:

1) The guardian system in Saudi Arabia should be the first to be eliminated. All Saudi females, from the day of their birth to the day of their death, are under the rule of a male family member who makes all decisions affecting their lives; they are treated like children. Until the guardian system is eliminated, women cannot function as adults. Our lives are lived as those of perpetual minors. Our guardian has the right to say if we go to school, if and whom we marry, if and where we travel, and if and when we can see a doctor. Women die in Saudi Arabia when the male guardian cannot be found to sign documents at hospitals giving approval for treatment. In fact, there was a recent case where a car accident caused the death of the husband and father. The wife and daughter were grievously wounded, but without a guardian present to sign the proper papers the wife died for need of an amputation. Mothers are not allowed to make the most trivial decisions on behalf of their children.

The only aspect of our lives not determined by our guardian is when we die. Our guardian does not have that power to determine the date and time of our death, which is in the hands of Allah only. In the past, Saudi women were confined in purdah, trapped in their homes, and had no inkling of how to survive or participate in public life without the men of their family. But those days are no more. The vast majority of females in Saudi Arabia are educated at least through the primary grades, with many more graduating from secondary educational institutions. With education, women are able to make their own decisions as to where to work and whom to marry. The guardian system is so ridiculous that most people living outside Saudi Arabia can scarcely believe that it is still thriving in my country.

2) Women should be allowed to drive! The men in my family have been promising to look into the possibility of women driving since mid-1970. But still nothing has been done; all we do is

talk about change. Too many women are stranded, unable to get to work, to the doctor or to purchase groceries. Saudi Arabia is the only country in the world where women are not allowed to drive.

3) The Committee for the Promotion of Virtue and the Prevention of Vice should be eliminated. The committee consists of approximately five thousand very angry men who are given authority to roam the streets of our cities looking for sinners. They are searching for the most mundane reasons to harass women, and sometimes men; they arrest unrelated men and women who might be together, as my country insists upon the strictest separation of sexes. Men and women who are not related or not married cannot dine in a restaurant together, or even ride in a car with one another. (Drivers hired to transport women are exempt from this rule.)

Members of the committee enforce what they believe to be the dress code for all women, which is to be covered from head to toe in dark colours. Although they sometimes ignore women foreign to our land, they are an achingly painful thorn in the side of Saudi women. Females in my country are afraid of these men, who have full power to arrest them for the way they look, dress or talk. I have known three women who were terrorized by these men, then arrested for wearing high heels that made a clicking sound on the payment. The charge was 'enticing innocent men whose hearts were pure' – until they heard the high heels clicking! They also patrol the stores, making certain all are closed for *salat*, the prayer times, and that men do not miss going to a mosque during prayer. These men used to be armed with sticks or canes and took the greatest pleasure in beating women who dared to show their hair, or failed to cover their bodies in the abaya or a similar costume. They were often armed with cans of red spray paint and would, with great enthusiasm, mark the legs of 'offending' women.

Thankfully, reform came in 2007 after a number of the most brutish incidents caught the attention of the foreign press. I have paid special attention to these men and I believe that most are uneducated brutes empowered by archaic laws to harass innocent Saudis. Like most of the uneducated, they seek such power so that they might harm others, appointing themselves as judge and jury over the innocents of our land.

4) All adult Saudis should be allowed to vote, whether male or female. Although there has been endless talk and empty promises about women voting, in reality neither men nor women have a true voice in the Saudi Arabian legal or social systems. The rules are there, and we are made to follow them or else! Some men are allowed to vote in local elections, but these elected officials can do little but follow the rules themselves. As far as women voting, I will believe it when I see it. For a woman to vote, she must get to the polls. She cannot drive, as I have mentioned. Most Saudi men will refuse to transport their wives to the polls to vote. It's a mind-numbing merry-go-round, and the losers are, once again, Saudi women.

5) All Saudis should have the right to free expression. Should any Saudi Arabian lightly criticize the government or the religious clerics, they are arrested, tried and most often given a long prison sentence and many lashes. This has happened to the 'worthy man' Raif Badawi, as well as his own attorney, a young man named Waleed Abulkhair – who happens to be married to Raif's sister – who was imprisoned and given a fifteen-year sentence for defending his client.

There are a number of Saudi journalists who have dared criticize the men in my family, or the religious authorities, and these men have been convicted on ridiculous charges, such as 'breaking allegiance with the ruler' or 'contact with a foreign journalist', or for 'insulting the judiciary' or 'gossiping about the ruler'. Other charges include 'calling for atheist thoughts', 'disloyalty to the king' and 'harming the reputation of the kingdom'. Any exposure of human-rights abuses occurring in Saudi Arabia – and there are ample abuses – will win an activist a long term in prison and many painful lashes. This should stop *now*!

6) Children should be exempt from arrest and torture. Saudi

judges are allowed to order the arrest and detention of children if the judge sees any sign of puberty. Since judges are not doctors, I question such a right. How does a judge know if a child has entered puberty? Besides, puberty is coming earlier to children these days, as early as eight years in some cases. Should these children be arrested, tortured and imprisoned for any crime? *No* country should arrest and torture children.

There are other things that must change in my country, but those abuses I will save to describe on another day, as I have listed six of the most important abuses Saudi citizens are suffering.

While there are many wrongs being committed in Saudi Arabia, and so many changes that are needed in this land, only the men are in a position to bring change: one of these men is my husband, another is my father, and another is my son.

Sadly, even I, a Saudi princess, would be imprisoned for compiling this list of abuses and calling for their end. And none of the men of my family would have the power to save me from severe punishment.

The 'thought police' are now ruling Saudi Arabia.

*　　*　　*

I considered displaying my feminine wiles when meeting with Kareem, pondering over what pretty dress I might wear and how to style my hair, but common sense prevailed. I realized that I should not have to seduce my husband with an attractive look and sweet smile when attempting to convince him to understand my views on the serious topics I wished to raise with him. I know that my husband loves me for my compassionate character and meticulous mind, so that is enough. It is wonderful that he considers me to be a physically attractive woman, but one has nothing to do with the other.

And so I wore my most comfortable turquoise lounging gown, with my hair loosely draping on my shoulders. I wore no jewellery and little make-up. My lips were pink and my brows were straightened, and I sprayed my favourite perfume on my hair and wrists, but this was nothing special, rather my daily regime when I am at home with no plans to go out or to entertain guests.

I was keen to see my husband, for hope was building in my heart that he, as I, was discontented with the increased security measures being taken against innocent Saudi citizens for merely speaking their minds.

When he arrived, he did not appear too pleased to see me and seemed physically weary. Although he smiled sweetly and settled into his easy chair, waiting for his Arabic coffee and a plate of dates to be served, I could see that something was troubling him.

I felt uneasy about his weariness because I worried that his smile was concealing a cranky mood. My husband is naturally irritable when he is tired.

I considered postponing our conversation until the morning, but then remembered that Kareem and his brother Assad were travelling to Switzerland for a four-day business trip the following day.

I would have to speak with him tonight, or delay for nearly a week, and I did not wish to wait so long to seek to alleviate the suffering of the worthy Raif Badawi. Truthfully, I was fearful that the floggings would start once again and that the frail-bodied Badawi would depart his life on earth as a result of this torture. I agreed with Dr Meena, should such a thing happen, that it would be a shame that forever lived in the pages of the history of Saudi Arabia.

However, I decided that the best course of action was to stall, but only for a few hours. I would wait until after our dinner before approaching the delicate topic.

Our meal was exceptional, with our favourite foods prepared by our French chef. Many of our cousins envied us our divine chef, despite the fact that most had French chefs in their kitchens, although all told us that no one was more talented than our own. Several of our cousins had inflamed Kareem's temper when they attempted to lure our chef to work in their palaces to create desirable dishes for their own families.

We started dining with a shrimp cocktail, followed by fresh snapper from the Red Sea, with a savoury rice dish and grilled vegetables. For dessert, there was a rich French crème brûlée with fresh fruits. Although we both enjoyed the fabulous dishes, our talk was strained, for Kareem was concerned about what it was I needed to say to him, and I was apprehensive as to how the evening would end. Would Kareem feel strongly enough to approach his most powerful cousins, the sons of the recently deceased King Abdullah, or the sons of our new king, Salman, or perhaps the grandsons of the long-deceased King Faisal? All those royal cousins had extra influence and one day some of them would be kings, sitting at the pinnacle of Saudi power. If Kareem might influence the cousins of his age, they might influence our king to try a different tactic with those pushing for the freedom to speak their minds.

Once we finished with our meal, we sat on the balcony overlooking our beautiful swimming pool. While sipping a glass of cold buttermilk, which Kareem always drinks at the end of his evening meal, my husband looked at me with curiosity flashing in his eyes. 'All right, Sultana. I am here. I will be quiet. Tell me this important news that you wish to share with me.'

'One moment, husband,' I said, as I stood and walked to the antique Windsor cabinet we had purchased in England several years before. I had placed the reference papers for Badawi in the top drawer.

Kareem looked at me in amusement. 'So, you require notes, darling? I have never known you to be short of words!'

'True, husband,' I said with a little smile. 'But this situation is very different.'

Kareem sat up straight, his eyes fixed on the papers in my hand. I knew my husband's plan. He was trying to read the papers from an upside-down angle. My husband had perfected that ability years before when we were young and I kept many secrets. It was a way of knowing my secrets before I confessed them. And so I intentionally kept the papers slanted so he could not see clearly enough to examine the words I was hiding.

I moved my chair and sat at a distance. 'Let me read you something, husband,' I said. I cleared my voice and spoke distinctly. '*The only way to deal with an unfree world is to become so absolutely free that your very existence is an act of rebellion.*'

Kareem stared at me in bemusement. 'And?'

'What do you think of that statement?'

'Nothing much. Did you write it?'

'No, Kareem. I did not write it! A man named Albert Camus said it.'

'Should I know this Mr Camus?'

'He is dead now, but he was a French Nobel prize-winning author and a philosopher.'

'Why are you quoting him to me?'

'Kareem, this quote was used by someone important in our world.'

'Sultana, you are speaking in riddles. I do not know of what you speak.'

'All right, let me read you something else, husband. "For me, liberalism simply means, live and let live. This is a splendid slogan. However, the nature of liberalism – particularly the Saudi version – needs to be clarified. It is even more important to sketch the features and parameters of liberalism, to which the other faction, controlling and claiming exclusive monopoly of the truth, is so hostile that they are driven to discredit it without discussion or fully understanding what the word actually means. They have succeeded in planting hostility to liberalism in the minds of the public and turning people against it, lest the carpet be pulled out from under their feet. But their hold over people's minds and society shall vanish like dust carried off in the wind."'

'That sounds like something a young person would dream up. Did one of our children write those words?' Kareem asked with alarm.

My husband so astonished me with his lack of knowledge about the blog writings of Raif Badawi that I sat slack-jawed, staring at him.

'No, Kareem,' I finally said. 'This conversation has little to do with our children, other than my concern for the future of the entire Al Sa'ud family and the country which we love.'

Kareem raised his hands, gesturing his confusion. 'Please speak plainly, Sultana. I have no crystal ball. I cannot read your mind.'

I stared into my husband's eyes. 'Kareem, do you find it ironic that Saudi Arabia is a member of the United Nation's top human-rights body? And that earlier in the year they tried to assume the head of the council?'

Kareem stiffened. 'Ironic? No. No more than Cuba, Russia and China, all of whom are or have been members.'

'Well, husband, I find it ironic that the land we love is a member of such a council that was supposedly formed to stop human-rights abuses, even as we are imprisoning, torturing and destroying the lives of young non-violent activists.'

Kareem stood up and went to the entry to the balcony before returning to me. With a lowered voice, he spoke. 'Sultana, what are you getting at?'

'Darling husband, I am getting at Raif Badawi, Waleed Abulkhair, Abdulrahman al-Subaihi, Bander al-Nogithan, Abdulrahman al-Rumaih and Mikhlif al-Shammari. All of these men are peaceful tweeters, bloggers, journalists or attorneys. None have raised a hand to another human being. Now they are either in prison or being tried for the most meaningless charges, like producing something that harms public morals. Really, Kareem!'

'You do not know of what you speak, Sultana,' Kareem re-peated, maddening me with his attitude that he was Mr Wisdom.

'Do not insult your wife, Kareem.'

'I know of these men,' he confessed with a loud sigh.

'Are you certain? You seemed rather mindless to me about very important people in Saudi Arabia. Young men who are standing up for personal freedoms.'

'I really did not want to enter this conversation with you, Sultana. Take this message from me. All these men are a danger to the peaceful reign of our government.'

'How are they a danger? They only long for the freedom to speak the thoughts in their heads. Is that a danger to anyone?'

'*Let me repeat, Sultana. You do not know of what you speak.* Look at history. Remember 1979 in Iran? The Shah of Iran was pushed by his allies to allow an easing of security. Within a year he was pushed once again – pushed out of power! The Iranian people believed their lives would improve but with the fanatical religious clerics at the helm they have suffered a hundred times more than during the days of the Shah. We can look to many other nations that are undergoing the most violent upheavals after their leaders – repressive leaders, I admit – were ousted. Saudi Arabia is far from perfect, Sultana, but if the government allows such men to arouse the people into anger, we will be driven out of our country too. There are times when governments must tighten restrictions, rather than loosen them.' Kareem made a little sound as he shuddered. 'Do you wish for your family to be ousted, some of us murdered while others live in exile in another nation? Think back. Our land has been ruled mainly very peacefully since our grandfather formed this country. What would you like to see in place of our Al Sa'ud rulers?'

'I want no one besides our family, Kareem. For the most part, all has been well, but this is more serious. How can we punish men who are non-violent and want nothing more than to tackle the social problems plaguing our country? That is a good goal for anyone, Kareem. I've been doing it for years.'

Kareem grunted but did not reply.

'Kareem, you say you know about these men. The men I am speaking about are intelligent, kindly, soft-spoken and harmful to no one. These men are suffering, and none more than Raif Badawi. He is going to die in prison, Kareem. He has the mind of a scholar, not the body of an athlete. One more flogging and he will die, Kareem. He will die! Such a black mark on our family will never be erased. At the very least, I beg you, please encourage our ruler to release these men and allow them to leave Saudi Arabia. Release them from the torture they experience every day. We would be much wiser not to punish such men. Although I sincerely believe that if they remain, and work with the government to slowly bring in democratic change, we would all benefit. Look at the wisdom shown by the Jordanian rulers. They allow dissent, at least to a degree, and for the most part their citizens love them and would seek no other ruler.'

'You cannot compare Jordan to Saudi Arabia, Sultana.'

'And why not?'

'You cannot. It is too complicated to explain.' Kareem sat and stared at me for many long moments. 'Sultana, all right. I admit that I have read every word written by Raif Badawi. Although he seems a good man, his words do incite. If he was allowed to leave Saudi Arabia and live in Canada with his wife, he would be much more vocal about the things he disagrees with in our country. I feel that he would create a big following with a consensus to shame and discredit King Salman and those who will follow him in years to come. Saudi Arabia is best ruled by the Al Sa'ud. I cringe to think what might follow if our family were ousted.'

'So you will do nothing?'

'What *can* I do, Sultana? I am not the king. I am not the king-in-waiting. I am not even the crown-prince-in-waiting. I will never be appointed to a high position in our government. All I can do is support our rulers because without them we will end up living as exiles. Can you not see how vulnerable we would be? Is that what you want, Sultana?

'This topic has been discussed until there is no more discussion left. As you know, the king does not decide alone. The minds of all the royals in high positions are probed to get ideas. Raif Badawi is a "hot potato", as they say in the United States. He is a threat to our rule, regardless of what happens. If he is released and is allowed to travel and live abroad, he will never stop harassing us with his words. If he is released and lives in Saudi Arabia with a travel ban, he will be a thorn in our side – and we will be the same in his. This is not a man who can be bought, or threatened. He is unusual, there is no doubt.

'If he dies in prison, it will be a huge shame. You are right about that one point. But once he made the decision to attack all that is Saudi Arabia, this complicated issue was instantly unsolvable.'

Kareem was right about Raif Badawi. He had the highest and most impeccable ethics. Money would not buy his silence. He would die first.

'So you will speak to no one?'

'I cannot.'

'You must! We *must* get this young man released, Kareem.' I was fighting back tears. I was failing. Kareem, I knew, was going to do nothing. Although from his words I felt that he would be unsuccessful, I longed for my husband to take a stand, to show the same bravery being shown by Raif Badawi.

Kareem's face reddened and his expression became very firm, reminding me of my father in one of his nastiest moods. 'Sultana, I know you well. You are a stubborn woman. You accept no advice. You plunge ahead into the forest, even when there is danger behind every tree. But, Sultana, I am warning you. If you do not burn those papers, there will be trouble, and if you ignore my counsel on the issue of the activists I will be forced to take the strongest action. You cannot destroy the lives of your family by thrusting yourself into this political quagmire.' He stood up. 'I will not allow you to destroy all that we have built. I will not allow you to ruin the lives of our children and grandchildren. If you do not cease with this foolish and dangerous behaviour, I will divorce you. I will.'

Tingles of shock ran throughout my entire body. My husband was menacing me by threatening to divorce me for the first time in our married life. While I had pushed him to the limit on a number of occasions, he had never resorted to warnings of a divorce.

Kareem strode purposefully to the door, turned at the last minute and threatened me once again. 'Do not doubt that I will divorce you over this. I love you, but I will divorce you. My children's lives cannot be destroyed by your reckless acts. There is nothing you, or I, can do to change the circumstances of this young man's life. His fate is in his hands, and in the hands of our king.'

Kareem had a sadness in his eyes. He parted with these words: 'Do not make me divorce you, Sultana. We will both have regrets, but I will divorce you over this.'

I sat as motionless as an ancient mummy in a museum in Egypt as my husband disappeared from my view.

I really could not move a muscle. And so I sat for more than an hour, ignoring the servants who were whispering behind the door, worried over my silence and stillness.

I was facing the biggest challenge of my life, facing painful, unsolvable problems of marriage and divorce, for Kareem and me, and of life and death for Raif Badawi.

How could I abandon the cause of the very worthy man Raif Badawi?

Yet how could I grow old without Kareem by my side?

I slowly got to my feet. I gathered all the papers I had on Raif Badawi and with a heavy heart I walked slowly to my quarters.

As I sat quietly, my thoughts were pulled back in time to the days when I was a young wife and mother. I remembered the first day I watched my husband and son enter the mosque without me. On that day, the haunting sound that lifts the heart of every Muslim with joy filled the air. The faithful were being called to pray.

'God is great, there are no other Gods, but God; and Muhammed was his prophet. Come to prayer, come to prayer. God is great; there is no God, but God.'

It was dusk on that day. The big yellow circle that was the sun was slowly sinking. For faithful Muslims, the time had come for the fourth prayer of the day.

I had stood on the bedroom balcony and watched my husband and son leave our palace grounds and walk, hand in hand, to the mosque. I saw that many men were gathering and greeting each other with the spirit of brotherhood.

The turbulent memories of my childhood had come back to me, and once again I was a young girl, shut out from the love my father expressed to his beloved son, Ali. Nearly thirty years had passed, yet nothing had changed. My life had come full circle. Father and Ali, Kareem and Abdullah, yesterday, today and tomorrow, immoral practices passed from father to son. Men I loved, men I detested, leaving a legacy of shame in their treatment of women.

And on this night those same emotions assaulted me.

I was a lonely figure in a world where wrongs should be righted but rarely were.

I knew then that if Raif Badawi died I would never forgive Kareem and indeed would welcome a divorce.

As I lay silent and unmoving upon my bed, my thoughts turned back to that worthy man. I wondered what he was doing in his tiny prison cell. I imagined that his thoughts were on his wife, and his three precious children, aching to see them, to hold them. I felt a great certainty that Raif Badawi felt himself the loneliest man in the world.

My heart was breaking for him, and all the brave and worthy Saudi men who are risking their freedom and life, languishing in prison, enduring painful lashes, for doing nothing more than expressing their thoughts and ideas.

There was an added sting to my pain. I had to acknowledge that it was members of my own family, those who share with me the blood of the same grandparents, who were committing the gravest of sins by punishing such worthy men.

Perhaps one day Raif Badawi would be free to express his feelings and ideas, but the shame of imprisoning and torturing such a man would forever follow the history of the Al Sa'ud.

My thoughts were jumbled as my tears flowed for the bravest men in all of Saudi Arabia.

May Allah be with you all, was my heartfelt prayer.

Chapter Ten

Saying Goodbye

Tʜᴇ ᴛᴀsᴛᴇ ᴏғ ᴅᴇғᴇᴀᴛ was as bitter on my tongue as the dandelion bulb I once ate when only a child. Few people know that the dandelion is native to the Middle East. They have been known for hundreds of years as being important medicinal plants, and so their seeds were carried all over the world, so now the plant is thought to be native in many countries. The dandelion begins its flowering cycle with golden petals followed by round fluffy heads with hundreds of seeds that sprout from a single puff ball. That feathery puff ball is a natural magnet to children, a trigger for kids all over the world, who take a moment to blow at the ball, watching with glee as the small seeds scatter with the wind.

Our family was travelling in the Middle East, exactly where I no longer recall, when we temporarily halted our journey along the roadside at a beautiful meadow. Since we are a desert people, flowering meadows hold enormous appeal. I remember tugging at one of the many hundreds of dandelions that seemed to blanket the meadow. I had no knowledge of the length and size of the dandelion root, but to pull the plant was impossible for me. My older sisters helped me pull until a long stem and root gave way, a stem nearly as long as I was tall, finally releasing the plant from the ground. A large fleshy root bulb popped into view. I eagerly brushed away the soil and took a big bite, believing that it would be sweet.

It was the time of the year when the milk juice of the root was very thick, and extremely bitter. I startled the entire family when I began to screech while spitting and jumping around on my small feet.

Mother came to my rescue, very roughly wiping out my mouth with the hem of her skirt, for she was afraid that the fluid might be poisonous. My father, as was his way, ignored his most irritating and youngest child. Ali, I remember, laughed loudly, ridiculing my baby ways, but I never forgot his shocked expression after he made a big production of tasting the root himself. To show he was a big, brave boy, he didn't spit but instead turned quietly, wiping his mouth and hurrying away to express interest in a bird that had landed in the meadow.

Now, after experiencing one of the most stinging defeats of my adult life, acidity seeped into my throat and into my heart just as bitter as that long-ago pungent dandelion, an unpleasant memory I had not revisited in many years.

I have suffered setbacks many times in life, for loss is no stranger to any woman of Saudi Arabia. But to face defeat in the quest to free the worthy men of Saudi Arabia was unbearably heartrending. I once heard that a kingdom is not lost by a single defeat, but I do not believe this old saying. A small voice inside warned that the death of Raif Badawi could alter the fate of my entire family, as well as negatively revise the history of the desert kingdom so carefully formed by my grandfather.

I am a woman who has always looked upon defeat as victory deferred, for I do not easily yield. But my experience as a member of the Saudi royal family warned me that this time was different. Even if I refused to accept this depressing setback, and rebuilt my plans to try even harder to reach the coveted goal of freedom for Raif Badawi, I knew that I would never succeed.

This defeat would live on for ever in the hearts and minds of all who *knew* Badawi, who *knew of* Badawi, or had even *read about* Badawi. He was a man not easily forgotten. I also felt with a frightening certainty that Badawi would never survive his ten-year sentence and his thousand lashes. The man was not in the best of health; he was frail medically, suffering from diabetes at an early age.

The men of my family were being stubborn, and even cruel, to continue on with the punishment of a kindly man who only wanted to discuss social issues.

Raif Badawi's senseless death would never be forgotten by the world.

And my family would be to blame, and rightfully so.

Such an idea put me to bed.

The night passed slowly, but the morning finally came. Kareem made no effort to check on me. My husband was showing his Al Sa'ud stubbornness.

That's when I had a splendid idea. I thought perhaps I might file for divorce before Kareem could divorce me. Although divorce for women in Saudi Arabia is not easy, with my royal position I knew that no judge would deny me the right to divorce. Although Kareem might attempt to bribe the judge, I decided that I, too, could play his bribery game. I would make a bribe for the first time in my life and spend much more money than Kareem would imagine.

I was thinking to surprise my husband with a divorce decree, as he lightly tapped on the door and asked, 'Sultana, may I come in, please?'

Feeling resentful, I raised my voice, not caring who might hear me. 'You have an ill-gotten key. Use it.'

Kareem was quiet for so long that I believed he had walked away, but then I heard the lock turn and my husband walked in with a self-conscious expression on his face.

'Sultana, I came to apologize,' he quickly said, as he walked towards me. 'I will not divorce you, darling.'

I was feeling rather callous, so I sneered. 'I wish you would,

Kareem. You would save me the trouble of divorcing you.' I raised my voice as I braced my body, moving upward, leaning on my right elbow. 'Go ahead and say it: I divorce you. I divorce you. I divorce you.'

I have always loathed the manner in which so many Saudi men rudely divorce their unsuspecting wives by saying the words three times, then notifying the clerics. With those words, and a simple action, a woman is removed from her husband and home in Saudi Arabia and there is *nothing* she can do to halt an un-wanted divorce. After the divorce, the husband generally takes the children from his wife, too, leaving a shattered mother in the wake of divorce. The inequality of life for women in my country added to my day's fury.

Kareem exhaled, then sat on the edge of my bed. 'Darling. Stop. I know, and you know, that we are better together than apart. I do not want a divorce. I spoke in the heat of the moment.'

'And I am speaking in the cool of the morning,' I replied, my anger mounting with every second. I had decided that I would be better off without a man who has no empathy in his heart for the very good men such as Raif Badawi who are languishing in prison.

'Sultana, I am not divorcing you. And you are not divorcing me. Think of the joy we shall miss together while watching our grandchildren grow and become adults. The journey will not be nearly so entertaining if we do not share what we have brought to life together.'

I said nothing.

'Sultana, just think of what we have built. Then consider what a divorce will do to hurt others, those innocent ones we love.'

I sat silently, although I was thinking. I was thinking of Little Sultana and her brother Prince Faisal. Then my thoughts went to Amani's son Prince Khalid and her daughter, Princess Basinah. All four of our grandchildren were secure in their family life and devoted to both grandparents, although due to the time I spent with them, they appeared to be closer with their grandmother.

Seeing their grandfather was a treat, but being with their grandmother was a beloved routine. Rarely a day passed when I did not spend some time with all four grandchildren, even if only briefly, at least when we were all in the country or taking holidays together.

While my adult children could better bear a divorce, all three would be distraught if their parents went separate ways.

When Kareem lifted my chin with his finger and looked into my eyes, I knew then that the heated argument would pass and we would reignite the passion in our relationship, a love that had been with us both since we were very young newlyweds.

Kareem smiled sweetly.

I smiled in return.

He brushed my face with his fingertips, and then with his lips, telling me, 'You are more beautiful today than the day we married, Sultana.'

Over the next hour, all thoughts of divorce were pushed aside.

But before Kareem left my quarters, I felt I had to say something, however it might upset my husband. 'I remain disappointed with the Badawi situation, Kareem.'

Kareem sat down, his eyes downcast as he spoke. 'As am I, Sultana, but this is a problem that the ruler of our land will not allow interference. Even if I were to attempt to contact and convince my cousins to go with me to intervene, none would, and if we did, we would fail. Then we would be out of favour for a very long time, possibly for ever, and unable to have influence over anything in the kingdom. Nothing would be accomplished other than our children and grandchildren would be scorned for ever as the offspring of a man who tried to harm the security of our family.'

He paused, shaking his head in dismay. 'Perhaps we can do good things in the future if we stay in a positive place in this family. This is a very tricky situation and I know that I do not have the power to bring change. There are times in life when one has to acknowledge a disagreeable reality and bend to it.'

'But he is such an exceptional man, Kareem. He is suffering for the good of all Saudis. He is our Nelson Mandela, husband. One day we will all be judged harshly for the lack of courage to allow citizens of our land to speak their minds.'

Kareem exhaled again. 'I know. I know. But there is nothing that you, or I, can do. Only the king can pardon Badawi and the other men you speak of. Only the king.'

I sat quietly, pondering the fact that the fates of the worthy men depended solely upon my uncle, my father's half-brother. I had known Uncle Salman since I was a young girl and, other than King Fahd, I had always found him to be the most lighthearted of the Sudairi brothers, of whom there were seven. I had always felt anxiety when in the presence of Sultan and Naif, both very stern-faced men, but felt at ease around King Fahd, and King Salman.

Of those seven uncles, two rose to the peak of power in a monarchy. First, there was the oldest of the Sudairi boys, Uncle Fahd, who had several high-ranking positions before being appointed Crown Prince under King Khalid. At Uncle Khalid's death, he became king. Now Uncle Salman was king, and he too had had many high positions. My father says that Salman was the most effective deputy governor and then governor of Riyadh for nearly fifty years. He was defence minister in 2011, and was named Crown Prince in 2012 when Uncle Naif died. At King Abdullah's death in January 2015, he was crowned the new king.

Uncles Sultan and Naif held very high offices as well, and both would have reached the supreme position of king but for dying while serving in the post of Crown Prince. Had they not passed away, then four of the Sudairi boys would have served as king. Uncle Ahmed held important posts, too. Only uncles Turki and Abdel-Rahman (of the Sudairi Seven) chose not to hold formal offices, but both were very close to their brothers.

Indisputably, the most dominant family in the entire Al Sa'ud clan, thus in the kingdom, is the Sudairi family.

The mother of our grandfather King Abdul Aziz was Sara Sudairi. She was best known for her considerable size. Family members say that she was the largest woman they had ever seen, with a very tall stature and massive bones. For sure, she contributed to the massive six-foot-four-inch frame of her son, Abdul Aziz.

Our grandfather married a Sudairi as well. In fact, he married many women during his lifetime, most for the purpose of solidifying peace between various tribes, for without reconciliation between warring tribes there would have never been a Saudi Arabia.

It is reported in Western newspapers that Grandfather married more than twenty women and took innumerable concubines, but the number of wives is much higher, according to his sons. Of his multiple wives, Grandfather had 103 children and forty-five sons.

But of all the wives, it is said that he best loved Hassa bint Ahmad al-Sudairi. She was very young when first married to our grandfather, but during the early years of their marriage he chose to divorce her. Some say it was because their only son, Sa'ad, had died at age five and she did not become immediately pregnant. Grandfather lived to regret the divorce, but by that time Hassa had married our grandfather's half-brother. In time, Grandfather spoke persuasively with his half-brother, who agreed to divorce Hassa so that she could return to the king.

Their marriage lasted happily until my grandfather died in 1953.

During their second marriage, Hassa gave birth to seven sons and four daughters. The seven Sudairi sons formed an unbreakable bond. Their intelligence and loyalty to one another ensured their power.

Now the Sudairis are back in full power, with the reign of King Salman. Once Uncle Salman became king, he promptly appointed younger Sudairis to the most powerful positions in the government. Two specific Sudairis are now the kings-in-waiting, one of whom is a son of Naif, the other a son of Salman. Most likely, so long as Saudi Arabia remains a monarchy, Sudairis will always rule supreme in my country, for so long as there is a Sudairi in power, they will appoint other Sudairis to rule.

But the affection I had felt for my uncle Salman meant that I was now experiencing intense disappointment that he was being so severe with the young Badawi and other Saudi men who were asking for the right to express their ideas. Of all the kings we have had, it is now clear that King Fahd was the most sentimental of our kings and tended to overlook little annoyances. Uncle Fahd did not like punishing anyone other than hardcore criminals and murderers.

Uncle Salman was revealing a different stripe. He was ruling harshly, something I would have never believed.

Kareem and I talked until there was nothing left to say. I felt less anger than before at my husband because with his words I came to see that he could do little to change the course of history when it involved the young men pushing for reform. The only way for the men to survive would be to forgo all demands and live quietly without expressing their opinions. This I knew they would never do. Their ethics were strong, even if their bodies were not. While I understood their inability to give in, I fervently wished that they would, so that their lonely imprisonment could cease and the deadly floggings would stop.

Should any of these worthy men die while in prison, it will be the saddest day for them, their families and for Saudi Arabia.

After Kareem left, my heart nearly ceased to beat, for I remembered that Dr Meena would soon return to the kingdom and I knew that she would be eager to hear the progress I had made with my husband. How I dreaded to tell my dear friend that Kareem and I could do nothing. We were as helpless as any ordinary citizen living in our country.

*   *   *

Dr Meena is an angel. When she saw my tears forming as I explained the hopeless situation, she embraced me for the first time in our friendship. 'Dear princess, do not weep for what you cannot change. I pondered many times about my request while on this trip, and I reprimanded myself for putting you in a position that was bound to cause a disagreement with your husband. I know how it is in this world of ours. Even powerful princesses and princes in our land can do little if the king is not of the same mind.

'I know that you tried, and from what you are telling me your efforts nearly cost you a good husband, something rare in this world. All we can do is pray for Raif Badawi, and the other worthy men in our land. While we can do nothing political, we can pray for them all.'

'Yes, we shall pray,' I said, my voice breaking with the emotion of it all. 'Every day. I will pray.'

'And we can also pray for the outsiders who are protesting. I hear that our royal family, at least the men at the top, are stunned and horrified that the world is turning out in such numbers to support Raif Badawi.' She thought for a moment, before telling me, 'Are you aware that eighteen Nobel Laureates have written a letter to our ruler, a letter that makes it clear that so long as Badawi is imprisoned the entire world of academics will consider the marginalization of Saudi Arabia? We all know that our government wishes to market Saudi Arabia as a research hub. These Nobel Laureates will stop that advance. Such protests have more power than if half the population in Saudi Arabia were to march.'

Dr Meena's words gave me hope. Although sad that outsiders might make a more powerful impact than the citizens of our land, I would take anything at this point that would free the young men whose names were now forever engraved in my mind.

Dr Meena left my home but not before I advised her that she would soon receive two additional roomy automobiles and a group of drivers, all to be at her disposal. I would be responsible for full expenses, with the cars to be used as needed without concern for any costs. The drivers would live at my palace but report to her, their supervisor. This one small effort on my part meant that many more carless and driverless Saudi ladies could freely travel throughout the city. These are the small gifts I can provide that give me much joy.

Her grateful, happy smile soothed me, at least a little.

But I had little time to enjoy the moment because within ten minutes of Dr Meena's departure, a sombre Sara telephoned, whispering that our father had returned from Europe the previous day and had taken an unexpected turn for the worse overnight. In fact, Sara said, 'Sultana, I believe that he is dying. Come at once, if you wish to see him alive.'

I was startled because I did not even know that my father was in the kingdom. I was aware that the month before he had travelled to Europe for specialized healthcare for the terminal illness that was slowly taking his life, but Sara had told me that the physicians had informed him that they believed he had at least another six months to a year of life. I had not fretted because I know that doctors these days tell sick patients the truth and do not give them false hopes or impossibly lengthy promises of life when they are dying. I had spoken with Kareem the previous week about taking our entire family to Europe to visit with Father. Now that would not come to pass, I realized, with a stabbing sadness. I had envisioned a lengthy visit with all my children so that my father might derive some satisfaction from my impressive children and fetching grandchildren.

Just then I remembered a verse in the Koran: 'Nor does anyone know what it is that he will earn tomorrow: nor does anyone know in what land he is to die. Verily with Allah is full knowledge and Allah is acquainted with all things.' (Koran: 31:34.)

We are warned by these words that we shall not know when and where we will die. So perhaps my father had become introspective in his ageing years and knew that even doctors cannot say where or when one will die. The important time of our passing from this life is something that only God knows.

*   *   *

Kareem agreed to meet me an hour later at my father's palace. I rushed to call Abdullah and Amani, and both promised to leave their palaces quickly. Maha could not be immediately located, as she was visiting a royal cousin, but I left two assistants in charge of finding my eldest daughter and to alert her regarding my father's ill health. I knew that Maha would come the moment she heard the news, despite the fact that she, as I, had a rocky relationship with my father.

I was sitting in the back seat of my car, being driven to my father's palace, within fifteen minutes. The drive took an agonizingly slow thirty minutes in Riyadh's notoriously busy traffic, but finally we arrived just as I was fighting the urge to scream.

The huge gates did not swing open immediately for me – I have so rarely visited my father over the years that I was not recognized. The guardsmen took long moments telephoning security inside the palace to receive clearance that I was, indeed, the daughter of my father. My father has too many sons and daughters by a number of wives, although he is not aligned closely to any of his children but those born to his first wife, my mother. He has always been especially fond of Ali, for what reason none can imagine, because Ali has been obnoxious since he was born. Nura, the first child of my mother, always connected nicely with Father. Now that Nura had left this earth more than seven years before, Father had concentrated his affections on Sara, who was now his favourite daughter.

For far too many reasons to list, I was never my father's preferred child. In fact, I was never a favoured child at any point in my life. Only on the occasion several years ago when he had presented Mother's picture to me did we reach out to each other for a memorable evening of affable conversation and kindly feelings.

Just when I was about to telephone Sara to complain, we were finally allowed entrance. I looked stoically at the stern-faced guards as we passed through the opulent gates. I noticed real gold glimmering on the exterior of the metal gates. Real gold is unmistakable. Of all the royal princes, my father's palaces and grounds are some of the most lavish, although he had been cautious not to arouse envy by spending more money than his half-brothers, the men who ruled as kings or the kings-in-waiting.

There appeared to be hundreds of vehicles arrayed around the huge entrance to the palace. I wondered if all the people transported in those cars were royals who had come to see my father die. From what I know, my father has never been a particularly popular son of our grandfather. He was never interested in government, but instead enjoyed accumulating enormous wealth, which he has done. He had an interest in new technology, and Kareem had told me several years ago that Father had invested in some of the soundest of the technology companies, so his wealth had increased mightily over the years.

For certain, his many palaces displayed his wealth. At last count Sara told me that our Father had more than twenty palaces around the world, with seven located in Saudi Arabia and the rest in Europe and Asia. I heard that he had visited some of his palaces only once but kept them fully staffed in case he had a sudden desire to visit.

When I hear such stories, I fear for our future, for how long will our citizens continue to accept such extravagance when many Saudis are poor? Perhaps because most of the Al Sa'ud are discreet with their passion for spending most Saudis do not know the extent of the money spent on impractical items, such as a luxurious palace one never visits.

These are well-kept secrets known only to members of the royal family.

*   *   *

I was escorted through various wings of the palace, each more elaborate than the next. I wondered what my father did with all those endless rooms, as he lived alone only with his servants, while his three living wives each had their separate palaces, all located in a semi-circle around Father's palace.

219

Finally, we arrived at the specially constructed medical unit where my father was fitfully resting. No one noticed that I had arrived. After glancing at the occupants of the medical area, I saw that neither Kareem nor my children were in attendance. I stood quietly, familiarizing myself with the room, which was much larger than I could have imagined, until I realized it was similar to an intensive-care unit in a large hospital, with enough beds for twenty people. Was my father expecting a catastrophe when he planned the medical unit?

Father was in one of those beds, located in the right-hand corner of the room. Surprisingly, he was not connected to any machinery, or even to any tubes. For that I was glad, as I have heard that the most peaceful deaths come naturally.

I saw Sara and Ali standing closely by his side. Doctors in white coats were hovering. Several half-brothers and half-sisters whom I do not know well were standing in line to walk past Father to say their goodbyes.

I looked intently at my father's face. He was pale. But he was not grimacing in pain, to my relief. I watched as he opened and closed his eyes several times.

My idea of sharing a quiet goodbye with my father was not going to happen. I continued to stand alone, my eyes focused on his face, wondering what thoughts were going through his mind.

We are told in the Koran that every soul shall have the taste of death, and now my father was tasting his death. I felt terribly sad for him. Muslims are taught that death involves agony and hardship. There is an authentic Hadith that says, 'When Prophet Muhammad was dying, he put his hands in a large cup of water near to him and wiped his face with it, saying, "Oh Allah, help me over the hardship and agony of death."'

Although my father and I had never been close, I did not want to see him in agony or enduring hardship during the last moments of his life.

Perhaps the hardship was knowing that he was living his last few hours on earth, and that soon he would be taken to be washed and wrapped in a white shroud, then placed into a simple dirt grave, a frightening idea for most human beings.

I saw Sara and Ali speaking to Father, and so I moved closer so that I might know what was being said.

'There is no God but Allah,' Sara was saying in a very kind manner. She asked Father to repeat the words, because Muslims are taught that they should encourage the dying to repeat these words more than once. Father's lips moved in response to Sara's plea, but I could not hear his voice, faint from the weakness that signifies death.

Father's family was doing exactly what Muslims are taught to do when a loved one is at the point of death, which is to never leave the dying person alone. We are also told to ask them to repent their sins, but also to remember their good deeds. And that is when I overheard Ali, in a very quiet voice, urge Father to repent of any bad deeds he might have done. He quickly followed this up by reminding Father of his good deeds, which were to give generously at Ramadan to the poor and needy.

I was close enough to see Father close his eyes in acknowledgement of what his first-born son was saying before slightly nodding his head. Father was still aware: he had not yet gone to that middle place where he could not hear or see the living yet had not crossed over to Paradise.

At this point Sara saw me and gestured with her hand for me to come, to stand beside her. I hesitated, because I knew that my half-brothers and half-sisters had been waiting for a moment to say their goodbyes, but Sara is so revered in all the family that they, too, nodded in agreement and signalled for me to do as Sara said.

And so the day came that I never imagined, the day I would bid my dying father a final farewell.

Taking a step back, Sara pushed me closer to Father. 'Father,' she said, 'here is your baby daughter, Sultana, the daughter Mother most loved in this world.'

I looked at Sara, wondering if she really believed that I was the most loved. I did not agree, although I know as the baby of the family I was greatly loved and protected by my mother and older sisters.

My father made no response, not at first.

'Father? I am here. I am your daughter, Sultana.'

In a rare generous moment, my brother Ali squeezed Father's hand, saying, 'It is the little one, Father. Sultana is here. Look upon her.' Then he spoiled the moment by saying too enthusiastically, 'Sultana is no longer young. The baby girl is a grandmother.'

I glanced up to glare at my brother, but he was smiling, thinking his words amusing, so I let it pass and did not say what I was thinking, that the young son was an obese grandfather who looked twice my age, or at least that is what people tell me.

Father lay so quietly that I was afraid he had taken his last breath, but then I saw shallow breathing, with his chest slowly rising and falling.

I stared at his face, this man once so young who had now grown so old, with deep furrows on the flesh of his face and multiple lines around his eyes. Foamy spittle was dripping from the sides of his thin lips. His moustache was still dark black, as was his hair, but that was because my father, like most men in the Al Sa'ud family, dyed his hair. I saw grey hairs peeking from his ears and wondered why his barber did not dye those, too.

My memory took me back to the stories I had heard of his youth. He was one of the younger sons of our grandfather and he had been spoiled by his parents because he was the only son born to his mother, although she had several daughters, much in the same way Ali was surrounded by sisters. Father was a young boy when Grandfather King Abdul Aziz was fighting to form a kingdom for his family to rule, and so he did not fight in the battles fought by his older brothers Muhammad, Faisal and Saud. He was, however, taught to be a skilled horseman and his great love was to collect Arabian horses.

Now I was upset with myself, for I had failed to question my father closely about his youth, not that he would have answered but perhaps he might. Sadly, I only remember him as a father to be feared. When I was a child, he was a handsome young man filled with confidence but he was quick to anger, particularly with me, the daughter who created scenes and caused him to break his word to my mother not to physically strike any of the children. But in my stubbornness and determination to get my way I tried his patience many times, and he struck me hard with an open hand as a result.

That young man's life, filled with excitement, the love of horses, numerous wives and many children, was gone in a flash, and here he was, helpless with his adult children looking on with sympathy and care.

Finally, just as I had despaired of his acknowledging my presence, Father opened his eyes and looked into my own. There were no words spoken, but I saw a light of affection and when I pulled his hand into my own I felt a gentle squeeze. I felt with a great certainty that it was my father's way of telling me that despite all the ire in our past he did love me.

That's when I felt tears fall from my eyes, and watched as they fell on my father's face.

The tears were felt because he appeared startled, fully looking at me. I will always believe that my tears told him that he was loved by the daughter who had once hated him.

My father tried to smile, but his lips could only quiver.

I knew then that his time was brief, so I took one last, long look and pulled away, giving my siblings a chance for their own goodbyes.

Sara gave me a hug and then began to pull in the other children of my father.

As I was walking away, I heard my full-sister Dunia screech so loudly that all in the room took heed, knowing instantly that Father had stopped breathing and that he had left his life on earth.

I turned back to see my brother Ali use his fingertips to gently close Father's eyes.

That's when I saw Kareem and my three children in the crowd, standing quietly with sad expressions, watching as I had said goodbye to a man I once hated. That hate had now evaporated and I felt the greatest sorrow that I had not enjoyed a loving relationship with the man who gave me life.

I was truly an orphan, for neither of my parents were with the living.

Surrounded by my loving children and my husband, I wept for what never was.

*   *   *

And so the time came for my father to be buried in the ground. Prophet Muhammad said, 'You should hasten with the burial.'

There was much to be done, for our Islamic faith teaches us to quickly ready the body of the deceased for burial. Islam is very precise as to the burial procedures.

My father's sons would be in charge to ensure that all was accomplished as it should be for a Muslim.

I knew that these things would happen to my father's body.

They would bind his lower jaw to his head.

They would cover his body with a clean white sheet.

They would ask Allah to forgive him for all sins.

They would prepare the body for washing.

It was the responsibility of Father's family to wash him. Only males can wash the body of a male, other than the wives, who are allowed. I was told that Father's sons selected three among his sons to wash him. There can be no comment made about the body by the ones washing him.

After the washing, Father would be shrouded in white. Shrouding requires three white sheets made from an inexpensive material, which can be perfumed. This is because it was related that 'When the Prophet Muhammad died, he was shrouded in three white sheets from Yemen.'

After the shrouding, the body should be prayed for and then buried as soon as possible.

A box, or coffin, is not allowed unless the body is damaged, or if the grave is wet.

In Father's case, he was buried in his shroud, without a box.

In Islam, women are not allowed at funerals. Thus, my father's funeral was strictly a male affair.

He was buried in Riyadh's al-Oud cemetery, which is a public cemetery in the capital, near to the famous Batha Street. In Arabic, the world *oud* means elder, as in an old person.

The cemetery is famous in Saudi Arabia. All the men who have ruled as king of Saudi Arabia are buried there. This includes my grandfather, Abdul Aziz, and all his sons who became king: Saud, Faisal, Khalid, Fahd and Abdullah. Many other sons of my grandfather are buried there as well, and my father is one of those sons. The cemetery is public, with commoners and royals alike buried in its grounds. In the eyes of God, no man is above another.

However, there is an area reserved for members of the royal family, so there are many senior royals there, too.

After the body is totally covered with the earth, it is usual for three handfuls of soil to be thrown onto the grave.

It is forbidden to decorate the grave.

In Islam there is a saying, 'To God we belong, and to God we shall return.'

My father had returned to God.

Epilogue

How I longed to attend my father's funeral. I have heard of desperately miserable women who hide behind bushes or buildings to watch the proceedings from a distance, but I obeyed the rules of Islam and kept away, however much I wished to say a final goodbye. I felt keen pain and grief that while my husband and son could, and did, attend my father's funeral, my daughters and I could not. But there was nothing to be done, so I accepted with the best temper possible.

While I felt the urge to wail and cry loudly, I did not. Islam demands believers to show patience and acceptance of Allah's will when faced with the calamity of the death of any relative. All acts that show discontent and dissatisfaction with Allah's verdict, such as wailing or tearing clothes or hair, are forbidden. Only the calmest displays of sorrow are permitted.

And so I remained at home in my quarters, alone and praying quietly for my father. I knew from our teachings that he had already met with the angels to discuss his deeds, both good and bad, while he lived on earth. So his new life was opening up to him, whatever form it might take, although I prayed that my father was on his way to Paradise. Although I found him lacking as a husband to my mother, and as a father to his daughters, I know that he never took anything that did not belong to him, and he never murdered another person, and as far as I know he never tried to harm others in an intentional and cruel manner.

Some hours after the funeral had ended, and the family men had dispersed, Kareem came to me. I was greatly comforted by my husband, the person who knows me best. Kareem is so familiar with the thoughts in my mind that I feel he has known me for my entire life, although I had lived sixteen years on this earth before we first met. But knowing me from that age, and through the heartbreak of losing my mother, there is nothing of my past of which my husband is unaware. This long history between us means that Kareem is a great consolation in my life.

I looked at him and, with my voice breaking with emotion, said, 'I am glad we are not divorcing.'

Kareem pulled me into his arms and nuzzled my ear, whispering, 'I love you more than I could love any other woman on earth. You may try my patience, my love, but you are my life, Sultana.'

How glad I was to hear his words.

I knew that I must remain in mourning for three days, which is the time allotted for a woman who loses her father, so my behaviour could not be unseemly.

Muslims are instructed: 'It is not legal for a woman who believes in Allah and the Last Day to mourn for more than three days for any dead person except her husband, for whom she should mourn for four months and ten days. During this three days of mourning, women are supposed to abandon all that is normal when it comes to adornments or ornaments.' And so I did as taught. I was wearing the most basic black dress. I had on no perfume. My face was bare of make-up. No jewellery decorated my body. I had even removed my wedding ring.

Kareem and I pushed our emotions to a quiet place in our hearts and left my quarters arm in arm. To our great relief, our three children and four grandchildren were waiting for us in the largest of our sitting rooms. Abdullah was sitting beside Little Sultana, who looked very much the young lady at age eight, soon to be nine. Prince Faisal and Prince Khalid were playing with a tent and camel set Kareem had found for sale in Qatar when he was there for business, and had given to them a few months before. Both were cute toddlers and had no idea that it was a time of sorrow. Amani was sitting in front of her brother, Abdullah, and beside her sister, Maha, who was cooing at Princess Basinah. I felt Kareem cringe beside me when Amani exclaimed, 'Little Kitten, smile darling, for your grandparents.' I knew that my husband wished to reprimand her, to tell her to please call Basinah by her proper name, but thankfully he ignored her habit of calling our granddaughter a kitten, something that irritated us both.

We have nothing against kittens or cats, for Prophet Muhammad himself was tender and kind to cats. He even kept cats, and his favourite was named Muezza. In fact, once when the time to pray was called, Muezza happened to be asleep on one of the sleeves of the Prophet's robes. While the Prophet wanted to wear the robe to prayers, he could not bear to disturb the sleeping Muezza. So he surprised those around him with his kindness when he cut off the sleeve where Muezza was sleeping and went to prayers with a one-sleeved robe, while Muezza slept peacefully.

There are other witnesses who said that the Prophet gave sermons while Muezza rested upon his lap. Most surprising, he did his ablutions from the same water where Muezza drank.

Islam teaches Muslims to treat cats respectfully, and to cherish and love them. If one mistreats a cat, then that is considered a severe sin in Islam.

So, Kareem and I tried to temper our responses to Amani's nickname for our greatly loved granddaughter, for we felt that the Prophet would approve of Amani's great love for cats.

Little Sultana was sweetly subdued, getting up from her seat to come to her grandparents. Without speaking a word, she clung to us both, with one arm around Kareem's legs and the other around my waist. The forlorn expression in her little eyes said all that she needed to say. If those she loved were sad, then she was sad. Little Sultana was of the age to know that when someone died, we would not see them again, so she knew the sobering implications of death. And although she had never enjoyed a relationship with my father, she had never forgotten the night at our palace when Father showed obvious delight at her appearance and her behaviour. She had been reminded of that evening many times when we were making an effort to let her know that she was as important as any male child in our family.

I felt miserable that of all my grandchildren only Little Sultana would have a memory of my father. Prince Faisal and Prince Khalid were still toddlers on the evening Father had visited my home, so he would never feel alive in their thoughts. And so the two continued playing happily, unaware that death had visited our family and that their maternal great-grandfather was a man they would never know other than through the memories of the generations before them. Princess Basinah had been so recently born that Father would always be a distant figure in our family's past, no more alive than Al Sa'ud ancestors who had lived and died hundreds of years before our time.

I felt doubly sad that my father had never expressed a true interest in coming to know my children or grandchildren. Yet who could blame him, for he had been married many times, and had taken a number of concubines, and most had given him children. There are too many direct family members to know them all!

A huge negative of a man having many wives, and numerous children by those wives, is that there is little time to give specific attention to the individual children and grandchildren. Most men select their first-born son, and sometimes their first-born daughter, to lavish much attention and all the rest are merely a number in a long line of numbers.

Thankfully Kareem and I were the parents of only three children and four grandchildren, so we had time for all; none were numbers for us, but real live and breathing individuals whom we cherished.

On that evening, Kareem and I sat and derived some joy from being with them.

My children showed an interest in their maternal grandfather for the first time, pleading with me to share some little stories. I was taken aback, for most stories embedded in my mind about my father were unpleasant and not stories one would relish sharing. I thought of a few titbits regarding my father and his beloved horses, and a few trips he had taken our family on when I was young. My children most enjoyed the story of my eating the bitter dandelion root and could not believe that I was so foolish about such a thing. All claimed to know that the dandelion was not to be eaten when most bitter, but I doubted them on this point and asked where they had heard such. All claimed not to remember from where they got their knowledge.

After a time, we sat quietly and had tea and ate a few dates to give us strength.

I was so tired from the emotions of the past twenty-four hours that I soon retired, leaving Kareem to be with our children. My children promised to return the following day, for they wished to be with me during the three-day mourning period. Little Sultana volunteered to remain the night and sleep with me. 'Jadda,' she said, 'I will tickle your back so you can sleep better.' I held in my laughter. Little Sultana has long, delicate fingers that feel wonderful when she runs them over my back. She had done this for me in the past when I was stricken with a headache, which I had assured her was cured by her tickling, so since that time she believed that her fingers could cure all maladies.

'Darling, thank you. But on this night I will sleep soundly. Your father will take you home to your mummy, where you will rest well too.'

The little darling nodded solemnly and clasped her father's hand in her own.

And so I went to my bed and slept more soundly than I had believed possible. Exhaustion, I think, made this so.

*   *   *

The three days of mourning for my father passed quickly and I attempted to return to a normal place in my life, although there is never a good time to lose a parent. There is a sense of true loss for a child when a parent leaves this earth, even if the child is of an older age.

One week after my father passed away I was sitting in my office organizing one of my charities when Maha and Amani walked in together. My daughters had seemingly developed a more cordial relationship since the huge blow-up when Maha had been forced to return from Turkey.

Both daughters had charity on their mind, and for this I was glad, as I believe that there is no better good or greater pleasure than that which one finds from helping others.

Amani had interested Maha in their cousin Princess Sabrina's project in Pakistan. Maha, in fact, was planning to travel to that country soon and work closely with Sabrina. Amani, the mother of two young children who needed their mother on a daily basis, was unlikely to spend time there.

Maha had also piqued Amani's interest in the desperate refugees who had lost everything – their homes, their jobs, their countries and in too many cases the lives of those they loved. Amani and Maha were discussing how best to help, as both liked to know the individual stories of those they assisted rather than donate money to organizations which sometimes fail to notice the individuals behind the need.

I was pleased and happy with both my girls. Just as I was telling them about my own charity, Little Sultana walked in the door holding a single piece of paper in her small hands. Her little face appeared sad, which immediately caused me to stand and walk towards her.

'Jadda,' she said, 'am I old enough to have my own charity?'

'Darling, I do not think so.' I smiled at the precious girl. 'What charity are you thinking to begin?'

'I want to be like you, Jadda. I want to help girls and women.' Little Sultana held out the paper for me to see. 'Like this poor girl. She needs a lot of help, Jadda,' she said.

I felt a tingling in my head and shoulders, worried that

somehow or other Little Sultana was in possession of some of the photographs of the acid-scarred women from Pakistan. I took the paper from Little Sultana's hand and gasped. There was a hideously injured young woman sprawled across a bed, with a swollen head and face, both partially covered in blood-stained bandages.

'Where did you get this?'

'I found it in some papers in Mummy's office.'

I did not know that Zain was taking up a charity, or even had the time to consider doing such work. Zain was a very active and busy mother, and was also a devoted wife to my son. Abdullah did not like to travel without Zain, and he was an enthusiastic traveller. This was the first time I had heard a single mention that Zain might be interested in working in any kind of assistance programme.

Little Sultana enlightened me. 'This poor girl was attacked by some very mean men.'

'How do you know that, sweetheart? Perhaps she was in a car accident.'

'No. Some men did some bad things to her and threw her off a bus.'

'Let me take this from you, darling. I will investigate.'

'Once you investigate, I must help,' she insisted. 'I want to help.'

I had not noticed her little purse hanging from her shoulder. With her words, she took her small handbag and laid it on a chair, opening it to reveal many thousands of riyals, which would certainly be hundreds of British pounds or US dollars when converted.

'Little Sultana, what is this?'

Amani and Maha exchanged looks of surprise, but said nothing.

'Little Sultana, where did you get this money?'

'I have a safe that my father gave me. Anytime anyone gives me money, I put it in that safe. I have lots more there, but I wanted to show you and ask how many girls we might help with this money.'

'Darling, you can help, but it is best for you to be a bigger girl before you think of such serious issues,' I suggested.

'No, Jadda. I want to help now. I am a big girl. You told me that I am a big girl.'

I really did not know what to do because such decisions about their daughter should be left to Abdullah and Zain. 'Where is your father, darling?'

'He is sitting by the pool and eating fruit.'

'Does he know about this picture?' I waved the photograph of the injured women.

'No, Jadda. But you can tell him. He will be glad that I care about girls and women because he told me that you are a special person who helps women all over the world. He told me that one day I could do the things that you do, which is to make many sad girls very happy.'

I felt very pleased that my son appreciated the work I do, but I was at a loss about Little Sultana. She really was too young to know anything about such horrific stories. She was still a child, and I wanted her childhood to be innocent and free of the knowledge that one learns soon enough when one becomes an adult.

I looked quickly around the room and found a nice pink stationery box. I removed the stationery and held the box out to Little Sultana. 'All right, darling. Auntie Maha will help you to count your money and note the amount. Then put your money in this pretty pink box and we will keep it in my safe until we decide the best thing you can do with it.'

I looked at Maha. 'Maha, help Little Sultana. I need to speak with Abdullah.'

My two daughters and Little Sultana were counting the rumpled riyal bills as I left the room with the photograph of the injured woman in my hand.

Abdullah was startled to hear the story, although he explained to me the source of the photograph. Zain's cousin was firmly in-

234

volved with an organization in India and she had spoken with Zain about contributing money to help with women in need in that country. Clearly one of the papers she had presented to Zain had accidentally been left for Little Sultana to find. Abdullah gave Zain a quick call and she was clueless as to how Little Sultana had found the paper, but she did say that her daughter had been playing in a nearby room when Zain was talking to her cousin. Evidently, Little Sultana had done less playing than her mother believed, and much more listening. She had absorbed the conversation and knew that there were women in India who were being grievously harmed. She wanted to help.

I knew something of the ongoing violence against women in India. There had been a rash of news reports over the past year about the callous rape of girls in that country who were doing nothing more than taking a bus or walking home. The Government of India wanted to brush the outrages under the carpet, saying that all the stories did were humiliate their country.

It appeared to me that the governments of both Pakistan and India refused to address the problem behind the rising instances of rape and violence against their women, and the problem was that the men who did the criminal deeds were not punished. It was a free-for-all against innocent women in Pakistan and in India.

What is wrong with the men of this world, I silently screamed to myself. Women's needs are ignored. Violence against women is ignored. The murder of innocent women is ignored. The only wish of the Pakistani and Indian governments is for women to accept whatever happens to them and to remain quiet. Any uproar about the harmful discrimination against women is met with silence, or even disapproval. It is a scandal and a shame against the men of both countries.

Abdullah said that he and Zain would speak with Little Sultana, and if she wanted to contribute money to the cousin's charity in India, she would be allowed to do so, although it would be some years before they would consent for her to know further details of the abuse.

My precious granddaughter had enormous empathy in her heart for others. She had always had a unique kindness, noticing when people were in need of a sympathetic word. For this I was most happy, and looked forward to the day when she could join me in my quest to relieve the pain, grief and anguish that so commonly visits women.

But for now, she was too young.

While walking to my quarters to advise Little Sultana that her father wished to speak with her, and that she would be allowed to contribute funds, I was pleasantly surprised to see Fatima walking down the hallway, with Afaf and Abir, her two precious twin daughters, following closely behind. Fatima once called herself the unhappiest woman who had ever lived, and she had reason for her unhappiness. But after keeping custody of her two daughters, and obtaining a position working in our summer palace in Taif, she now wore a bright smile and laughed constantly about one thing or another. I could easily name her the happiest woman I knew. She was a woman whose life had gone from one extreme to the other, from bad to good.

She was exceedingly intelligent as well. She basically ran the entire household staff at Taif with a perfection none could have guessed. I only wish I had a Fatima managing all my homes. Fatima's two daughters were enrolled in a good school and both were excellent students. The girls were two years younger than Little Sultana and from the beginning the three children had enjoyed an instant rapport.

'Fatima, how lovely to see you. What are you doing in Riyadh?'

'Princess, I had an important medical appointment today that could not be missed, so the driver was kind enough to travel with us. I wished to see you while I was here so that I could tell you that I thought of you many times since I heard about the loss of your father.'

I thanked Fatima for her kindness. I was very happy that she was so efficient that none had to organize her life. With the Taif driver accompanying her, she was free to travel all over the country without a problem, for Kareem had provided her with a letter granting travel permission so she had no need to ask for special authorization each time. In Saudi Arabia, a single woman must have such a paper. Since we are members of the royal family, Fatima never had any difficulties with officials once she had shown them Kareem's seal and signature.

'Are you unwell, Fatima?' I asked with true concern. When Fatima came to us, she was very sickly, and due to beatings at the hand of her husband she had extensive dental and facial work that was necessary.

'No, Princess. I am not moving to death, as far as I know. I only had some pain in my teeth and there needs to be more work done so that I can eat properly. I hope it is not too expensive for you, Princess.'

'Fatima, we told you. Have your dental and medical work and do not think about the expense. Your health expenses are fully paid for in this family.'

Fatima smiled broadly. 'You are too good to me, Princess. Too good.'

'You are a treasure, Fatima.'

'Thank you, Princess.'

'Fatima, Amani is here, as is Little Sultana. Come with me, so they can see you and your girls. Little Sultana will be very happy to see them.'

And so only a week after the sad time of family death, the evening unfolded in a beautiful way. Little Sultana insisted that Fatima's daughters go with her to the children's room. I looked in to see the three of them looking very serious, with Little Sultana telling the twins that when she became old enough she was going to help women all over the world. And most fun of all, Afaf and Abir could assist her in doing this good work.

'Little Sultana,' I intervened, 'why don't you play with your new dolls? Afaf and Abir might like some of them to take to Taif.'

Little Sultana smiled at me, then turned back to the girls. 'Let us play. Jadda says that I must play until I am older.' With a big squeal, she and the twins rushed to gather the dolls and started play-acting, the way little girls are supposed to play.

I was satisfied, and happy that those coming after us were already thinking of the good they might do for others.

Fatima was visiting some of the employees in our home, joking that she had the best job of all because she was living in the cool of Taif, whereas they were coping with a hot desert city. She felt badly for them all, she said, with a big laugh. Fatima had become a normal working single mother, knowing that she could care for her twins by her own labour and that she had no worries ever again of being beaten, or of having her daughters forcibly taken from her. She was secure and happy.

Abdullah, Maha and Amani were sitting together at a table by the pool. All three of my children were smiling, joking and enjoying each other's company as I have never seen before. It was as though each had discovered goodness in the others and they were pleased to be siblings. This was a scene I had never expected to see even if I lived a hundred years.

That was when Kareem came home and found me standing quietly, watching my children.

'Sultana, darling,' he whispered in my ear. 'Are you spying on your children?'

'No, husband, but I am enjoying their joy at being together without discord. When have we ever seen these three sitting happily and relishing the others' company?'

'I would say . . . never,' Kareem said with a satisfied laugh.

'What do you think caused this marvellous change?' I pondered.

'They were bound to find the good in each other,' Kareem said. 'You have been a mother like no other. You feel with your heart. You react with your heart. After living with you, I know that the best things in the world are often overlooked. You have always been here for me, and for our children. But when someone is there all the time, she oftentimes becomes invisible. We took you for granted, Sultana. When you were so distraught after the incident with Maha, your extreme distress brought about a fear in all of their hearts that one day you would no longer be around. That fear opened a door for them to see how fortunate they all are to have a mother like you, Sultana. This appreciation has brought them to a new place of love and care for their family.'

'Really? Is that what you think, husband?'

'It is what I *know*, Sultana.'

I did not know how to respond, for Kareem is not a man who easily gives compliments. His words so warmed my heart that I was silent, but when I looked up and into his eyes I gasped. The love in my husband's eyes was overwhelming. I knew at that moment Kareem and I would never again consider divorce. I knew at that moment that one day, one of us would close the eyes of the other in a final act of love. At that moment, I wanted to be the one to go first, because I knew that I would be forever sad and lost without my husband by my side.

I have been guilty of taking my husband for granted, for seeing him each day and knowing that he is there for me made him invisible, too.

But from this day forward, he will be always be visible to me.

At that moment I felt myself the luckiest wife, mother and grandmother in the world.

Despite the loss of my mother, father, sisters Nura and Reema, I know this truth: God is good.

Glossary

abaya: a black, full-length outer garment worn by Saudi women

abu: father

Al Sa'ud: ruling family of Saudi Arabia

Bedouin: a nomadic desert people, the original Arabs

Committee for the Promotion of Virtue and the Prevention of Vice (also known as the Morals Police): religious authorities in Saudi Arabia who have the power to arrest those they believe commit moral wrongs or crimes against Islam or go against the teachings of Islam

Dhu al Hijjah: the twelfth month of the Hejira calendar

Dhu al Qi'dah: the eleventh month of the Hejira calendar

haji: person who makes the pilgrimage to Mecca (a title that denotes honour)

hajj: annual pilgrimage to Mecca made by those of the Islamic faith

Hejira: Islamic calendar, which started on the date that Prophet Muhammad fled Mecca and escaped to Medina (622)

ibn: means 'son of' (Khalid ibn Faisal, son of Faisal)

ihram: special time during hajj when all Muslims refrain from normal life and dwell on nothing but religious matters

imam: person who leads communal prayers and/or delivers the sermon on Fridays

infanticide: practice of killing an infant. In pre-Islamic times, a

common practice in Arabia, thereby ridding the family of unwanted female children

Islam: religious faith of Muslims of which Muhammad was the
Prophet. Islam was the last of the three great monotheistic religions to appear

Kaaba: Islam's holiest shrine, a sacred sanctuary for all Muslims.
The Kaaba is a small building in the Holy Mosque of Mecca,
nearly cubic in shape, built to enclose the Black Stone, which is
the most venerated Muslim object

kohl: a black powder used as eye make-up by Saudi Arabian
women

Koran: the Holy Book of all Muslims, it contains the words of
God as they were given to the Prophet Muhammad

la: Arabian word meaning 'no'

mahram: males to whom a woman cannot be married, such as
her father, brother or uncle, who are allowed to be a woman's
escort when travelling. Must be a close relative

Mecca: holiest city of Islam. Each year, millions of Muslims travel
to Mecca to perform the annual pilgrimage

Medina: second holiest city of Islam. The burial place of Prophet
Muhammad

monotheism: belief that there is only one God

muezzin: the crier who calls the faithful to pray five times a day

Muslim: adherent of the religion founded by Prophet Muhammad
in the year 610

mut'a: temporary marriage allowed to those of the Islamic faith

Mutawah: the religious police, also known as the Morals Police.
Men who seek out, arrest and punish those who do not abide
by Saudi religious law

Najd: the traditional name for central Arabia. The inhabitants of
this area are known for their conservative behaviour. The ruling
family of Saudi Arabia are Najdis

polygamy: marriage to more than one spouse at the same time.
Men of the Muslim faith are legally allowed four wives at one
time

purdah: a practice of confining women to their homes. This total seclusion of females can occur in some Muslim countries

purification: the ritual of cleansing prior to offering prayers to God practised by Muslims

riyal: Saudi Arabian currency

Rub al Khali: an enormous desert wilderness that occupies the south-east portion of Arabia. It is often referred to as the Empty Quarter

secular: not religious

Shiite: the branch of Islam that split from the Sunni majority over the issue of Prophet Muhammad's successor. One of two main sects

Sunna: traditions of the Islamic faith, as addressed by Prophet Muhammad

Sunni: the majority orthodox branch of Islam. Saudi Arabia is 95 per cent populated by those of the Sunni sect. The word means 'traditionalists'. One of two main sects

thobe: a long shirt-like dress that is worn by Saudi men. It is usually made of white cotton but can be made of heavier, darker-coloured fabric for the winter months

Umm Al Qura: 'Mother of Cities' or 'the Blessed City' that is Mecca

umrah: a short pilgrimage (to Mecca) undertaken by those of the Muslim faith that can be made any time of the year

woman's room: room in a man's house used to confine Saudi Arabian women who go against the wishes of their husbands, fathers or brothers. The punishment can be for a short period or a life sentence

zakat: obligatory alms giving required of all Muslims that is the third pillar of Islam

Appendix A

Facts about Saudi Arabia

Head of State: HM King Salman ibn Abdul Aziz Al Sa'ud
Official Title: Custodian of the Two Holy Mosques

Main Cities

Riyadh – capital
Jeddah – port city
Mecca – holiest city of Islam, towards which Muslims pray
Medina – burial place of Prophet Muhammad
Taif – summer capital and summer resort area
Dammam – port city and commercial centre
Dhahran – oil industry centre
Al Khobar – commercial centre
Yanbu – natural gas shipping terminal
Hail – trading centre
Jubail – industrial city
Ras Tanura – refinery centre
Hofuf – principal city of the Al Hasa Oasis

Religion

Islam: it is a crime to practise other religions in Saudi Arabia.

Public Holidays

Eid al-Fitr – five days
Eid al-Adha – eight days

Short History

Saudi Arabia is a nation of tribes who can trace their roots back to the earliest civilizations of the Arabian Peninsula. The ancestors of modern-day Saudis lived on ancient and important trade routes and much of their income was realized by raiding parties. Divided into regions and ruled by independent tribal chiefs, the various warring tribes were unified under one religion, Islam, led by the Prophet Muhammad, in the seventh century. Before the Prophet died, aged sixty-three, most of Arabia was Muslim.

The ancestors of the present rulers of Saudi Arabia reigned over much of Arabia during the nineteenth century. After losing most of Saudi territory to the Turks, they were driven from Riyadh and sought refuge in Kuwait. King Abdul Aziz Al Sa'ud, father of the present-day king, returned to Riyadh and fought to regain the country. He succeeded and founded modern Saudi Arabia in 1932. Oil was discovered in 1938 and Saudi Arabia rapidly became one of the world's wealthiest and most influential nations.

Geography

Saudi Arabia, with an area of 864,866 square miles, is one-third the size of the United States and is the same size as Western Europe. The country lies at the crossroads of three continents: Africa, Asia and Europe. Extending from the Red Sea in the west to the Persian Gulf in the east, it borders Jordan, Iraq and Kuwait

to the north, and Yemen and Oman to the south. The United Arab
Emirates, Qatar and Bahrain lie to the east.

A harsh desert land, with no rivers and few permanent streams,
Saudi Arabia is home to the Rub al Khali (Empty Quarter), which
is the largest sand desert in the world. The mountain ranges of
Asir Province rise to more than 9,000 feet in the south-west.

Calendar

Saudi Arabia uses the Islamic calendar, which is based on a lunar
year, rather than the Gregorian calendar, which is based on
a solar year. A lunar month is the time between two successive
new moons. A lunar year contains twelve months but is eleven
days shorter than the solar year. For this reason, the holy days
gradually shift from one season to another.

Lunar year dates are derived from AD 622, the year of the
Prophet's emigration, or Hejirah, from Mecca to Medina. The
Islamic holy day is Friday. The working week in Saudi Arabia
begins on Saturday and ends on Thursday.

Economy

More than one-quarter of the world's known oil reserves lie
beneath the sands of Saudi Arabia. In 1933, Standard Oil
Company of California won the rights to prospect for oil in
Saudi Arabia. In 1938, oil was discovered at Dammam Oil Well
#7, which is still producing oil today. The Arabian American Oil
Company (Aramco) was founded in 1944 and held the right to
continue to search for oil in the kingdom. In 1980, the Saudi
government assumed ownership of Aramco.

The kingdom's oil wealth has ensured that the citizens of Saudi
Arabia live the kind of opulent lifestyle enjoyed by few. With
free education and interest-free loans, most Saudis prosper. All
Saudi citizens, as well as Muslim pilgrims, receive free healthcare.
Government programmes provide support for Saudi Arabians

in the case of disability, death or retirement. The entire country is an impressive socialist state. Economically, Saudi Arabia has developed into a modern, technologically advanced nation.

Currency

The Saudi riyal is the basic monetary unit in Saudi Arabia. The riyal consists of 100 halalas and is issued in notes and coins of various denominations. The riyal is 3.7450 to the US dollar.

Law and Government

Saudi Arabia is an Islamic state and the law is based on sharia, the Islamic code of law taken from the pages of the Koran, and the Sunna, which are the traditions addressed by Prophet Muhammad. The Koran is the constitution of the country and provides guidance for legal judgments.

Executive and legislative authority is exercised by the King and the Council of Ministers. Their decisions are based on sharia law. All ministries and government agencies are responsible to the King.

Religion

Saudi Arabia is home to Islam, one of the three monotheistic religions. Muslims believe in one God and that Muhammad is his Prophet. As the heartland of Islam, Saudi Arabia occupies a special place in the Muslim world. Each year, millions of Muslim pilgrims journey to Mecca in Saudi Arabia to pay homage to God. For this reason, Saudi Arabia is one of the most traditional Muslim countries and its citizens adhere to a strict interpretation of the Koran.

A Muslim has five obligations, called the Five Pillars of Islam. These obligations are:

1) Profession of faith: 'There is no god but God; Muhammad is the messenger of God.'

2) A Muslim should pray five times a day, facing the city of Mecca.

3) A Muslim must pay a fixed proportion of his income, called *zakat*, to the poor.

4) During the ninth month of the Islamic calendar, a Muslim must fast. During this time, called Ramadan, Muslims must abstain from food and drink from dawn to sunset.

5) A Muslim must perform the hajj, or pilgrimage, at least once during his lifetime (if he has the economic means).

Saudi Arabia – Timeline

570	*19 January*. Prophet Muhammad, the founder of Islam, is born in Mecca.
632	*8 June*. Prophet Muhammad dies in Medina. After his death, his companions compile his words and deeds in a work called the Sunna, which contains the rules for Islam. The most basic are the Five Pillars of Islam, which are 1) profession of faith 2) daily prayer 3) giving alms 4) ritual fast during Ramadan 5) hajj, the pilgrimage to Mecca.
1400s	The Sa'ud dynasty is founded near Riyadh.
1703	Muhammad ibn Abd al-Wahhab (d.1792), Islamic theologian and founder of Wahhabism, is born in Arabia.
1710	Muhammad Ibn Al Sa'ud is born.
1742–65	Muhammad bin Sa'ud Al Sa'ud joins the Wahhabists.
1744	Muhammad Ibn Al Sa'ud forges a political and family alliance with Muslim scholar and reformer Muhammad ibn Abd al-Wahhab. The son of Ibn Sa'ud marries the daughter of Imam Muhammad.
1804	The Wahhabis capture Medina.
1811	Egyptian ruler Muhammad Ali overthrows the Wahhabis and reinstates Ottoman sovereignty in Arabia.
1813	The Wahhabis are driven from Mecca.
1824	The Al Sa'ud family establishes a new capital at Riyadh.

1876	Sultana's grandfather, Abdul Aziz ibn Sa'ud, founder of the kingdom, is born.
1883	*20 May*. Faisal ibn Hussein is born in Mecca. He later becomes the first king of Syria (1920) and Iraq (1921).
1890	Muhammad bin Rasheed captures Riyadh, forcing the Al Sa'ud family out of the area.
1890–1902	The Al-Sa'ud family leave the area to live in exile (from Qatar to Bahrain and finally to Kuwait) until 1902 when they regain control of Riyadh.
1901	Abdul Aziz leaves Kuwait to return to Arabia with family and friends with plans to attack Riyadh.
1902	*January*. Abdul Aziz attacks Mismaak fort and recaptures Riyadh.
	Sa'ud ibn Abdul Aziz, son of Ibn Sa'ud, is born. At his father's death, he will rule Saudi Arabia from 1953 to 1964.
1904	Faisal ibn Abd al-Aziz, who one day will be a king of Saudi Arabia, is born.
1906	Abdul Aziz Al Sa'ud regains total control of the Nejd region.
1906–26	Abdul Aziz Al Sa'ud and his forces capture vast areas and unify much of Arabia.
1916	Mecca, under control of the Turks, falls to the Arabs during the Great Arab Revolt.
1916	British officer T.E. Lawrence meets Faisal Hussein, forging a friendship.
1916	T.E. Lawrence is assigned as the British liaison to Arab Prince Faisal Hussein.
1917	*6 July*. Arab forces led by T.E. Lawrence and Abu Tayi capture the port of Aqaba from the Turks.
1918	*1 October*. Prince Faisal takes control of Syria when the main Arab force enters Damascus.
1918	Lawrence of Arabia blows up the Hejaz railway line in Saudi Arabia.
1921	At the Cairo Conference, Britain and France carve up

Arabia and create Jordan and Iraq, making brothers Faisal and Abdullah kings. France is given influence over what is now Syria and Lebanon.

1923   Abdul Aziz's son Fahd is born in Riyadh. He will one day reign as king of Saudi Arabia.

1924   Ibn Sa'ud, king of the Nejd, conquers Hussein's kingdom of Hejaz. He rules over Saudi Arabia, later taking Mecca and Medina.

1926   *January*. Abdul Aziz is declared King of Hejaz and the Sultan of Nejd.

1927   Saudi Arabia signs the Treaty of Jeddah and becomes independent of Great Britain.

1927–28   King Abdul Aziz crushes the fanatical Islamist tribes of central Arabia.

1931   Mohammed bin Laden (one day will be father of Osama bin Laden) emigrates to Saudi Arabia from Yemen. He works hard to establish his business, later building a close relationship with King Abdul Aziz and King Faisal.

1932   The kingdoms of Nejd and Hejaz are unified to create the Kingdom of Saudi Arabia under King Abdul Aziz Ibn Sa'ud. Saudi Arabia was named after King Ibn Sa'ud, founder of the Saudi dynasty, a man who fathered forty-four sons who continue to rule the oil-rich kingdom.

1933   Saudi Arabia gives Standard Oil of California exclusive rights to explore for oil.

1938   Standard Oil of California strikes oil at Dammam #7.

1945   *14 February*. Saudi King Abdul al-Aziz and American President Franklin D. Roosevelt meet on a ship in the Suez Canal, where they reach an understanding whereby the US will protect the Saudi royal family in return for access to Saudi oil.

      22 March. The Arab League is formed in Cairo, Egypt. Saudi Arabia becomes a founding member of the UN and the Arab League.

1953   King Abdul Aziz, Sultana's grandfather, dies, aged seventy-seven. He is succeeded by his son, Sa'ud.

1953–64	King Sa'ud rules.
1957	*Friday, 15 February*. Osama bin Laden is born in the early hours in Riyadh, Saudi Arabia. His parents are Yemen-born Mohammed Awad bin Laden and Syrian Alia Ghanem.
1962	Saudi Arabia abolishes slavery.
1964	*2 November*. Faisal ibn Abdul Aziz Al Sa'ud (1904–75) succeeds his older brother, Sa'ud bin Abdul Aziz, as king of Saudi Arabia.
1964–75	King Faisal rules.
1965	King Faisal defies Islamist opposition when he introduces television and later women's education. Riots ensue. Later senior clerics are convinced by the government that television could be used to promote the faith.
1967	*6 June*. An Arab oil embargo is put into effect after the beginning of the Arab–Israeli Six Day War.
	3 September. Mohammed bin Laden, the wealthy father of Osama bin Laden, dies in a plane crash, leaving the well-being of his children to King Faisal.
1973	An embargo against Western nations is announced, lasting until 1974. Gasoline prices soar from 25 cents per gallon to $1. As a result, the New York stock market falls.
1975	*25 March*. King Faisal of Saudi Arabia is assassinated by his nephew.
	Crown Prince Khalid becomes king.
	18 June. Saudi Prince Faisal Ibn Musaid is beheaded in Riyadh for killing his uncle, King Faisal. Crown Prince Khalid is declared king.
	November. Armed men and women seize the Grand Mosque in Mecca. They denounce the Al Sa'ud rulers, demanding an end to foreign ways. The radicals are led by Saudi preacher Juhayman al Utaybi. The siege goes on until French special forces are flown to Mecca to assist. The extremists are shot and killed or captured, later to be beheaded.
1980	Osama bin Laden starts his struggle of fighting against the

Soviets in Afghanistan. This is where he will found his Al-Qaeda network.

Saudi Arabia executes the remaining radicals for the siege of the Grand Mosque. The radicals are beheaded in various towns across the country.

1982	*13 June.* King Khalid dies. He is succeeded by his half-brother, Crown Prince Fahd.
1983–2005	Prince Bandar bin Sultan Al Sa'ud, one of King Fahd's favourite nephews, serves as Saudi Arabia's Ambassador to Washington.
1985	Great Britain signs an $80 billion contract with Saudi Arabia to provide 120 fighter jets and other military equipment over a period of twenty years.
1987	*31 July.* Iranian pilgrims and riot police clash in the holy city of Mecca. The Iranians are blamed for the death of 402 people.
1988	Saudi-born Osama bin Laden founds Al-Qaeda (the base), a Sunni fundamentalist group with a goal of establishing an Islamic caliphate throughout the world.
1990	*July.* The worst tragedy of modern times occurs at the hajj in Mecca, when 1,402 Muslim pilgrims are killed in a stampede inside a pedestrian tunnel.

6 November. A group of Saudi women drive cars in the streets of Riyadh in defiance of a government ban. The protest creates enormous problems for the women drivers: they are arrested and fired from their jobs, banned from travelling and named as prostitutes. This event led to a formal ban on driving for women.

Saudi Arabia and Kuwait expel a million Yemen workers as the government of Yemen sides with Saddam in the first Gulf War.

1991	*January.* US-led forces attack the Iraqi military in Kuwait. The ground war begins between Iraq and the Coalition forces. Iraqi forces are routed from Kuwait and are no longer a danger to Saudi Arabia.
1992	King Fahd outlines an institutional structure for the

country. A law is passed that allows the king to name his brothers or nephews as successors and to replace his successor at will.

1994   *23 May*. Two hundred and seventy pilgrims are killed in a stampede in Mecca, as worshippers gather for the symbolic ritual of 'stoning the devil'.

Osama bin Laden is disowned by his Saudi family and stripped of his Saudi citizenship. His fortune is estimated at $250 million.

1995   One hundred and ninety-two people are beheaded in Saudi Arabia over the year – a record number.

1996   Osama bin Laden is asked to leave Sudan after the Clinton administration puts pressure on the Sudanese government. Osama takes his son Omar with him to return to Afghanistan. The rest of his family and close associates soon follow.

An ailing King Fahd cedes power to his half-brother, Crown Prince Abdullah.

1997   Three hundred and forty-three Muslim pilgrims die in a fire outside the holy city of Mecca. More than a thousand others are injured.

1998   One hundred and fifty pilgrims die at the 'stoning of the devil' ritual during a stampede that occurs on the last day of the annual pilgrimage to the holy city of Mecca.

1999   The Saudi Arabian government claims it will issue travel visas into the kingdom to upscale travel groups.

2001   *26 January*. A UN panel angers the Saudi government and citizens when it criticizes Saudi Arabia for discriminating against women, harassing minors and for punishments that include flogging and stoning.

5 March. Thirty-five Muslim pilgrims suffocate to death during the 'stoning of the devil' ritual at the annual hajj in Mecca.

March. The Higher Committee for Scientific Research and Islamic Law in Saudi Arabia says that Pokémon games and cards have 'possessed the minds' of Saudi children.

September. After 9/11, six chartered flights carrying Saudi nationals depart from the US. A few days later, another chartered flight carrying twenty-six members of the bin Laden family leave the USA.

2002   *17 February*. Saudi Crown Prince Abdullah presents a Middle East peace plan to *New York Times* columnist Thomas Friedman. The plan includes Arab recognition of Israel's right to exist if Israel pulls back from lands that were once part of Jordan, including East Jerusalem and the West Bank.

March. There is a fire at a girl's school in Mecca, but the police block the girls from fleeing the building because they are not wearing the veil. A surge of anger spreads across Saudi Arabia when fifteen students burn to death.

13 April. Saudi Arabian poet Ghazi Al-Gosaibi, Saudi Ambassador to Britain, publishes the poem 'The Martyrs' in the Saudi daily *Al Hayat*, praising a Palestinian suicide bomber.

25 April. American President George Bush meets with Saudi Crown Prince Abdullah. Crown Prince Abdullah tells the American president that the country must reconsider its total support of Israel. Abdullah gives Bush his eight-point proposal for Middle East peace.

April. The Saudi Arabian government closes several factories that produce women's veils and abayas that are said to violate religious rules. Some of the cloaks are considered too luxurious, with jewels sewn on the shoulders.

May. There is a disagreement between Saudi diplomats and members of the UN Committee Against Torture over whether flogging and the amputation of limbs are violations of the 1987 Convention Against Torture.

December. Saudi dissidents report the launch of a new radio station, Sawt al-Islah (the Voice of Reform), broadcasting from Europe. The new station is formed with the explicit purpose of pushing for reforms in Saudi Arabia.

2003   *February*. Mina, Saudi Arabia: fourteen Muslim pilgrims are trampled to death when a worshipper trips during the annual hajj pilgrimage.

29 April. The United States government announces the withdrawal of all combat forces from Saudi Arabia.

12 May. Multiple and simultaneous suicide car bombings at three foreign compounds in Riyadh, Saudi Arabia, kill twenty-six people, including nine US citizens.

14 October. Hundreds of Saudi Arabians take to the streets, demanding reform. This is the first large-scale protest in the country, as demonstrations are illegal.

2004   It is discovered that Libya planned a covert operation to assassinate Crown Prince Abdullah the previous year (2003).

1 February. During the hajj, 251 Muslim worshippers die in a stampede.

10 April. Popular Saudi Arabian TV host Rania al-Baz is severely beaten by her husband, who thought he had killed her. She survived, suffering severe facial fractures that required twelve operations. She allowed photos to be broadcast and opened discussions of ongoing violence against women in Saudi Arabia. She travelled to France, where she wrote her story. It was reported that she lost custody of her children after her book was published.

May. In Yanbu, Saudi Arabia, suspected militants spray gunfire inside the offices of an oil contractor, the Houston-based ABB Ltd. Six people are killed. Many are wounded. Police kill four brothers in a shoot-out after a car chase in which the attackers reportedly dragged the naked body of one victim behind their getaway car.

6 June. Simon Chambers (thirty-six), an Irish cameraman working for the BBC, is killed in a shooting in Riyadh. A BBC correspondent is injured.

8 June. An American citizen working for a US defence contractor is shot and killed in Riyadh.

12 June. An American is kidnapped in Riyadh. Al-Qaeda post the man's picture on an Islamic website. He is identified as Lockheed Martin businessman Paul M. Johnson, Jr. Islamic militants shoot and kill American Kenneth Scroggs in his garage in Riyadh.

13 June. Saudi Arabia holds a three-day 'national dialogue' in Medina on how women's lives could be improved and the recommendations are passed to Crown Prince Abdullah.

15 June. Al-Qaeda threatens to execute Paul M. Johnson, Jr within seventy-two hours unless fellow jihadists are released from Saudi prisons.

18 June. Al-Qaeda claim to have killed American hostage Paul M. Johnson, Jr. They post photos on the Internet showing his body and severed head.

June. The Saudi parliament pass legislation overturning a law banning girls and women from participating in physical education and sports. In August, the Ministry of Education announces that it will not honour the legislation.

20 July. The head of slain American hostage Paul M. Johnson, Jr is found during a raid by Saudi security forces.

30 July. In the United States, in a Virginia court, Abdurahman Alamoudi pleads guilty to moving cash from Libya to pay expenses in the plot to assassinate Saudi Prince Abdullah.

28 September. The use of mobile phones with built-in cameras is banned by Saudi Arabia's highest religious authority. The edict claims that the phones are 'spreading obscenity' throughout Saudi Arabia.

6 December. Nine people are killed at the US Consulate in Jeddah when Islamic militants throw explosives at the gate of the heavily guarded building. They force their way into the building and a gun battle ensues.

2005   *13 January.* Saudi judicial officials say a religious court has sentenced fifteen Saudis, including a woman, to as many as 250 lashes each and up to six months in prison for participating in a protest against the monarchy.

10 February. While women are banned from casting ballots, Saudi male voters converge at polling stations in the Riyadh region to participate in city elections. This is the first time in the country's history that Saudis are taking part in a vote that conforms to international standards.

3 March. Men in eastern and southern Saudi Arabia turn out in their thousands to vote in municipal elections. It is their first opportunity to have their say in decision-making in Saudi's absolute monarchy.

1 April. Saudi Arabia beheads three men in public in the northern city of al-Jawf; in 2003 the three men killed a deputy governor, a religious court judge and a police lieutenant.

15 May. Three reform advocates are sentenced to terms ranging from six to nine years in prison. Human-rights activists call the trial 'a farce'.

15 May. Saudi author and poet Ali al-Dimeeni is sentenced to nine years in prison for sowing dissent, disobeying his rulers and sedition. His 1998 novel *A Gray Cloud* centres on a dissident jailed for years in a desert nation prison where many others have served time for their political views.

27 May. King Fahd, Saudi Arabia's monarch for twenty-three years, is hospitalized for unspecified reasons.

1 August. King Fahd dies at the King Faisal Specialist Hospital in Riyadh. His half-brother Crown Prince Abdullah is named to replace him.

8 August. Hope rises in Saudi Arabia after the new king, Abdullah, pardons four prominent activists who were jailed after criticizing the strict religious environment and the slow pace of democratic reform.

15 September. The Saudi government orders a Jeddah chamber of commerce to allow female voters and candidates.

21 September. Two men are beheaded in Riyadh after being convicted of kidnapping and raping a woman.

17 November. A Saudi high-school chemistry teacher, accused of discussing religion with his students, is sentenced to 750 lashes and forty months in prison for blasphemy following a trial on 12 November.

27 November. To the delight of Saudi women, two females are elected to a chamber of commerce in Jeddah. This is the first occasion when women have won any such post in the country, as they are largely barred from political life.

8 December. Leaders from fifty Muslim countries promise to fight extremist ideology. The leaders say they will reform textbooks, restrict religious edicts and crack down on terror financing.

Saudi Arabia enacts a law that bans state employees from making any statements in public that conflict with official policy.

2006

12 January. Thousands of Muslim pilgrims trip over luggage during the hajj, causing a crush in which 363 people are killed.

26 January. Saudi Arabia recalls its Ambassador to Denmark in protest at a series of caricatures of the Prophet Muhammed published in the Danish *Jyllands-Posten* newspaper. Discontent spreads across the Muslim world for weeks, resulting in dozens of deaths.

19 February. Following the publication of the twelve cartoons of the Prophet – highlighting what it described as self-censorship – the *Jyllands-Posten* newspaper prints a full-page apology in a Saudi-owned newspaper.

6 April. Cheese and butter from the Danish company Arla are returned to Saudi Arabian supermarket shelves following a boycott sparked by the country's publication of offensive cartoons.

April. The Saudi Arabian government announces plans to build an electrified fence along its 560-mile border with Iraq.

16 May. Newspapers in Saudi Arabia report that they have received an order from King Abdullah telling editors to stop publishing pictures of women. The king claims that such photographs will make young Saudi men go astray.

18 August. According to the *Financial Times*, Great Britain has agreed to a multi-billion-dollar defence deal to supply seventy-two Eurofighter Typhoon aircraft to Saudi Arabia.

20 October. In an attempt to defuse internal power struggles, King Abdullah gives new powers to his brothers and nephews. In the future, a council of thirty princes will meet to choose the crown prince.

The kingdom beheaded eighty-three people in 2005 and thirty-five people in 2004.

2007   *4 February.* A Saudi Arabian judge sentences twenty foreigners to receive lashes and prison terms after convicting them of attending a mixed party where alcohol was served and men and women danced.

17 February. A report published by a US human-rights group reveals the Saudi government detains thousands of prisoners in jail without charge, sentences children to death and oppresses women.

19 February. A Saudi court orders the bodies of four Sri Lankans to be displayed in a public square after being beheaded for armed robbery.

26 February. Four Frenchmen are killed by gunmen on the side of a desert road leading to the holy city of Medina in an area restricted to Muslims only.

February. Ten Saudi intellectuals are arrested for signing a polite petition suggesting it is time for the kingdom to consider a transition to constitutional monarchy.

27 April. In one of the largest sweeps against terror cells in Saudi Arabia, the Interior Ministry says police arrested 172 Islamic militants. The militants had trained abroad as pilots so they could duplicate 9/11 and fly aircraft in attacks on Saudi Arabia's oil fields.

5 May. Prince Abdul-Majid bin Abdul-Aziz, the governor of Mecca, dies, aged sixty-five, after a long illness.

9 May. An Ethiopian woman convicted of killing an

Egyptian man over a dispute is beheaded. Khadija Bint Ibrahim Moussa is the second woman to be executed this year. Beheadings are carried out with a sword in a public square.

23 June. A Saudi judge postpones the trial of three members of the religious police for their involvement in the death of a man arrested after being seen with a woman who was not his relative.

9 November. Saudi authorities behead Saudi citizen Khalaf al-Anzi in Riyadh for kidnapping and raping a teenager.

Saudi authorities behead a Pakistani for drug trafficking. This execution brings to 131 the number of people beheaded in the kingdom in 2007.

14 November. A Saudi court sentences a nine-year-old girl who had been gang-raped to six months in jail and 200 lashes. The court also bans the lawyer from defending her, confiscating his licence to practise law and summoning him to a disciplinary hearing.

17 December. A gang-rape victim who was sentenced to six months in prison and 200 lashes for being alone with a man not related to her is pardoned by the Saudi king after the case sparks rare criticism from the United States.

2008   *21 January.* The newspaper *Al-Watan* reports that the Interior Ministry issued a circular to hotels asking them to accept lone women as long as their information was sent to a local police station.

14 February. A leading human-rights group appeals to Saudi Arabia's King Abdullah to stop the execution of a woman accused of witchcraft and performing supernatural acts.

19 May. Teacher Matrook al-Faleh is arrested at King Saud University in the Saudi capital Riyadh after he publicly criticized conditions in a prison where two other human-rights activists are serving jail terms.

24 May. Saudi authorities behead a local man convicted of armed robbery and raping a woman. The execution brings the number of people beheaded in 2008 to fifty-five.

20 June. Religious police arrest twenty-one allegedly homosexual men and confiscate large amounts of alcohol at a large gathering of young men at a rest house in Qatif.

8 July. A human-rights group says domestic workers in Saudi Arabia often suffer abuse that in some cases amounts to slavery, as well as sexual violence and lashings for spurious allegations of theft or witchcraft.

30 July. The country's Islamic religious police ban the sale of dogs and cats as pets. They also ban owners from walking their pets in public because men use cats and dogs to make passes at women.

11 September. Sheik Saleh al-Lihedan, Saudi Arabia's top judiciary official, issues a religious decree saying it is permissible to kill the owners of satellite TV networks who broadcast immoral content. He later adjusts his comments, saying owners who broadcast immoral content should be brought to trial and sentenced to death if other penalties do not deter them.

November. A US diplomatic cable says donors in Saudi Arabia and the United Arab Emirates send an estimated $100 million annually to radical Islamic schools in Pakistan that back militancy.

10 December. The European Commission awards the first Chaillot Prize to the Al-Nahda Philanthropic Society for Women, a Saudi charity that helps divorced and underprivileged women.

2009   *14 January*. Saudi Arabia's most senior cleric is quoted as saying it is permissible for ten-year-old girls to marry. He adds that anyone who thinks ten-year-old girls are too young to marry is doing those girls an injustice.

14 February. King Abdullah (eighty-six) dismisses Sheik Saleh al-Lihedan. King Abdullah also appoints Nora al-Fayez as deputy minister of women's education, the first female in the history of Saudi Arabia to hold a ministerial post.

3 March. Khamisa Sawadi, a seventy-five-year-old widow, is sentenced to forty lashes and four months in jail for talking with two young men who are not close relatives.

22 March. A group of Saudi clerics urges the kingdom's new information minister to ban women from appearing on TV or in newspapers and magazines.

27 March. King Abdullah appoints his half-brother, Prince Naif, as his second deputy prime minister.

30 April. An eight-year-old girl divorces her middle-aged husband after her father forces her to marry him in exchange for $13,000. Saudi Arabia permits such child marriages.

29 May. A man is beheaded and crucified for slaying an eleven-year-old boy and his father.

6 June. The Saudi film *Menahi* is screened in Riyadh more than thirty years after the government began shutting down theatres. No women were allowed, only men and children, including girls up to ten.

15 July. Saudi citizen Mazen Abdul-Jawad appears on Lebanon's LBC satellite TV station's *Bold Red Line* programme and shocks Saudis by publicly confessing to sexual exploits. More than 200 Saudi Arabians file legal complaints against Abdul-Jawad, dubbed a 'sex braggart' by the media, and many Saudis say he should be severely punished. Abdul-Jawad is convicted by a Saudi court in October 2009 and sentenced to five years in jail and 1,000 lashes.

9 August. Italian news agencies report that burglars have stolen jewels and cash worth eleven million euros from the hotel room of a Saudi princess in Sardinia, sparking a diplomatic incident.

27 August. A suicide bomber targets the assistant interior minister Prince Mohammed bin Naif and blows himself up just before going into a gathering of well-wishers for the Muslim holy month of Ramadan in Jeddah. His target, Prince Naif, is only slightly wounded.

23 September. A new multi-billion-dollar co-ed university opens outside the coastal city of Jeddah. The King Abdullah Science and Technology University, or KAUST, boasts state-of-the-art labs, the world's fourteenth fastest supercomputer and one of the biggest endowments worldwide. Currently enrolled are 817 students representing sixty-one different countries, with 314 beginning classes in September 2009.

24 October. Rozanna al-Yami, aged twenty-two, is tried and convicted for her involvement in the *Bold Red Line* programme featuring Abdul-Jawad. She is sentenced to sixty lashes and is thought to be the first female Saudi journalist to be given such a punishment. King Abdullah waived the flogging sentence, the second such pardon in a high-profile case by the monarch in recent years. He ordered al-Yami's case to be referred to a committee in the ministry.

October. The bin Laden family go under the spotlight in *Growing Up Bin Laden – Osama's Wife and Son Take Us Inside their Secret World*, written by American author Jean Sasson. The book is based on interviews which Sasson conducted with Omar bin Laden and his mother, Najwa bin Laden.

9 November. A Lebanese psychic, Ali Sibat, who made predictions on a satellite TV channel from his home in Beirut, is sentenced to death for practising witchcraft. When he travelled to Medina for a pilgrimage in May 2008, he was arrested and threatened with beheading. The following year a three-judge panel said that there was not enough evidence that Sibat's actions had harmed others. They ordered the case to be retried in a Medina court and recommended that the sentence be commuted and that Sibat be deported.

2010

19 January. A thirteen-year-old girl is sentenced to a ninety-lash flogging and two months in prison as punishment for assaulting a teacher who tried to take the girl's cell phone away from her.

11 February. Religious police launch a nationwide crackdown on shops selling items that are red, as they say the colour alludes to the banned celebration of Valentine's Day.

6 March. The Saudi Civil and Political Rights Association says that Saudi security officers stormed a book stall at the Riyadh International Book Fair and confiscated all work by Abdellah Al-Hamid, a well-known reformer and critic of the royal family.

20 April. When Ahmed bin Qassin al-Ghamidi suggests that men and women should be allowed to mingle freely, the head of the powerful religious police has him fired.

10 June. After a Saudi man kisses a woman in a mall, he is arrested, convicted and sentenced to four months in prison and ninety lashes.

22 June. Four women and eleven men are arrested, tried and convicted for mixing at a party. They are sentenced to flogging and prison terms.

15 August. Ghazi Al-Gosaibi, a Saudi statesman and poet, dies from colon cancer after a long illness. Al-Gosaibi was close to the ruling family, although his writings were banned in the kingdom for most of his life. The Saudi Culture Ministry lifted the ban on his writings the month before his death, citing his contribution to the nation.

26 August. T. Ariyawathi, a housemaid from Sri Lanka working in Saudi Arabia, is admitted to hospital for surgery to remove twenty-four nails embedded in her body. Her Saudi employer hammered the nails into her body as punishment.

17 November. King Abdullah steps down as head of the country's National Guard. His son assumes the position.

20 November. A young woman in her twenties defies the kingdom's driving ban and accidentally overturns her car. She dies, along with three female friends who were passengers.

22 November. King Abdullah visits New York for medical treatment and temporarily hands control to Crown Prince Sultan, his half-brother.

23 November. Saudi media announces that a Saudi woman accused of torturing her Indonesian maid has been sent to jail, while the maid, Sumiati Binti Salan Mustapa, is receiving hospital treatment for burns and broken bones.

An estimated four million Saudi women over the age of twenty are unmarried in a country of 24.6 million. It is reported that some male guardians forcibly keep women single, a practice known as *adhl*. The guardians have the right to keep the salaries of the women for themselves. Saudi feminist Wajeha al-Huwaider describes male guardianship as 'a form of slavery'.

2011   *16 January*. A group of Saudi activists launches 'My Country', a campaign to push the kingdom to allow women to run in municipal elections scheduled for spring 2011.

24 January. New York-based Human Rights Watch says in its World Report 2011 that Saudi Arabia's government is harassing and jailing activists, often without trial, for speaking out in favour of expanding religious tolerance and that new restrictions on electronic communication in the kingdom are severe.

9 February. Ten moderate Saudi scholars ask the king for recognition of their Uma Islamic Party, the kingdom's first political party.

15 February. The Education Ministry says the kingdom plans to remove books that encourage terrorism or defame religion from school libraries.

24 February. Influential intellectuals say in a statement that Arab rulers should derive a lesson from the uprisings in Tunisia, Egypt and Libya, and listen to the voice of disenchanted young people.

5 March. Saudi Arabia's Interior Ministry says demonstrations won't be tolerated and its security forces will act against anyone taking part in them.

11 March. Hundreds of police are deployed in the capital to prevent protests calling for democratic reforms inspired by the wave of unrest sweeping the Arab world.

2 May. Osama bin Laden, the founder and head of the Islamic militant group Al-Qaeda, is killed in Pakistan shortly after 1 a.m. PKT by US Navy Seals of the US Naval Special Warfare Development.

18 March. King Abdullah promises Saudi citizens a multi-billion-dollar package of reforms, raises, cash, loans and apartments in what appears to be the Arab world's most expensive attempt to appease residents inspired by the unrest that has swept two regional leaders from power.

22 May. Saudi authorities re-arrest activist Manal al-Sharif, who defied a ban on female drivers. She had been detained for several hours a day by the country's religious police and released after she'd signed a pledge agreeing not to drive. Saudi Arabia is the only country in the world that bans women, both Saudi and foreign, from driving.

18 June. Ruyati binti Satubi, an Indonesian grandmother, is beheaded for killing an allegedly abusive Saudi employer.

28 June. Saudi police detain one woman driving in Jeddah on the Red Sea coast. Four other women accused of driving are later detained in the city.

25 September. King Abdullah announces that the nation's women will gain the right to vote and run as candidates in local elections to be held in 2015 in a major advance for the rights of women in the deeply conservative Muslim kingdom.

27 September. Saudi female Shaima Jastaina is sentenced to be lashed ten times with a whip for defying the kingdom's prohibition on driving. King Abdullah quickly overturns the court ruling.

29 September. Saudi Arabian men cast ballots in local council elections, the second-ever nationwide vote in the oil-rich kingdom. Women are not allowed to vote in the election. The councils are one of the few elected bodies in the country, but have no real power, mandated to offer advice to provincial authorities.

29 September. Manssor Arbabsiar, a US citizen holding an Iranian passport, is arrested when he arrives at New York's Kennedy International Airport. Mexico worked closely with US authorities to help foil an alleged $1.5 million plot to kill the Saudi Arabian Ambassador to Washington. On 11 October, Arbabsiar is charged in the US District Court in New York with conspiring to kill Saudi diplomat Adel Al-Jubeir.

22 October. Saudi Crown Prince Sultan bin Abdul Aziz, heir to the Saudi throne, dies in the United States. He had been receiving treatment for colon cancer, first diagnosed in 2009.

27 October. Saudi Arabia's powerful interior minister, Prince Naif bin Abdul Aziz, is named the new heir to the throne in a royal decree read out on Saudi state television.

30 November. Amnesty International publishes a new report accusing Saudi Arabia of conducting a campaign of repression against protesters and reformists since the Arab Spring erupted.

6 December. Saudi Arabia sentences an Australian man to 500 lashes and a year in jail after being found guilty of blasphemy. Mansor Almaribe was detained in Medina on 14 November while making the hajj pilgrimage and accused of insulting companions of the Prophet Muhammad.

10 December. Saudi Arabia's *Okaz* newspaper reports that a man convicted of raping his daughter has been sentenced to receive 2,080 lashes over the course of a thirteen-year prison term. A court in Mecca found the man guilty of raping his teenage daughter for seven years while under the influence of drugs.

12 December. Saudi authorities execute a woman convicted of practising magic and sorcery. Court records state that she had tricked people into thinking she could treat illnesses, charging them $800 per session.

15 December. Police raid a private prayer gathering, arresting thirty-five Ethiopian Christians, twenty-nine of them women. They later face deportation for 'illicit mingling'.

Seventy-six death row inmates are executed in Saudi Arabia in 2011.

Indonesian maid Satinah Binti Jumad Ahmad is sentenced

to death for murdering her employer's wife in 2007 and stealing money. In 2014, the Indonesian government agree to pay $1.8 million to free Satinah.

2012

2 January. Saudi Arabia announces that on 5 December it will begin enforcing a law that allows female workers only in women's lingerie and clothes stores.

12 February. Malaysian authorities deport Hamza Kashgari, a young Saudi journalist wanted in his home country over a Twitter post about the Prophet Muhammad, defying pleas from human-rights groups who say he faces execution. His tweet read: 'I have loved things about you and I have hated things about you and there is a lot I don't understand about you.'

February. A royal order stipulates that women who drive should not be prosecuted by the courts.

22 March. Saudi Arabia media reports say single men in Riyadh will be able to visit shopping malls during peak hours after restrictions aimed at stopping harassment of women are eased.

4 April. A Saudi official reiterates that Saudi Arabia will be fielding only male athletes at the London Olympics. However, Prince Nawaf bin Faisal announces that Saudi women taking part on their own are free to do so but the kingdom's Olympic authority would 'only help in ensuring that their participation does not violate the Islamic sharia law'.

A man found guilty of shooting dead a fellow Saudi is beheaded. His execution in Riyadh brings the total number of beheadings to seventeen for 2012.

23 May. An outspoken and brave Saudi woman defies orders by the notorious religious police to leave a mall because she is wearing nail polish and records the interaction on her camera. Her video goes viral, attracting more than a million hits in just five days.

16 June. Saudi Crown Prince Naif bin Abdul Aziz, a half-brother of King Abdullah, dies. Naif is the second crown prince to die under King Abdullah's rule.

18 June. Saudi Arabia's Defence Minister Prince Salman bin Abdul-Aziz, a half-brother to the king, is named the country's new crown prince.

24 June. In Saudi Arabia, a man dies from severe pneumonia complicated by renal failure. He had arrived at a Jihad hospital eleven days earlier with symptoms similar to a severe case of influenza or SARS. In September, an Egyptian virologist says it was caused by a new coronavirus. Months later the illness is named MERS (Middle Eastern respiratory syndrome).

June. Blogger Raif Badawi is jailed for ridiculing Islamic religious figures.

20 July. Saudi authorities warn non-Muslim expatriates against eating, drinking or smoking in public during Ramadan, or face expulsion.

30 July. Saudi Arabia implements a ban on smoking in government offices and most public places, including restaurants, coffee shops, supermarkets and shopping malls.

2013 *9 January*. Saudi authorities behead a Sri Lankan domestic worker for killing a Saudi baby in her care. Rizana Nafeek was only seventeen at the time of the baby's death and proclaimed her innocence, denying strangling the four-month-old boy. Many agencies and individuals worldwide pleaded with the boy's family, and with the Saudi government, to pardon the girl.

11 January. King Abdullah issues two royal decrees granting women thirty seats on the Shura Council. The council has 150 members. Although the council reviews laws and questions ministers, it does not have legislative powers.

15 January. Dozens of conservative clerics picket the royal court to condemn the recent appointment of thirty women to the 150-member Shura Council.

1 April. A Saudi newspaper reports that the kingdom's religious police are now allowing women to ride motorbikes and bicycles, but only in restricted recreational areas. They also have to be accompanied by a male relative and be dressed in the full Islamic abaya.

16 May. Riyadh vegetable seller Muhammad Harissi sets himself on fire after police confiscate his goods after he was found to be standing in an unauthorized area. He died the next day.

29 July. Raif Badawi, editor of the Free Saudi Liberals website, is sentenced to seven years in prison and 600 lashes for founding an internet forum that violates Islamic values and propagates liberal thought. Badawi has been held since June 2012 on charges of cyber-crime and disobeying his father.

20 September. US prosecutors drop charges against Meshael Alayban, a Saudi princess accused of enslaving a Kenyan woman as a housemaid, forcing her to work in abusive conditions and withholding her passport. Lawyers for the Saudi royal accused the thirty-year-old Kenyan, who has not been named, of lying in an attempt to obtain a visa to stay in the US.

8 October. A Saudi court sentences a well-known cleric convicted of raping his five-year-old daughter and torturing her to death to eight years in prison and 800 lashes. The court also orders the cleric to pay his ex-wife, the girl's mother, one million riyals ($270,000) in 'blood money'. A second wife, accused of taking part in the crime, is sentenced to ten months in prison and 150 lashes.

18 October. Angered by the failure of the international community to end the war in Syria and act on other Middle East issues, Saudi Arabia says it will not take up its seat on the UN Security Council.

22 October. A source says that Saudi Arabia's intelligence chief revealed that the kingdom will make a 'major shift' in relations with the United States in protest at its perceived inaction over the Syria war and its overtures to Iran.

24 October. Saudi women are warned that the government will take measures against activists who go ahead with a planned weekend campaign to defy a ban on women drivers in the conservative Muslim kingdom.

26 October. Saudi activists say more than sixty women claimed to have answered their call to get behind the wheel in a rare show of defiance against a ban on female driving. At least sixteen Saudi women received fines for defying the ban on female driving.

27 October. Saudi police detain Tariq al-Mubarak, a columnist who supported ending Saudi Arabia's ban on women driving.

3 November. A Kuwaiti newspaper reports that a Kuwaiti woman has been arrested in Saudi Arabia for trying to drive her father to hospital.

12 December. Saudi Arabia's Grand Mufti, the highest religious authority in the birthplace of Islam, condemns suicide bombings as grave crimes, reiterating his stance in unusually strong language in the Saudi-owned *Al Hayat* newspaper.

20 December. Saudi Arabia beheads a drug trafficker. So far in 2013, seventy-seven people have been executed, according to an AFP count.

22 December. Saudi Arabia's official news agency says King Abdullah has appointed his son, Prince Mishaal, as the new governor of Mecca.

2014   *20 February.* Rights groups criticize an agreement between Indonesia and Saudi Arabia aimed at giving Indonesian maids more protection in the kingdom, with one saying 'justice is still far away'.

New anti-terrorism law is introduced which critics claim will further stifle peaceful dissent in the kingdom.

16 March. The local *Okaz* daily reports that organizers at the Riyadh International Book Fair have confiscated 'more than 10,000 copies of 420 books' during the exhibition, which began on 4 March. Organizers had announced ahead of the event that any book deemed 'against Islam' or 'undermining security' in the kingdom would be confiscated.

Saudi government designates Islamic groups as terror organizations. The government bans any support or funding for these groups, which are the Islamic State (ISIS), the Muslim Brotherhood and the al-Nusra Front.

8 April. Saudi Arabia's Shura Council recommends that a long-standing ban on sports in girls' state schools, which was relaxed in private schools in 2013, be ended altogether.

September. Saudi Arabia (along with other Arab States) joins with the United States in air strikes against the Islamic State's sanctuaries in Syria.

2015   *23 January.* King Abdullah ibn Al Sa'ud dies. He was the sixth king to rule. King Salman ascends the throne as the seventh king of Saudi Arabia.

March. Saudi Arabia attacks Houthi rebels in neighbouring Yemen. Other Arab states join them in air strikes.

April. King Salman donates more than $30 billion to his people.

April. King Salman creates a potential crisis in the kingdom when he breaks with King Abdullah's plan to move away from the Sudairis (King Abdullah had appointed a half-brother (and youngest son of the first king) as Crown Prince). King Salman quickly reverses King Abdullah's appointments, pushing out the Crown Prince and moving to the third generation (the grandsons of the first king), and appoints Interior Minister Mohammed bin Naif as the new Crown Prince. The king then appoints his own son, Mohammed bin Salman, as Deputy Crown Prince. With this unexpected move, King Salman moves the crown closer to the next generation of Al Sa'ud, and specifically to the Sudairi clan, as both his nephew and son are descendants of the Sudairi side of the family.

May. Two suicide bomb attacks on Shiite mosques in the Eastern Province kill at least twenty-five people, claimed by the Saudi branch of Islamic Group, a Sunni extremist group.

May. Saudi Arabia's King Salman announces that he will not attend the summit meeting called by President Obama.

The Deputy Crown Prince, Mohammed bin Salman, will represent Saudi Arabia instead. This decision signals a huge shift in the relationship between the United States and Saudi Arabia.

May. King Salman and other leaders in the Gulf Cooperation Council countries go public with their displeasure at President Obama's Middle East policies.

May. The government of Saudi Arabia advertises job openings for executioners for beheadings and limb amputations in public squares in the country.

May. The coalition led by Saudi Arabia resumes air strikes against the Houthi rebels in Yemen shortly after the five-day ceasefire ends. This renewed bombing threatens the ongoing relief efforts in Yemen.

May. Eighty people in Yemen are killed in one day from air strikes by the Saudi-led coalition against Houthi rebels.

May. The World Health Organization reports that approximately 2,000 Yemenis have died in the conflict since March. Millions of civilians are in urgent need of medical care for war-related injuries or other medical issues.

June. The Saudi royal family announces that it is building a theme park attraction in the old capital of Diriyah. The park will feature museums and restaurants.

June. The Saudi Arabian military coalition fighting against the Houthi rebels in Yemen kills more than fifty people. Reports claim that most of the dead are civilians.

June. The conflict with Yemen escalates. Houthi rebels fire a Scud missile into Saudi Arabia. Saudi Arabia shoots it down.

June. Despite the Saudi-led bombing campaign, Houthi rebels have taken the capital city of Yemen's Jawf Province, further consolidating their control over the country.

June. Saudi Arabia's Supreme Court upholds the verdict against Raif Badawi, who was previously found guilty of insulting Islam. Its Foreign Ministry rejects all criticism for the conviction and sentence of ten years and 1,000 lashes for the liberal blogger. Badawi is lauded worldwide for his bravery in the face of government harassment, arrest, imprisonment and torture by lashing.

July. Prince Saud al-Faisal ibn Faisal ibn Abdul Aziz Al Sa'ud dies at age seventy-five. The prince served as Saudi Arabia's foreign minister for four decades. He was a highly educated and sophisticated man who was respected worldwide.

July. Reports say that 3,000 Yemenis have died in the past three months of fighting.

July. Prince Al-Waleed bin Talal of Saudi Arabia says he will donate his entire $32 billion fortune to help eradicate disease, empower women and for relief for disasters.

Appendix B

Yemen

An Update on Yemen – and the lives of two brave women, Italia and Fiery

The *Yemen Times* has continued reporting online, although their print edition has been suspended, so it is possible to keep up with daily news coming out of Yemen. The reporters on the *Yemen Times* make it clear that life for the average Yemeni has deteriorated until it is nearly impossible for Yemenis to live any kind of normal life. Electricity and other basic services have collapsed. There is a humanitarian crisis that is developing that is setting the poorest country in the Middle East back for decades.

The *Yemen Times* reports that more than one million people have been displaced across all governorates in Yemen since the Saudi-led coalition started their campaign on 26 March 2015, with more than 500,000 of the newly displaced people coming from the provinces of Al-Dalea, Ibb and Hajjah.

Most Yemenis have been forced to flee their city or their homes due to the war. Many families are seeking shelter with other families, meaning that small homes are sheltering four or five families under one roof. When the conflict becomes intense in one area, people will flee to another area. There has also been a tragic loss of many historical sites.

The Mayor of Hadramawt has reported that approximately 39,000 refugees have arrived in his governorate. There is true concern about health issues, as dengue fever is spreading.

It's estimated that 2,000–3,000 civilians have been killed and 10,000 injured. Nearly 50,000 people have fled the country and at least 10,000 refugees are living in a coastal camp in Djibouti. Others are fleeing the country by boat.

Um Fahd, one of the former residents of Mualla district in Aden, reported to the *Yemen Times* that 'We are living in the time of funerals, we lost three of our neighbours in Mualla and my aunt's husband got shot in Khormaksar.'

Another Yemeni civilian, Adnan Al-Qasas, reported, 'My mother's cousin Shawqy Abdulqader passed away this morning, their house fell on top of their heads, we can't even imagine what they went through, he was a good man never held a gun.'

Every Yemeni has a story, and most are tragic.

With the crisis building, two courageous women continue their fight for their people, and their country. Neither Italia nor Fiery have fled their country. The two women lived in Italia's boat and worked from there until it was accidentally shelled by some local fighters. They were sad to see the boat sink, but then shrugged off the loss and moved back into the old city of Sanaa where they both claim to be happier. They are too busy to worry about their own safety, as they rise early in the mornings and look for supplies and food to purchase so that they can distribute it to those in greatest need in their neighbourhood, and beyond.

Italia has made several exciting trips back to her old village and each time takes supplies. Once she had to travel with a donkey and a cart, but she said it brought back memories of the days of her youth when her parents travelled in the same manner.

Fiery is no longer working as a professor, but instead assists Italia with her charity work. Both women scorn any talk of danger, saying that only Allah knows when they will leave this earth.

And Yemen is a better place because of these two women.

Yemen Timeline (2011–15)

(Houthis follow a branch of Shiite Islam which is known as Zaidism. Zaidis governed North Yemen for nearly a thousand years until 1962. The Houthis seized Sanaa in 2014, setting off the current crisis in that country and bringing air attacks from Saudi Arabia.)

2011	*27 January.* Revolution in Yemen begins when protesters in Sanaa call for President Ali Abdullah Saleh to resign after thirty years in power.
	12 September. President Saleh gives Vice-President Abed Rabbo Mansour Hadi special powers for negotiating transition of power with the Gulf Cooperation Council (GCC) and Yemen's political opposition parties.
	November. President Saleh agrees to hand over power to his vice president, Abed Rabbo Mansour Hadi. A unity government is formed.
2012	*January.* Former President Saleh leaves Yemen. The parliament votes to grant him and his family full immunity from prosecution. Thousands of protesters take to the streets.
	February. Abed Rabbo Mansour Hadi is inaugurated as president of Yemen after a one-man election.
	May. With Yemen on the brink of a food crisis, international aid is pledged.
	June. The Yemen army recaptures three Al-Qaeda sanctuaries in the south.
	September. Violence escalates. Eleven people are killed in a car bomb attack in Sanaa. A local Al-Qaeda deputy is killed in the south.
	November. Militants attack the Saudi diplomat's convoy

in Sanaa. The diplomat and his bodyguard are killed. Witnesses say that the militants were policemen.

2013   *March.* A National Dialogue Conference convenes with the purpose of drafting a new constitution.

April. The son of the ex-president Saleh is fired. He was the head of the Yemen Republican Guard.

July. The United States intensifies their drone attacks against Yemen Al-Qaeda.

December. Mass protests commence in the eastern province of Hadramawt after a tribal leader is shot at a military checkpoint.

2014   *January.* After nearly a year of deliberation, the National Dialogue Conference agrees to a document on which the new Yemen constitution will be based.

February. Presidential panel votes to give approval for Yemen to become a federation of six regions.

July. Disgruntled Yemeni tribesmen destroy Yemen's largest oil pipeline. Oil supplies are disrupted.

August. Yemen President Hadi fires his entire cabinet.

After two weeks of anti-government protests led by the Houthi rebels against a fuel price hike, President Hadi overturns the fuel mandate.

September. In a stunning turn of events, Houthi rebels take control of the capital Sanaa. The UN negotiate a peace deal. Houthis consent to withdraw their fighters if they approve of a new national unity government.

2015   *January.* After rejecting the new constitution proposed by the government, the Houthis seize the Yemen state TV. Fights break out between the Houthis and government troops in the capital. Yemen President Hadi and his government resign at the occupation of the capital by Houthi rebels. Hadi later withdraws his resignation.

February. Houthi leaders seize power. Houthi leaders form a transitional five-member presidential council to replace President Hadi.

The UN Security Council condemns Houthi action. The UN demands that the Houthi negotiate under the aegis of the Gulf Cooperation Council.

Yemen President Hadi flees Sanaa and escapes to Aden.

March. The Islamic State targets two Shiite mosques in Sanaa. More than 130 people are killed.

The Houthi rebels advance towards southern Yemen.

A Saudi-led coalition of Arab states launches air strikes against Shia Houthi rebel targets. The coalition imposes a naval blockade.

Iran condemns the coalition.

The UN warns that Yemen is 'on the verge of total collapse'.

June. Talks on the conflict in Yemen open in Geneva.

Appendix C

Syria

Syria Timeline (2011–15)

2011   *March*. Protestors in Deraa, Syria, demand the release of political prisoners. Syrian President Bashar Assad's security forces shoot and kill the protesters. The protest prompts violent demonstrations that spread across the entire country.

President Assad broadcasts peacemaking measures, freeing dozens of political prisoners, discharging government and finally, lifting a forty-eight-year-old state of emergency.

May. Ongoing anti-regime protests continue in Homes, Deraa, Banyas, and some suburbs of Damascus. Syrian tanks try to crush protesters. The United States and the European Union tighten sanctions.

President Assad announces amnesty for political prisoners.

July. After mass demonstrations in the province of Hama, President Assad fires the governor. When protests continue, Syrian troops go in to restore order and many Syrian civilians are killed.

October. The Syrian National Council announces that it has formed a communal group of internal and exiled opposition activists to seek peace.

November. The Arab League suspends Syria, and imposes sanctions.

The uprising against the Assad government is now recognized as a full-scale civil war.

December. Bombs outside security buildings in Damascus kill forty-four. These blasts are the first of many to come in the capital of Syria.

2012   *February.* The Syrian government increases the bombardment of Homs.

March. The United Nations Security Council endorses a non-binding peace agreement drafted by the UN envoy Kofi Annan.

May. Australia, France, the United Kingdom, Italy, Germany, Canada, and Spain all expel senior Syrian diplomats in protest after more than a hundred civilians are killed in Houla, near Homs.

July. The Free Syria Army kills three security chiefs in Damascus. The also seize the city of Aleppo.

August. Syrian Prime Minister Riad Hijab defects.

August. President Obama warns Syria that if they use chemical weapons, then the United States will consider intervention in the ongoing war.

October. There is a huge fire in Aleppo that destroys that city's historical market.

December. The United Kingdom, the United States, France, Turkey and the Gulf States formally recognize the opposition National Coalition as legitimate representatives of the Syrian people.

2013   *January.* Syria claims that Israeli jets have attacked a military research centre near Damascus.

February. International donors pledge $1.5bn (£950m) to help Syrian civilians affected by the conflict.

March. After Syrian rebels seize control of the city of Raqqa, the city is bombed by Syrian government military planes.

The Syrian government denies all allegations of chemical weapons use.

June. The Syrian government, joined by the Lebanese Hezbollah forces, recaptures the strategically important city of Qusair located between Homs and the Lebanese border.

October. Syrian President Assad surprises the world when he agrees for international inspectors to start destroying Syria's chemical weapons earlier agreed upon between the United States and Russia.

December. Great Britain and the United States break off 'non-lethal' support for Syrian rebels in northern Syria after it is learned that Islamist rebels have seized bases of the Western-backed Free Syrian Army.

2014   *January/February.* When Syrian authorities refuse to discuss the option of a transitional government, the United Nations peace talks in Geneva collapse.

March. The Syrian government army and Hezbollah forces recapture Yabroud, which is the last rebel stronghold near the Lebanese border.

May. Hundreds of rebels fighting the Syrian government/military are remove from their last stronghold in the city of Homs. This disappointing withdrawal ends three years of resistance in the city.

June. The United Nations announces that all of Syria's chemical weapons have been destroyed or removed.

The Islamic State of Iraq and Syria militants announce that they have formed a 'caliphate' that stretches from the Syrian city of Aleppo to the eastern Iraqi province of Diyala.

August. After the Islamic State captures the Tabqa airbase, which is near the northern city of Raqqa, ISIS now controls all of Raqqa province.

September. Five Arab countries join the United States in launching air strikes against ISIS located near Raqqa and Aleppo.

2015   *January.* After a four-month battle, Kurdish fighters defeat the Islamic State, pushing them from the city of Kobane which is located on the Turkish border.

May. Fighters of the Islamic State seize the ancient city of Palmyra in central Syria and they proclaim that they will destroy the pre-Islamic World Heritage site.

June. Kurdish fighters intensify the fighting against the Islamic State in a region between the Turkish border and Raqqa.

ISIS in Iraq and Syria

ISIS began as a splinter group of Al-Qaeda. Former Iraqi soldiers serving under Saddam Hussein are said to be an important part of ISIS. The Islamic State is also known as the Islamic State in Iraq and the Levant.

The leader of ISIS is Abu Bakr al-Baghdadi. There are no proven facts about al-Baghdadi, but his biography, posted on jihadist websites, claims that he earned his doctorate in Islamic studies from a university in Baghdad.

Al-Baghdadi formed a militant group in Salaheddin and Diyala provinces, north of the Iraqi capital, before joining Al-Qaeda in Iraq. Al-Baghdadi was imprisoned for four years in a United States prison in southern Iraq, named Camp Bucca. He was released in 2009.

After ISIS declared the creation of the so-called 'Islamic State', al-Baghdadi took the name al-Khalifah Ibrahim.

The goal of ISIS is to create a caliphate across the Sunni areas of Iraq and in Syria. ISIS has conquered large regions of northern and western Iraq. It currently controls hundreds of square miles, ignoring all international borders. They now have a presence from Syria's Mediterranean coast to south of Baghdad.

ISIS rules by sharia law. It brags about carrying out crucifixions, public executions, and the rape and murder of women, girls, children and babies.

ISIS's tactic for acquiring revenue includes conquering oil fields, smuggling, selling ancient artefacts, demanding ransoms from kidnappings, and extortion.

ISIS announces and shows videos of their soldiers destroying ancient and irreplaceable relics.

Appendix D

Violence Against Women
in Pakistan

In Pakistan, violence against women is linked to the history of women being submissive to men. In Pakistan, the society sees women as the personal property of men. Many men believe that they have the right to control women and to make all their decisions.

In some rural areas, women are not even considered to be human beings; instead, they are used as personal property and can be bartered to settle debts or even to negotiate as property, in order to resolve family conflicts.

Pakistan's laws on rape too often treat the sexual assault of women as the theft of a man's property. Professor Shahla Haeri, whose speciality is women's studies, has said that rape in Pakistan is 'often institutionalized and has the tacit and at times the explicit approval of the state'. Human Rights Watch has written that in Pakistan 'there is a rape every two hours, and a gang rape every eight hours'. Women in custody of the police are even raped. Asma Jahangir, a lawyer and co-founder of the women's rights group Women's Action Forum, reported that in a 1988 study of detainees in Punjab, '72 per cent of the women arrested said that they had been sexually abused while in custody'. These are outrages against the women of Pakistan.

Many men in rural areas think of women as nothing more than servants for doing their command.

In Pakistani society, it is not considered wrong for a father to beat his daughter, or a brother to beat his sister, or a husband to beat his wife. These beatings often occur due to very minor issues, such as burning a meal or leaving the home to visit family without permission, or even for being late coming home from school.

Most Pakistani women are dependent on the male members of their family. The man takes care of their needs and they, in turn, obey the man. Only women who are educated and have economic independence push for equality in a marriage and freedom of choice, but even then there are problems and the women have to fight for gender equality. In Pakistan, girls are reared to be obedient and docile. In rural areas particularly, girls are led to believe that their role in life is to serve men.

From childhood, a girl's movements are restricted. She is controlled so that she will not do anything to dishonour the family. This linking of females with male honour is a major issue that creates many crimes against women. While men have no limitations, many young girls are not allowed to play outside the home; in fact, often grown women are not allowed to go outside the home.

Pakistani women are often victims of many forms of violence. The most dangerous place for a Pakistani woman is in her home. That is where she often endures domestic abuse; in some cases, women have had acid thrown on them by family members or they have been burned alive by their husbands. There are many other forms of known ritual honour killings.

Despite the high level of family violence against women, the judiciary considers family violence a 'family matter' and tries to avoid involvement.

Young girls do not escape this violence. Forced marriages are still common, particularly in rural areas. Additionally, girls and women are used to settle debts or even conflicts between families.

Tribal leaders have organized a parallel judicial system and these councils are often promoters of honour killings.

Religious scholars are also against the rights of women. These men of religion appear to detest women who demand rights. The scholars say that such women are following the agenda of the 'West', which is to secularize the Islamic society of Pakistan. A woman who struggles against gender discrimination is a woman who is against Islam. These men band together to oppose any new laws that might increase freedom for women.

Pakistan is a country of more than 150 million people. There is an extremely high rate of illiteracy, 70 per cent. In Pakistan, the definition of a person considered literate is someone who has the simple ability to write his or her name. While girls in Lahore, Islamabad, Karachi or other large cities generally go to school, this is not the case in rural areas.

The Pakistani judiciary's actions make it clear that the people in charge protect the patriarchal structure of Pakistani society.

All of these factions come together to mean that if a man is turned down for a marriage proposal, or a husband is unhappy with his wife, he can feel relatively safe to do anything he wishes to any woman, and he will not be punished. And that is why the horrific habit of acid-throwing by men goes unabated. Women and girls are left to suffer the consequences of a society that refuses to punish men who disfigure or even murder women.

ABOUT THE AUTHOR

Jean Sasson has travelled widely in the Middle East since 1978, living as a resident in Saudi Arabia for twelve of those years. She has spent much of her career as a writer and lecturer sharing the personal stories of courageous Middle Eastern women. Her book, *Princess: A True Story of Life Behind the Veil in Saudi Arabia*, became a classic, an international bestseller and formed the basis of a compelling series. *Princess: Secrets to Share* is Jean's thirteenth book. She has plans to write her own memoir, as well as several other books about courageous women of the world. She currently makes her home in Atlanta, Georgia.